Sexual Difference in European Cinema

Also by Fabio Vighi

Le ragioni dell'altro. La formazione intellettuale di Pasolini tra saggistica, letteratura e cinema (2001)
Traumatic Encounters in Italian Film: Locating the Cinematic Unconscious (2006)
Did Somebody Say Ideology? On Slavoj Žižek and Consequences (edited with Heiko Feldner, 2007)
Žižek: Beyond Foucault (with Heiko Feldner, 2007)

Sexual Difference in European Cinema

The Curse of Enjoyment

Fabio Vighi
School of European Studies, Cardiff University, UK

First published 2009 by
PALGRAVE MACMILLAN

Palgrave Macmillan in the UK is an imprint of Macmillan Publishers
Limited, registered in England, company number 785998, of Houndmills,
Basingstoke, Hampshire RG21 6XS.

Palgrave Macmillan in the US is a division of St Martin's Press LLC,
175 Fifth Avenue, New York, NY 10010.

Palgrave Macmillan is the global academic imprint of the above
companies and has companies and representatives throughout the world.

Palgrave® and Macmillan® are registered trademarks in the
United States, the United Kingdom, Europe and other countries

ISBN-13: 978–0–230–54925–8   hardback
ISBN-10: 0–230–54925–X   hardback

This book is printed on paper suitable for recycling and made from fully
managed and sustained forest sources. Logging, pulping and manufacturing
processes are expected to conform to the environmental regulations of the
country of origin.

A catalogue record for this book is available from the British Library.

Library of Congress Cataloging-in-Publication Data

Vighi, Fabio, 1969–
    Sexual difference in European cinema : the curse of enjoyment /
    Fabio Vighi.
        p. cm.
    Includes bibliographical references and index.
    ISBN 978–0–230–54925–8
    1. Sex role in motion pictures.   2. Motion pictures—Europe.   I.
    Title.
    PN1995.9.S47V54   2009
    809'.933538—dc22
                                                              2008041054

10   9   8   7   6   5   4   3   2   1
18 17 16 15 14 13 12 11 10 09

Printed and bound in Great Britain by
CPI Antony Rowe, Chippenham and Eastbourne

Contents

Introduction   1

Part I: The Comfort of Fantasies   15

1 Sublime Objects: the Antinomies of Masculine Sexuality
   from Fellini to Truffaut   17

2 Ethics of Drive: Beauty and its Enjoyment from
   Rohmer to Pasolini   57

3 Unbearable Freedoms: the Real of Sexual Difference from
   Rossellini to Fassbinder   96

Part II: Variations on Feminine Enjoyment   147

4 In the Beginning was Enjoyment: the Emergence of
   Feminine Desire in Bergman and Antonioni   149

5 About Nothing, with Precision: Femininity Unbound from
   Ophuls to Antonioni   176

6 In Film Beyond Film: the Ontological Primacy of Woman   203

Conclusion   237

Notes   242

Bibliography   250

Index   254

v

Introduction

Until now, psychoanalytic film theory has privileged the Lacanian category of the Imaginary and its corollary question of audience identification. It seems to me that despite their pioneering role in generating the right conditions for a long-term joint effort between psychoanalysis and cinema, the 1970s and 1980s appropriations of Lacan by film studies were (and still are) intrinsically reductive, as they resulted in the promotion of a discursive practice that concerned itself almost exclusively with the effects of cinematic production on the viewer (spectatorship theory). In so doing, these studies glaringly overlooked the order of the Real, especially in its symbiotic relationship with the symbolic texture of film. This means that the latter part of Lacan's teachings was practically ignored. Recently, it would appear that the potential for a fertile crossbreeding between psychoanalysis and cinema has either been absorbed by the depoliticised appeal of Cultural Studies, or reconsidered and eventually discarded by both cognitive-historicist approaches and conventional film theory. To my mind, Slavoj Žižek is the only theorist today who – despite being regularly criticised for not adhering to the standards of scholarship that define film studies as an academic discipline (see Bordwell 2005; Stamp 2007; Lebeau 2001) – advocates the convergence of psychoanalysis and film as part of a project for the radical re-politicisation of culture. It is within such a project that my work finds its scope. More precisely, I do not merely argue for the employment of psychoanalytic theory as yet another theoretical framework for the discussion of film narratives. Rather, by unravelling the Real of film – film's unconscious presuppositions – I aim to bring the political potential of Lacanian theory to full fruition.

The main criticism levelled against Žižek's use of film is that it ignores the specificity of the filmic medium and instead borrows from it to argue abstract theoretical points. While this is not entirely true (his book on Kieślowski engages directly and in a sustained manner with form, elaborating original readings of key concepts such as suture and gaze), perhaps we should approach this question from the opposite angle: what if it is precisely Žižek's seemingly "irresponsible" method that opens up the possibility of thinking cinema in a thoroughly alternative way, one that may challenge the depoliticised status of today's film studies? Žižek does not look at film as an end in itself, but as a means to unravel wider theoretical problems that he considers to be central to our socio-political reality. Perhaps, then, if we feel offended by the way he plunders world cinema to discuss psychoanalytic, philosophical and political points, we should take his unorthodox method as a provocation aimed at shaking the film studies community out of the insularity and politico-theoretical cul-de-sac in which it currently finds itself, especially with regard to the use of Lacanian theory.

As anticipated, one of the most prolific ways in which Lacan has been appropriated by film theory is through the notion of spectatorship, which first appeared within the "structuralist Marxism" of the 1970s and 1980s. I want to make it clear that with this book I do not intend to add another interpretative layer to the spectatorship or apparatus theories that have appeared in rapid succession since such essays as Christian Metz's 'The Imaginary Signifier' (Metz 1975) and Laura Mulvey's 'Visual Pleasure and Narrative Cinema' (Mulvey 1975). The problem with these theories is that they place excessive emphasis on the audience's imaginary identification, thus neglecting what from a Lacanian perspective is the key issue, i.e. the analysis of how film masters its own symbolic efficacy. Furthermore, it is not merely that audiences do not lend themselves to be categorised around normative lines of class, gender, ethnicity, etc., but rather that film itself is constantly "at war" with the Real surplus it produces. The use that spectatorship theories make of Lacan is flawed, for, to put it bluntly, they fail to realise that, around the mid-1960s, *Lacan moved beyond structuralism*. If it is plausible that the "cinematic apparatus" (the darkness of the theatre, the position of the projector behind the spectators' heads, etc.) contributes to creating the effect that what is being watched is a sealed reality; and if it is indisputable that such structural constraints are often strengthened by the formulaic and effectively static character of dominant film industries such as Hollywood, what is nevertheless missing is the simplest and yet most vital question: how does film construct its (ambiguous) meaning? I therefore agree with Žižek when he claims that

> authors usually referred to as Lacanians (from Laura Mulvey to Kaja Silverman) as a rule "engage with" Lacan: they appropriate some Lacanian concepts as the best description of the universe of patriarchal domination, while emphasising that Lacan remained a phallogocentrist who uncritically accepted this universe as the only imaginable framework for our socio-symbolic existence. [...] My response to this is, of course: what if one should finally give Lacan himself a chance? (Žižek 2001c: 2)

And, precisely to give Lacan a chance, it seems to me that the most important issue to address is not (the difficulty of) defining who a spectator is and how he or she makes sense of film (including unconscious identificatory processes), but actually to examine *how film makes sense of itself*: how it emerges by way of negotiating its symbolic consistency with its excessive and excluded surplus.

Here I shall add that it is not simply a matter of studying the relationship between the historical context and the textual inscription of specific meanings, gender roles, and so on (say, how feminine sexual identity is connoted in 1940s melodramas), for such an approach is based on the idea that film is a mere reflection of contingent historical determinants. Faced by the prospect of historicising film, a Lacanian theory of cinema should point out that history itself is the product of the dialectical rapport between the represented and what exceeds representation, and that therefore the only way film could reflect a given socio-historical context would be by reflecting the ahistorical split (the Real) that cuts across history and sustains its representability. An example of this paradoxical logic can be found in Pier Paolo Pasolini's over-identification with the Roman sub-proletariat in a film like *Accattone* (1961), where the excluded sub-proletariat is uncovered as the remainder/excess of Italy's post-war economic miracle. What we need to highlight here is not just that Pasolini's film reflects an important aspect of Italian history in the 1960s, but that through its obsessive attachment to the sub-proletariat the whole film effectively turns into a strange remainder of narrative symbolisation, something akin to a continuous deflagration of libido which disrupts narrative continuity. The paradox is that to historicise *Accattone* adequately, one is forced to explore the very nature of cinematic perception, i.e. cinema's ability to construct narrative meaning by disavowing its self-generated excess. Today's fashionable strategy of using cinema to outline or critically explore the development of socio-historical contexts is therefore deeply limited, for it ignores the dialectical complexity of both history and cinematic representation. The historicist relativism typical of Cultural Studies, for example, happily avoids the ontological and epistemological presuppositions through which the space for historical representation emerges. Rather than endorsing such an approach, I vindicate the thoroughly self-reflexive character of the filmic text, claiming that only by shifting the emphasis on the dialectics of cinematic representation can Lacan be saved from being 'a comically simplified caricature' (Žižek 2001c: 4), and cinema given a decisive political twist. To substantiate this claim, my Lacanian investigation deploys two concomitant strategies, looking at (1) the role of enjoyment in film, and (2) the representation of sexual difference.

(1) In approaching film from a psychoanalytic angle, I make use of the main critical implications of Lacanian theory, referring specifically to the key notion of enjoyment (*jouissance*, I use the two terms interchangeably). It is precisely with regard to enjoyment, however, that we encounter the first and crucial difference between my position and the film studies appropriations of Lacan: what if the term in question does not simply refer to the spectators' libidinal affects (visual pleasure), but, most importantly, to the ways in which the filmic text organises *its own* enjoyment? My central claim in this book is that before it can be used to describe the complex interrelation between film and audience, enjoyment ought to be seen as a self-reflexive cinematic category insofar as it is embedded in film and determines its conditions of possibility. Film theorists who draw on psychoanalysis have regularly overlooked how film itself is a split unit, divided between its explicit narrative level and a foreclosed kernel of libidinal pressure which constantly resurfaces in symptomatic mode. It is this elementary Lacanian point that forms the basis of my analysis. In order to draw out its consequences let us move to the actual definition of enjoyment.

Lacan conceives of enjoyment as an excessive, inherently disturbing dimension which, as such, is Real. We need to be precise when defining the status of the Real of enjoyment in Lacan. As Žižek has repeatedly argued, in its deepest configuration it is not a domain *beyond* the remit of language and signification (as the early, "structuralist" Lacan implied); it is not 'the terrifying primordial abyss that swallows everything'. Instead, it emerges as a traumatic formation *produced by language itself*, a troubling surplus of sense which distorts our perception of reality the very moment a perception begins to form. The Real is 'that invisible obstacle, that distorting screen, which always "falsifies" our access to external reality, that "bone in the throat" which gives a pathological twist to every symbolisation, that is to say, on account of which every symbolisation misses its object' (Žižek 2003: 67). From this perspective, the notion of cinematic enjoyment carries the decisive implication that the ultimate aim of the moving image is not the purposeful development of a given message towards an end. Film, in other words, is a-teleological, its aim as a linguistic act residing in the displaced and often imperceptible materialisations of *jouissance* that stain its text.

This emphasis on the presence of blots of enjoyment which skew cinematic communication does not, however, lead me to embrace a sceptical position towards the authority of fictions, and even less to reject fixed referential meanings. What qualifies my methodology is not a relativistic approach to film language but a reflection on its fundamental dislocation. I see filmmaking as the effect of its liaison with the Real that filmmaking itself produces whilst it struggles to attain a degree of symbolic consistency. Cinematic representation therefore emerges as a dialectical, mutually transformative rapport between its fictional domain (with all its complexities and ambiguities) and its negative/foreclosed underside, which from a Lacanian standpoint amounts to the invisible "pull" of the Real.

With respect to film studies, then, the proper wager of Lacanian psychoanalysis is that we have a chance to identify the Real of filmic representation, which is also the Real of representation as such. If there is a Lacanian lesson to apply to film, it concerns Lacan's key insight (articulated from the mid-1960s) that the Symbolic and the Real are consubstantial, fused into one another. As any other linguistic act, film produces a non-symbolisable libidinal remainder, or surplus, with which it enters into a symbiotic relationship. My specific Lacanian claim here is that this surplus works as the crucial anchoring point of filmic representation. Precisely because there is no film without the Real excess it generates, this very excess is film at its purest, the disavowed matrix of the moving image. Needless to say, only certain films will demonstrate the potential to express the deep-seated logic that governs their own representational status. The aim of film criticism, I argue, is to locate this potential.

But why, exactly, does this aim matter? First and foremost because it opens up a dimension which is profoundly political. The significance of unearthing the dynamics through which film and enjoyment interact has to do with what should be at the heart of every political discourse: the analysis of the rapport between the represented and what is excluded from, or simply exceeds, representation. It is not the narrative treatment of political themes that I am interested in, but the way in which the analysis of filmic representation may lead us to grasp the inner logic sustaining our socio-political space. What a Lacanian reading effectively tells us is that the field occupied by cinema is formally equivalent to any other representational field, insofar as its structural dynamics obey an embedded mechanism of displacement *which is also what determines the emergence of social reality*. My claim is therefore that through film we understand how reality as such is constructed around an excess of enjoyment, produced and simultaneously foreclosed in the very effort of generating meaning and communication. The political consequences of this analogy are immense, as well as self-evident, since the focus falls directly on the disavowal that opens up the space for representation, and by the same token allows us to conceptualise the formal outline of an intervention that may determine the collapse and subsequent redefinition of that space. The distinctiveness of a Lacanian politics of enjoyment is that it is able to delve into the ontological core of symbolisation, into what Žižek (2006a: 298) aptly terms 'the constitutive excess of representation over the represented'. What we see, hear, and make sense of never amounts to "the whole story", but relies on an invisible surplus (the Real of *jouissance*) which structures what we see, hear, and make sense of. There is no formal difference between cinema and reality, for both involve a series of representations articulated around the repression of their own inherent excess.

At the heart of this argument there is the assumption that, as Jacques Rancière (2004: 38) succinctly put it, 'the real must be fictionalized in order to be thought'. Thinking cinema, just as much as thinking social reality, is not a spontaneous activity. Rather, *thinking as such* is an epiphenomenon, a reflexive, secondary occurrence, for it is preceded by the unconscious act of foreclosure that sets up the fictional framework where thought intervenes. To be able to think something we must first exclude a part of it, relegating it into the reservoir of the Real. My Lacanian method targets this Real, in as much as its presence is detectable through the interpretation of the enjoyment that seeps through the filmic text. It follows that what matters politically is to locate those excluded, largely unacknowledged remainders of symbolisation whose function is both to cement and, once identified, undermine, the consistency of representation. And, again, let us remind ourselves that the intention is not to lament the spurious nature of representation (this is, rather, the postmodern/deconstructionist task), but to attempt to identify the disavowed truth of the field(s) of representation itself, without which there would be no reality.

Key to my approach is the recognition that the strictly speaking unattainable cause of cinematic fiction (*jouissance*) is locatable through the traces it leaves at the symbolic level, for these traces function as the exact equivalent of Lacanian symptoms. Here we should recall that from the start of the 1960s Lacan progressively moves away from his early idea that the symptom, like the unconscious, is structured like a language (see Lacan 1989: 65). From its status as a linguistic or ciphered message, "symptom" slowly evolves into *sinthome*, an opaque residue of *jouissance*, the trace of its pure, non-analysable presence through which the subject enjoys the unconscious insofar as the unconscious determines the subject. My aim is to identify the *sinthomes* that are sutured in the symbolic space of film so as to sustain the effect of self-enclosure. The main question, then, is not a hermeneutical one (concerning the interpretation of hidden meanings), but both epistemological (about the dynamics that determine the emergence of meaning) and ontological (since this radical epistemological perspective allows us to isolate the core of reality).

This point is worth expanding. The theoretical and practical goal of Lacanian psychoanalysis is to uncover the mechanism through which reality emerges for us, in as much as reality itself always coincides with an act of representation. Lacanian theory tells us why there is *something* instead of *nothing*, why and how we are able to represent the world to ourselves; ultimately, it tells us how representation materialises into a specific content. The fundamental question in Lacan is not "what does this mean?", but rather "through which mechanism of displacement did this signifying framework emerge?" Even in clinical terms, what matters is not simply to restore the patient's wellbeing, but to confront the patient with the impasse through which he or she emerges as a (disturbed) individual, i.e. a desiring human being. The self, Lacan claims, must come to be where the unconscious is, it must attempt to disturb the fantasmatic core of foreclosed enjoyment that an unconscious drive always is, for that is the only way to access the truth of the subject. This is why, in Lacan's reading, Freud's famous formula *Wo Es war, soll Ich werden* (the Ego should conquer the Id) is significantly changed into "I must approach that foreclosed site where the unbearable truth about me is located". My argument is that film analysis fulfils itself in the application of this injunction to locate film's own unconscious, excessive (and therefore traumatic) enjoyment. It is because of this radical epistemology encouraging us to probe the structuring causes of a given conceptual framework that Lacan's system of thought ought not be regarded as postmodern or deconstructionist (as in today's "cultural studies" appropriations) but rather as political in a way that we should not be afraid to link with the Marxist legacy.

After all, it was Lacan who claimed that Marx (and not Freud) invented the symptom (see Lacan 1975). He did so by highlighting how in the passage from feudalism to capitalism and the establishment of bourgeois society, the explicit character of social domination and servitude between human beings was suddenly repressed, only however to re-emerge in commodity fetishism. With the advent of capitalism human beings started perceiving themselves as free and independent subjects, emancipated from the fetishistic type of inter-subjective relations characteristic of feudalism (master and servant, etc.). However, Marx noticed that class domination does not simply disappear but rather *returns* in the shape of fetishistic relations between things: 'It is nothing but the definite social relation between men themselves that assumes here, for them, the fantastic form of a relation between things [...] I call this the fetishism which attaches itself to the products of labour as soon as they are produced as commodities' (Marx 1990: 165). This means that to understand capitalism and the social reality it creates and purports we need to look for its symptomatic and disavowed truth, which Marx caught more than a glimpse of when he realised that, once produced, commodities acquire a magical aura through which they control us: 'Their own [human beings as 'exchangers' of commodities] movement within society has for them the form of a movement made by things, and these things, far from being under their control, in fact control them' (Marx 1990: 167–8). It is insofar as he sees the commodity-form (its 'mystical character', 164) as a disavowed symptom of capitalism that Marx understands how commodities materialise the repressed truth of human relations under capitalism itself. What matters is that the truth of a given representational domain is embodied by its symptom, or rather *sinthome*: the *jouissance* of the commodities as they engage in their "mad dance". For this very reason, film criticism should look for *sinthomes*.

As for the specificity of cinematic communication, Freud's rejection of the moving image is well known. The quandary that convinced him of the impossibility of any productive interconnection between psychoanalysis and cinema is the thorny issue of the figurative/non-figurative nature of the unconscious (see Heath 1999: 30–1). To Freud, the obstacle between the two disciplines is insurmountable because of the plastic dimension of cinema, which relies too heavily on the assertiveness of images and is thus ill equipped to render the "invisible presence" of the unconscious. It is here, however, that we should look to Lacan, for he allows us to solve the problem by turning around its presuppositions, that is to say, by claiming that what we see is always-already impregnated with the Real of enjoyment. Shifting the emphasis on the interpenetrations of the Symbolic and the Real, Lacanian theory bridges the gap between the non-figurative and the figurative, suggesting that cinema's unacknowledged structuring kernel belongs in the "too-visual" of cinema, in the redundancy of the image.

As will be clear by now, my approach rejects the standard critical assumption of the autonomy of film as a self-entrenched, specialised academic discipline. The object of my investigation is not the history of cinema but the cinematic field insofar as it embodies a dimension that, in Žižek's words, is 'more Real than reality itself'. In *The Pervert's Guide to Cinema* (Žižek 2006b), for instance, he claims:

> In order to understand today's world, we need cinema, literally. It is only in cinema that we get that crucial dimension which we are not yet ready to confront in our reality. If you are looking for what is, in reality, more real than reality itself, look into cinematic fiction. [...] If you take away from our reality the fictions that regulate it, you lose reality itself. We need to perceive not the reality behind the illusion, but the reality in illusion itself.

What is at stake in this position is the persuasion that cinematic fiction has the potential to evoke or even embody the disavowed core that structures our perception of reality (the "reality in illusion", which is "more real than reality itself"). This question is crucial for Žižek's aspiration to popularise Lacanian theory and, simultaneously, politicise film. Along these lines, what interests me is the radical self-reflexivity at work in cinema: the fact that cinematic representation is sustained by the desire to exceed itself. Again, it is here that Lacan, film and politics meet, for in Lacanian terms the political emerges when we are able to identify that limit dimension where the symbolic field collapses into the Real, thus encouraging us to imagine the reconfiguration of the field itself. It is in relation to this limit dimension, and the way it undermines the traditional belief in representation, that sexual difference can be introduced...

(2) By conflating sexual difference and European cinema, my intention is to identify a specific cinematic context where the excess of representation becomes visible. At the beginning of Carl Theodor Dreyer's *Gertrud* (1964), the Danish director's last film, there is a long take where the eponymous heroine (played by Nina Pens Rode) confronts her husband Gustav (Bendt Rothe) about her decision to leave him. She articulates her argument in a memorable monologue, only occasionally broken by the husband's timid and dumbfounded replies:

> *Gertrud*: I no longer wish to be your wife... you love power and knowledge. You love your wisdom, your books, your cigars, and I don't doubt that you've loved me, occasionally... You think of your work only... it is worse than indifference, it is lack of feeling... a woman loves her husband above all else, but for him work comes first...
> *Gustav*: Isn't this a law of nature?

Gertrud: Naturally, it is in the nature of man to work, to create, but work mustn't expel woman from his thoughts. I often feel as if I haven't really got a husband, as if I'm meaningless to you... in a very humiliating way, you show me how little you care about me. Do I exist at all for you? You never guess my wishes or my thoughts, whether I am happy or sad makes no difference at all to you... the man I am to be with must be mine entirely. I must have precedence. I won't just be a toy to be played with now and again.
Gustav: But dear, love cannot fill a man's life, it would be ridiculous for a man.

What emerges with Gertrud's rebellion is the impossibility of the sexual relationship insofar as it is based on the incompatible modalities in which each sex structures its relation to the other by way of fantasy. Later, Gertrud's attempt to establish a viable relationship with Gabriel Lidman (Ebbe Rode), her lover, proves equally unsatisfactory, for she realises that he is just "another man", a younger version of her husband. Deeply frustrated, the heroine eventually decides to move to Paris with her friend Axel (Axel Strøbye) in order to study psychoanalysis. It is precisely in Paris, more or less around 1964, that my book begins – at the time, that is, when Jacques Lacan's psychoanalytic theories were entering their last, crucial stage of development.

The central question I investigate is the deadlock of sexual difference as conceptualised in Lacanian theory and represented in post-war European cinema. First and foremost, it concerns what Žižek has labelled the consubstantiality of sexual difference and universality:

> sexual difference is co-substantial with universal humanity. There is no neutral definition of the human being without a reference to sexual difference. What defines humanity is this difference as such. In this sense, sexual difference is a kind of zero-level definition of what a human being is. [...] to be human means precisely to be differentiated along the lines of sexual difference. In Lacan's theory, sexual difference is inscribed into the very structure of the symbolic order. It is not a difference between two modes of symbolization, but the difference that pertains to a certain fundamental deadlock of the symbolic order. This is more subtle than it may at first appear, because again the point is that difference as such is universal. (Žižek and Daly 2004: 81)

Sexual difference is therefore a *universal* antagonism that cuts across the socio-symbolic field, constantly threatening to throw it off balance. Because it is an ontological category, it is also a political one.

An investigation into the deadlock of sexual difference is simultaneously an investigation into the symbolic order (the invisible system of signs and conventions that determines our perception of reality) insofar as it is inseparable from the Real as *voiding effect*, failure of symbolisation, the point where the big Other as universe of sense disintegrates. The European cinema I invoke in this book can be thought of as the gaze of the camera fascinated by the non-existence of the sexual relationship and yet compulsively obliged to record it, as in the famous 30-minute domestic sequence in Jean-Luc Godard's *Contempt* (Le Mépris, 1963), which strives to capture the sudden, inexplicable deterioration of the rapport between Paul (Michel Piccoli) and Camille (Brigitte Bardot). My aim is to look at film as the place where 'the sexual relationship doesn't stop not being written' (Lacan 1998b: 94) – where we discover that it *can only be written as the impossibility of being written*, as a series of failures to inscribe it in the communicative domain.

In respect of the ambiguity of film as it endeavours to write the sexual relationship, I explore two main perspectives: firstly, in Part I, the ideological process of concealing the wound of sexual difference by displacing it onto woman *qua* sublime and forbidden cause (the logic of courtly love); secondly, in Part II, the uncovering of feminine enjoyment as correlative to the Real of sexual difference itself, and therefore to *difference* as such.

It will be immediately apparent that I do not wish to engage in a debate on the legitimacy of the various approaches to gender representation in cinema. My work does not fall into the category of gender studies as its purpose is not to examine cultural representations of gender. Rather, I explore Lacan's theory of sexuality by showing how European cinema offers itself as an ideal means through which that theory can be elucidated. Ultimately, my fascination with sexual difference in European cinema finds its *raison d'être* in the analysis of how Lacanian theory conceptualises the interrelation between the Symbolic and the Real, for the dynamics involved in this interrelation lead us to identify political strategies relative to our socio-symbolic sphere. This is why it is worth exploring what Lacan actually means by sexual difference.

"There is no such thing as a sexual relationship", Lacan's bombshell motto of the late 1960s, indicates that what we call "masculine" and "feminine" are each 'a specific modality of how the subject failed in his or her bid for identity which would constitute him or her as an object within phenomenal reality' (Žižek 1994: 159). Or, more precisely:

> Sexual difference is the Real of an antagonism, not the Symbolic of a differential opposition: sexual difference is not the opposition

allocating to each of the two sexes its positive identity defined in opposition to the other sex (so that woman is what man is not, and vice versa), but a common Loss on account of which woman is never fully a woman and man is never fully a man – 'masculine' and 'feminine' positions are merely two modes of coping with this inherent obstacle/loss. (Žižek 2000a, 272)

As a sexed being, the Lacanian subject designates an impasse in relation to its attempt to achieve a stable identity; ultimately, the Lacanian subject *is* this very impasse. In fact, it is only against the background of the universal deadlock of sexuality as such – the 'Real of the human animal' (Žižek 2003: 74) – that we are entitled to distinguish between masculinity and femininity. Apropos this distinction, the point to note is that man and woman, in Lacan, are split (inconsistent, "lacking") *in radically incompatible ways*. How? First of all, we should acknowledge that the obstacle to our reaching full sexual identity is none other than *the other sex*: ' "man" is that on account of which woman can never fully realize herself as woman, achieve her feminine self-identity; and, vice versa, "woman" materializes the obstacle which prevents man's self-fulfilment' (Žižek 2000a: 72–3). The Real of sexual difference, then, is predicated upon the assumption that the partner is, in its deepest configuration, a sexed other with whom all symbolic/communicative negotiations take place against a condition of fundamental impracticality, which might be concealed but not eliminated. The reason for this can be found in Lacan's formulas of sexuation (see Lacan 1998b: 78), which suggest that man relates to woman as *objet a*, the ever-elusive object-cause of desire, and woman to man as Phi, the fundamentally delusive image of a full phallic presence.

However, once we grant the radical incompatibility of these mutual constructions of the other sex, how do we account for the actual configurations of the two fields themselves? That is to say: are we authorised to surmise that, feminine fantasy aside, the masculine field is actually characterised by the phallic function; and that the feminine field, irrespective of the masculine fantasy, truly relies on radical elusiveness? The problem is that this *is* the wrong question, for the simple reason that the two fields are not autonomous and self-sufficient. Rather, as anticipated, they forge themselves around each other, coming into being *through* the sexed other. The upshot is that masculinity and femininity can only be defined as (incompatible) failures to come to terms with the gap separating subjectivity from subject, i.e. the fictional yet fully-constituted self (subjectivity) from its empty frame (subject). While man can only define himself by positing a fantasised about and libidinally-invested point of exclusion (woman *qua objet a*), woman constructs her own identity by submitting it to the phallic order. It is precisely apropos the definition of femininity, however, that we encounter the key problem, for, according to Lacan, woman (unlike man) has a chance to connect with the Symbolic *also* by "dissolving" her link with the other sex. I am referring to the crucial Lacanian theme of feminine enjoyment, which is fully unravelled in Part II of this book. Let us summarise the argument.

There are two standard ways to read Lacan's articulation of femininity within the wider question of sexual difference. The first is best represented by Luce Irigaray, who agrees with Lacan that sexual difference is ontological but claims that his conceptualisation of femininity bears witness to his own chauvinistic phallocentrism (see Irigaray 1985). The second, represented by Jane Gallop (1985), Judith Butler (1989, 1993) and others, holds that, on the one hand, gender difference is culturally/discursively constructed and therefore a performative matter, and on the other hand femininity is capable of reaching "beyond the phallus", actually embodying an external point of resistance to it. Following Žižek's critique, I argue that both these positions are misleading.

As for the first approach, it is enough to recall that Lacan's formulas have nothing to do with biology, but instead refer to sexuality in psychological terms. This also indicates that the passage from the masculine position to the feminine one (and vice versa) hinges merely on a formal shift. Thus every attempt to define sexuality as a context filled with positive/substantial features, whether in relation to man or to woman, misses the point. As for the second, more interesting, option, I argue that it overlooks Lacan's decisive account of the fact that the Symbolic and the Real over-determine each other totally.

The typical argument concerning Lacan's theory of feminine enjoyment goes as follows: since the masculine field coincides with the phallus as guarantee of symbolic authority, the feminine one bears witness to a position which, no matter how ambiguously, manages to defy the rule. While no woman is fully exempted from the phallic function, at the same time a part of her eludes it and thus potentially subverts it. Žižek's argument here is that in Lacan's formulas *no part of woman resists the phallic order*, i.e. she is fully submitted to the phallus. Woman is immersed in the symbolic order *without exception* (see Žižek 1993: 58), in other words she dissolves the exception through which man universalises the symbolic domain. It is from this theoretical perspective that I look at cinematic representations of femininity. Ultimately, if woman is "split" in a different way from man – if her subjective division is incompatible with his – it is because she embodies the possibility of the dissolution of the "knot" through which man constitutes the symbolic field and totalises its function. If masculinity sets itself up through the exclusion of a surplus object (*objet a*), in femininity the surplus is brought back where it originally belongs: in the very self-fracture of the symbolic order. Consequently, as we shall see in Part I, the reference to an ever-elusive, mysterious essence of femininity should be unmasked as a deeply delusive masculine strategy through which man seeks to assert his own position of authority. In contrast to this logic, and in a way that challenges it profoundly, woman has the chance to demonstrate to man that 'there is no Other of the Other' (Lacan 1998b: 81) – that the symbolic field is always-already inconsistent, traumatically erected upon its own lack (since the phallus in Lacan is the signifier of lack).

Taking seriously Lacan's stance on the non-biological nature of sexuality, I do not distinguish between male and female directors, but between directors who focus predominantly on the phallic position (such as Truffaut and Fellini) and directors who identify with feminine enjoyment (such as Bergman and Antonioni). Despite acknowledging the imbalance of power relations in the field of European cinema (traditionally, the majority of Europe's most influential directors are males) this book does not address the question of gender-related inequality. In fact, I prefer to argue that many of the male directors I take into consideration often manage to unravel feminine desire in such a way that it challenges the very masculine bias they are supposed to personify. As Lacan (1998b: 76) claims about feminine enjoyment, 'there are men who are just as good as women'. Ultimately, the selection of films in this book is dictated by my personal taste and not by the directors' gender, which also implies that this is not an anthological volume in any respect. The choice of post-war European cinema, finally, springs from my conviction that it represents an ideal terrain to examine the sexual relationship, if only because of its genealogical linkage with Europe's tradition of courtly love. Whatever the case, it is of course not meant to be prescriptive.

Part I
The Comfort of Fantasies

1
Sublime Objects: the Antinomies of Masculine Sexuality from Fellini to Truffaut

When the declared aim of cinema is the sublimation of woman, one can be assured that, at some point, sublimation will fail, and film will start speaking for something radically dissimilar. Directors who hide behind a reassuring fantasy screen so as to avoid confronting Woman, or sexual difference, more often than not end up producing in their films the very deadlock that had initially demanded the intervention of cinematic fantasy. In different ways, European film shows that, as a protective strategy against the nightmarish apparitions of the Real, the investment in sublimation does not necessarily pay off.

1.1 Courtly love as desiring machine

What is courtly love? It is a highly refined way of making up for the absence of the sexual relationship, by feigning that we are the ones who erect an obstacle thereto. (Lacan 1998b: 69)

Brought down to its essential, Lacan's analysis of courtly love tells us that sublimation serves the purpose of concealing the status of the Lady as "inhuman partner", an implicitly traumatic other with whom no successful relationship is possible. By elevating the object (of desire) to the status of the Thing (the uncanny Lady), sublimation obscures the inherently disturbing fact that "woman does not exist": 'The assertion "Woman does not exist" does not in any way refer to an ineffable feminine Essence beyond the domain of discursive existence: *what does not exist is this very unattainable Beyond.* [...] the "enigma of woman" ultimately conceals the fact that there is nothing to conceal' (Žižek 1994: 143). My investigation starts from the assumption that a number of highly influential European films miss Woman, in her radical Lacanian configuration, by embodying masculine desire in its sublimating mode. The idealisation of the Lady seeks to neutralise the Real of sexual difference through a substantial investment in fantasy – an operation which, as Lacan noted, 'is fundamentally narcissistic in character' (Lacan 1999: 151). However, the alternative to the narcissism of courtly love is definitely *not* the blissful enjoyment of transparent and harmonious relationships between the sexes; rather, what awaits us once we purify the relationship from its fantasy supplement is the abyss of pure subjectivity: the lack, or self-relating negativity, that pervades the Lacanian subject.

It is with regard to this question that courtly love helps us clarify the dynamics at work in cinema. Insofar as it is governed by sublimation, cinema itself is, first and foremost, an attempt to keep the Real at a safe distance. As a fantasy screen, its aim is to safeguard and perpetuate its own logic, which is the logic of desire. In this respect, European cinema can be compared to an immense 'forest of desires' (Lacan 1999: 105) rummaged by Knights vainly searching for the Lady; if the search was successful, the forest, and the Knights, would instantly burst into flames. It is to protect us from these flames that courtly love occupies such a central role in European cinema. Suffice it to add, for the moment, that the Lady from time to time *does* materialise, as in the poem by the famous troubadour Arnaud Daniel quoted by Lacan in *Seminar VII*. In this poem,

> the woman responds for once from her place, and instead of playing along, at the extreme point of his invocation of the signifier, she warns the poet of the form she may take as signifier. I am, she tells him, nothing more than the emptiness to be found in my own internal cesspit, not to say anything worse. Just blow in that for a while and see if your sublimation holds up. (Lacan 1999: 215)

As we shall see, sublimation operates on the basis of an internalised instance of prohibition which "magically" replaces the impossibility of the sexual relationship. 'The techniques involved in courtly love', Lacan tells us, 'are techniques of holding back, of suspension, of *amor interruptus*' (Lacan 1999: 152) keenly perceived as prohibitions. This is how Žižek comments on this logic:

> the aim of the prohibition is not to 'raise the price' of an object by rendering access to it more difficult, but to raise this object itself to the level of the Thing, of the 'black hole', around which desire is organised. [...] What Lacan means by sublimation [...] is shifting the libido from the void of the 'unserviceable' Thing to some concrete, material object of need that assumes a sublime quality the moment it occupies the place of the Thing. (Žižek 1994: 96)

At a fundamental level, prohibition is therefore instrumental to sub-limation insofar as it changes *impossibility* into *a ban*, thus opening up the necessary fantasy space for the introduction of the sublime object (*objet petit a*) that triggers desire and subsequently erases the instance of prohibition itself.[1] Another way of putting this is by claiming that sublimation is rooted in "symbolic castration", whose basic paradox is that 'jouissance has to be refused in order to be attained on the inverse scale of the Law of desire' (Lacan 2007: 700). Ultimately, cin-ema itself is castrated: it has to do with the Law, with the sacrifice of *jouissance* that generates desire and its attendant fantasy – since 'desire is a defense, a defense against going beyond a limit in jouissance' (Lacan 2007: 699). The 'power of sublimation', therefore, accomplishes itself 'in an imaginary function, and, in particular, that for which we will use the symbolization of the fantasm ($\$\diamond a$), which is the form on which depends the subject's desire' (Lacan 1999: 99).

The key question, as far as my method is concerned, has to do with the way European cinema negotiates the outcome of its investment in fan-tasy, insofar as the fantasy occupies that 'slope' in between 'the object as it is structured by the narcissistic relation and *das Ding*', where 'the prob-lem of sublimation is situated for us' (Lacan 1999: 98). And, from Lacan's perspective, we should bear in mind that sublimation is not merely a cultural problem, but a question of ethics.

Marcello and Viagra

As a first and classic example of the masculine ruse called sublimation, let us turn to Federico Fellini's admittedly most famous work, *La dolce vita* (1959). When, before shooting, Marcello Mastroianni (who plays the film's hero named Marcello Rubini) asked the director to see the script, he was rewarded with a stack of blank pages containing only a drawing by Fellini himself showing a man swimming in the sea. Cru-cially, this man is endowed with an enormous penis that reaches almost to the seabed, where it appears surrounded by mermaids (Faldini and Fofi 1981: 8). The symbolism is self-evident: on the one hand the lost *jouissance* of the "maternal Thing" immersed in the depths of the sea *qua* amniotic liquid; on the other hand woman as interchangeable sub-stitute (the mermaids) for the primordially lost object. This drawing reflects faithfully a central aspect of the film, since Marcello's mother is significantly absent, while the leading character is faced by potential and frustratingly unsatisfactory relationships with (at least) three differ-ent women (the mermaids). These are Maddalena (Anouk Aimée), a rich and dissolute heiress dissatisfied with life, Emma (Yvonne Furneaux),

Marcello's possessive fiancée, and of course Sylvia (Anita Ekberg), the sensual Swedish-American movie star. At different points in the film the three women present for Marcello – Fellini's alter-ego – the prospect of the relationship. The first thing to do apropos these women is to detect in each of them a specifically masculine characterisation of femininity (often labelled as typically Italian or, by extension, Latin): Maddalena is woman *qua* prostitute; Emma embodies the opposite cliché of the faithful and maternal wife; Sylvia, finally, stands for a modern version of the Lady of courtly love, the radically elusive object of desire. This splitting of woman into three fantasy projections reveals that in each case we are confronted with an act of sublimation aimed at concealing the absence of Woman, i.e. the fact that she is intrinsically an "inhuman partner" who can only be approached through fantasy. Fellini's cinema is first and foremost a testament to the power of sublimation. This is how Žižek elaborates on Lacan's understanding of the term in question:

> the Object can be perceived only when it is viewed from the side, in a partial, distorted form, as its own shadow – if we cast a direct glance at it we see nothing, a mere void. [...] the Object is attainable only by way of an incessant postponement, as its absent point of reference. The Object, therefore, is literally something that is created – whose place is encircled – through a network of detours, approximations, near-misses. It is here that sublimation sets in – sublimation in the Lacanian sense of the elevation of an object into the dignity of the Thing: 'sublimation' occurs when an object, part of everyday reality, finds itself at the place of the impossible Thing. Herein resides the function of those artificial obstacles that suddenly hinder our access to some ordinary object: they elevate the object into a stand-in for the Thing. (Žižek 1994: 95)

We set up external hindrances not just to heighten our libido, as Freud had claimed, but most importantly to create the illusion that without these hindrances the Lady would be immediately accessible. In *La dolce vita* this is exactly what Marcello's conduct reveals, especially of course in relation to Sylvia, the woman-commodity produced by the Hollywood machine. However, we should add that it is insofar as we see Sylvia through Marcello-Fellini's eyes, rather than as a Hollywood star, that she appears objectified. Indeed, Sylvia is a typically Felliniesque caricature, a product of his fantasy structured around *objet a* – where this *a*, strictly speaking, is the way her curvaceous body inscribes itself in space (the same sinuous line we find endlessly rewritten in Fellini's drawings of female bodies). The paradox involved in this logic is that, although Marcello's conscious goal is to sleep with the Lady, what he truly expects and wants from the Lady 'is simply yet another new ordeal, yet one more postponement' (Žižek 1994: 96).

We need to insist that Sylvia is deliberately characterised as an *unattainable* object. Fellini's enjoyment in frustrating his character's desire is unmistakable, as for instance in the scene when, dressed up in a nun's clothes, Sylvia runs atop (a studio reconstruction of) St Peter's in Rome, while Marcello struggles to keep up with her pace. Sylvia's lightness here is directly proportional to Marcello-Fellini's investment in sublimation. In a way that reminds us of Judy's and Scottie's run atop the San Juan Bautista bell tower in Hitchcock's *Vertigo* (1958), the libidinal economy of this scene could not be any clearer: in relating to woman, the male character has erected a fantasmatic screen which allows him to find enjoyment, paradoxically, in missing the target (with St Peter and the San Juan Bautista bell tower as obvious phallic symbols). This suggests that sublimation involves, in Lacan's reading of Freud, 'a potential mode of satisfaction of the drive', which in turn means that 'the drive is able to find its aim elsewhere than in that which is its aim' (Lacan 1999: 110).

This paradox of drive as a conservative agency instrumental to the pacifying effect of sublimation is at the heart of courtly love and, consequently, of Fellini's universe. As we shall see, however, the Lacanian drive does not stop at the entropy of sublimation. Its lesson, rather, is far more disturbing, for it not only involves the impossibility of reaching the object (desire), but also the impossibility of getting rid of *jouissance*: 'whatever we do, *jouissance* will stick to it; we shall never get rid of it' (Žižek 2000a: 293). The central ambiguity concerns the fact that desire eventually emerges as inseparable from drive as a form of destabilising enjoyment *beyond* the pleasure principle. Drive is an agency through which the subject, by pushing desire to the outer limit of the pleasure principle, seeks, in vain, to recover 'the loss of life he has sustained due to the fact that he is sexed' (Lacan 2007: 720). The impossibility of this task implies that 'the satisfaction of a drive' (Lacan 1999: 209) can only be conceived as a 'direct will to destruction', a 'will to create from zero, a will to begin again [...] *ex nihilo*' (Lacan 1999: 212). Lacan's point is that the ultimate target of drive is *loss itself*: we are profoundly disturbed by the fact that our libido gets "stuck" onto a certain partial object, and there is nothing for us to do but see ourselves condemned to circulate hopelessly around this object. Because drive implies our getting caught into the compulsion to repeat endlessly the same gesture which misses the object, it cannot but be experienced as a *curse*, a disturbing event that ruptures our inner peace – in other words, drive belongs to the register of the Real.

In spite of this concept of drive, which I shall focus on more consistently in the next section, the famous Trevi Fountain scene in *La dolce vita* should be taken as paradigmatic of Fellini's resolution *not* to risk the confrontation with *jouissance*. Differently from other instances in his work, here sublimation works perfectly as a way to preserve or even buttress the protective distance between Marcello's desire and *objet a*. When Marcello joins Sylvia inside the famous fountain, something remarkable happens: he stops short of touching her, stares at her from close distance, as if hypnotised by the ecstasy that suddenly emanates from her body... 'Chi sei?' – who are you? – is all Marcello can conjure up when faced with Sylvia's display of what has often been described as mesmerising animal energy. As made explicit in other parts of the film, Sylvia seems able to "connect" with the world in a somewhat mystical way that fascinates Marcello to the point of paralysis. On such occasions she appears transfixed, inundated or traversed by enjoyment, as if Fellini were suggesting that in her the sublime coincides with vulgar frivolity. To fully understand the problem with the Trevi Fountain scene, however, we need to focus on its religious symbolism, which explodes when Sylvia symbolically baptises Marcello with the water of the fountain. *This* is cinematic sublimation at its purest, the transformation of *jouissance* into a narrative element which, in this specific case, is designed to convey Marcello's need to redeem himself. The encounter with Sylvia's enjoyment is gentrified into an encounter with the supernatural powers of a Hollywood sex goddess who is meant to embody grace. After such a trite narrative solution, which only attests to his desire *not* to get to the core of woman, the best Fellini can do (and, indeed, he does so) is to remove Sylvia entirely from his film.

It seems to me that with *La dolce vita*, as well as with Fellini's filmography as a whole, the main question at stake is *the fear of losing the fantasy* in its illusory, protective function. Social criticism is not alien to this question, albeit in an indirect way. Fellini's cinema amounts to an unbroken attempt, at times desperate and moving, to keep desire alive, to find a way to continue fantasising in an increasingly aseptic universe. Marcello's problem is in this sense a very modern one: his loss of desire, the waning of authentic passion for life, is presented as a result of modern society's injunction to enjoy. The more he finds himself involved in the hedonistic lifestyle of his contemporaries, the more he realises that he is losing the ability to desire. If *La dolce vita* was made today, Marcello would probably take Viagra, and perhaps Fellini's sketch of the man with the enormous penis previously referred to would have to be read as a prophetic forewarning on the sad state of contemporary masculinity, with its dependence on drugs and surgery.

The very failure of the paternal metaphor in *La dolce vita* is a clear indicator that Fellini's world is constructed around the need to inscribe a gap between the subject and the object of contemplation. Marcello is deeply disappointed when he realises that even his father has fallen prey to the hedonistic appeal of the advancing consumer society. At the opposite end, Steiner (Alain Cuny), the intellectual father figure upon whom Marcello projects his hopes for higher spiritual solidarity, also fails as a paternal metaphor since he fails (to feign) to occupy a position of authority: like Marcello's real father, he is guilty of *not* setting a limit, of *not* embodying the law. Perhaps this explains why, a decade or so after making *La dolce vita*, Fellini turned to representations of fascist Italy in such films as *Roma* (1972) and *Amarcord* (1973). What we should not miss is that behind the satirical intention the tone of these films is truly nostalgic. It is not nostalgia for the fascist regime as such, of course, but, perhaps unconsciously, for the idea of law it incarnated, an embodiment of authority that might be able to awaken desire. Ultimately, however, the only law Fellini acknowledges, outside history and politics, is woman. Like the Lady in courtly love, Fellini's woman must be elusive, cruel and sublime at the same time, thus truly authoritative. By paying homage to this woman, in a constant attempt to keep desire alive and the fantasy flowing, Fellini's cinema can also be seen, in Lacanese, as a 'highly refined way of making up for the absence of the sexual relationship'.

Fantasy gaps

Given *La dolce vita*'s overwhelming reliance on the logic of sublimation, perhaps the decisive psychoanalytic question to ask is the following: where can we find the film's repressed symptom? I suggest we look for it in the final sequence, where Marcello, having participated in yet another debauched party, wanders on the beach at dawn with his decadent friends and chances upon Paola (Valeria Ciangottini), the blonde, innocent-looking adolescent he had previously met in a restaurant outside Rome, when he had likened her to an angel in Umbrian painting. The presence of this asexual, ethereal girl in a film so crammed with sexually charged atmospheres and promiscuous characters can only be symptomatic, although not in the way this term is normally intended. Far from merely standing as a metaphor of purity, the ideal of moral rectitude Marcello vainly aspires to,[2] Paola embodies the repressed truth of the three sublimated "visions" of femininity previously highlighted. More specifically, her role is surprisingly compatible with that of Sylvia, who would seem to stand at the opposite end of Fellini's personal "graph of desire". In fact, Paola's virginal appearance is paradoxically closer to the empty set of femininity upon which masculine desire inscribes itself than Sylvia's "pneumatic" body. Similarly to the *donna angelicata* (angelic lady) in Italy's thirteenth-century literary movement "dolce stil novo", she functions as *objet a*, the barely substantial "objective correlative" to the very curvature of space defining Sylvia's voluptuousness. Effectively, Paola is the neutral flat surface Fellini is left with after dispelling his fantasy of woman (Sylvia). The key feature of Fellini's representation of femininity resides precisely in the axis connecting the grotesquely caricaturised ideal of woman and the flat, dematerialised surface of genderless femininity: Sylvia and Paola are two sides of the same coin.

There are a number of examples of this logic in Fellini's work, but perhaps none is more convincing than a key event from his own biography. Is not Giulietta Masina, Fellini's wife and leading actress in several of his films, the perfect obverse of the typical Felliniesque fantasy of the voluptuous woman beyond reach that inhabits his narratives as well as his notebooks? Similarly to Paola in *La dolce vita*, Giulietta Masina is precisely *what we cannot account for through Fellini's fantasy*. Here it is crucial to introduce once again the Lacanian notion of the excluded part sustaining the whole. What if the vital strategic function of a wife who does not fully fit the husband's fantasy scenario is, as it were, to keep the latter alive by denying the possibility of its concrete realisation? What if, by marrying Masina, Fellini's secret aim was to strengthen his potential for (pseudo-)transgression in fantasy (film) without however risking the confrontation with the object-cause of desire itself, since the place was already occupied by Masina, his life-time companion? Despite playing a whore named Cabiria in *The White Sheik* (Lo sceicco bianco, 1952) and *The Nights of Cabiria* (Le notti di Cabiria, 1957), for instance, Masina is as far as possible from the Felliniesque stereotype of the prostitute. In Sam Rohdie's words: 'She is small, neither boy nor girl, slightly deranged, with the movements of a puppet, wears dresses with horizontal stripes, loses interests in a client in order to watch instead, enraptured, a fire-eater. Cabiria is not sexy, nor tarty nor seductive' (Rohdie 2002: 89). As a sexless, childlike creature, Giulietta Masina is never used by Fellini as a fantasy-object. By circumventing the fantasy, she rather occupies that limit-position where, paradoxically, the traumatic/impossible dimension of the Thing transpires. Perhaps it is here that we find the reason of Fellini's obsession with clowns: insofar as they are sexless, clowns effectively sustain his sexualised fantasy universe.

This logic is also prominent in Fellini's *The City of Women* (La città delle donne, 1980). The film opens with Snaporaz (Marcello Mastroianni) sitting on a train, staring desirously at a woman in front of him. The woman then seduces him and leads him through a series of bizarre encounters in a feminist community. At the end of the film, however, we realise that the whole narrative was nothing but Snaporaz's dream, for we see him awakening on the same train on which he was initially travelling. The detail not to miss is that the fantasy woman opposite him has now been replaced by Elena (Anna Prucnal), his wife. From a psychoanalytic angle, this means that the entire vision/dream is actually sustained by the concrete presence of his wife, and it is therefore thanks to her that Snaporaz is able to produce his (adulterous) fantasy. How, then, do we account for the fact that the content of the dream is actually *unpleasant* for the hero, since it involves a series of frustrating confrontations with groups of "hard-core" feminists? As always with Fellini, it is advisable to move beyond considerations of social or political nature. While the feminists here undoubtedly reflect a significant aspect of the changing Italian society of the 1970s, their disturbing role speaks rather for Fellini's deep-seated awareness that, if fully endorsed, masculine desire leads to a "nightmare scenario". When Fellini described Snaporaz's fantasy as 'the nightmare aspect of Guido's dream in *8½*' (in Chandler 1995: 210), he only failed to add that such a scenario of frustration, impotence, and castration, is nothing but *the other side of the masculine ideal of sexual potency*. As Lacan put it in an exemplary definition, 'the phallus – that is, the image of the penis – is negativized where it is situated in the specular image' (Lacan 2007: 697); in other words, there is no arousal without the underlying threat of castration.

The overarching point is that for all its reliance on sublimation and fantasy, Fellini's cinema cannot avoid encroaching upon that traumatic dimension where sublimation *fails*, thus revealing the difference between the logic of desire and the logic of drive. At its most radical, Fellini's cinema testifies to the disturbing awareness that *there is nothing to enjoy apart from enjoyment itself* – apart from, that is, the loop of drive in its senseless repetitiveness. The enlightening paradox of the non-sexual, virginal object at the heart of the fantasy frame that uncovers the presence of drive is also what Luchino Visconti in *Death in Venice* (Morte a Venezia, 1971) is about. Here, the problem with the distinguished composer Gustav von Aschenbach, played by Dirk Bogarde, is that his fantasy-world is at risk of collapsing *before* he sees, and becomes obsessed with, the androgynous boy Tadzio (Björn Andresen). When he arrives in Venice for a period of convalescence, he is already facing artistic, intellectual (and physical) decline. His fixation on Tadzio, therefore, would seem to amount, first and foremost, to a strategy through which he aims to recover the ability to fantasise – to rebuild his damaged identity. However, we soon realise that the plan is undermined from the very beginning, for the real (unconscious) aim of the composer's attachment to Tadzio is not to find relief in sublimation, but rather to radicalise the initial deadlock through drive. This is confirmed by a simple observation: in his asexual nature, Tadzio (like Paola in *La dolce vita*) epitomises the purely aesthetic, formal, crystallised correlative of *objet a* (which is also why it would be misleading to see Aschenbach as a paedophile). The whole film is indeed centred on the radical estrangement of the object, to the extent that it soon becomes apparent that we are dealing with the object of drive in its merciless reflexivity. If, therefore, Aschenbach is terrified at the prospect that Tadzio might perish during the cholera epidemic, it is because his death would simply materialise for him the boy's true nature as object-cause of desire: it would confirm that the boy/object is nothing but a thinly disguised correlative of the threatening void at the heart of desire. Eventually, the composer's death, as he watches Tadzio departing (notice the detail of the abandoned still camera, on a tripod, by the sea, reinforcing the idea of film as the voyeuristic art by definition), can only be explained as the outcome of his stepping into drive. He does not die because the source of his longing departs, as a romantic reading would suggest, but because *he has got too close to it*, finally plummeting into its abyss – which also suggests that we read the cholera epidemic as a subjective event, a nightmare that takes place in Aschenbach's mind. Here we are reminded of Lacan's theory of the gaze in *Seminar VII*: so intensely has Aschenbach looked at the object that the object has turned into gaze, i.e. into the void that (su)stains the visual field. In its evocation of the gaze *qua* hole, *Death in Venice* effectively realises the potential of cinema; similarly to the dead man photographed accidentally by Thomas' camera in Antonioni's *Blow-up* (1966), Tadzio is indeed one of the cinematic names for the Lacanian gaze.

Double visions

The logic of masculine desire is captured in all its clarity in *the* classic European film about sublimation, Luis Buñuel's *That Obscure Object of Desire* (Cet obscure objet du désir, 1977). Let us recall Žižek's passage quoted above, 'the Object can be perceived only when it is viewed from the side, in a partial, distorted form', since it accounts for the most remarkable feature of the film, Mathieu's (Fernando Rey) "double vision". The reason why Mathieu sees and refers to two ladies, despite chasing one, conclusively demonstrates that woman *qua* object-cause of desire does not exist; or, put differently, she exists only as a fantasy projection, the product of a distortion, *anamorphosis*:

> We are dealing here with the interconnection between anamorphosis and sublimation: the series of objects in reality is structured around (or, rather, involves) a void; if this void becomes visible, 'as such', real-ity disintegrates. So, in order to maintain the consistent edifice of real-ity, one of the elements of reality has to be displaced on to and occupy the central Void – the Lacanian *objet petit a*. This object is the 'sublime object [of ideology]', the 'object elevated to the dignity of a Thing', and simultaneously the anamorphic object (in order to perceive its sublime quality, we have to look at it 'awry', askew – viewed directly, it looks like just another object in the series). (Žižek 2001a: 149)

It is crucial to notice that Buñuel's film is told in a series of flashbacks, as this makes the logic of sublimation/anamorphosis all the more evident. By verbalising his attempted love story with Conchita (Carole Bou-quet/Angela Molina), Mathieu is forced to externalise his hallucinated perceptions of the object. In this respect, his double visions confirm that hallucination is fully constitutive of the field of desire. The very sexu-alisation of reality, which involves the passage from demand to desire, is marked by the intervention of hallucinations through which the sub-ject attempts to satisfy the impossibility of desire itself (see Lacan 1998a: 154–5).

This is indeed courtly love at its purest, for the obstacles that emerge between the male character and the Lady are created by the former, whose main fear is to actually possess the Lady: 'although the thing should be easily within reach, the entire universe has somehow been adjusted to produce, again and again, an unfathomable contingency blocking access to the object' (Žižek 1994: 95). Similarly to most of Fellini's films, *That Obscure Object of Desire* deals exclusively with mas-culine desire, providing a perfectly concise illustration of its logic. What Conchita's supreme elusiveness makes absolutely palpable (she is "hot and cold", appeasing and cruel, etc.) is endless postponement as a mas-culine strategy rewarded with the perpetuation of desire. The obvious lesson of the film is that desire is self-reflexive, *the desire to desire*.

There is, however, also a more hidden and surprising question to high-light. It concerns the analogy between the impossibility of the sexual relationship and the impossibility of class relationship. From the incipit we are reminded that Mathieu's private frustrations are redoubled as society's own frustrations. In the first sequence Mathieu is on his way to the train station when a car explodes before his very eyes in what he immediately labels a 'terrorist attack'. The film is punctuated by such baffling explosions through to its end, when another bomb goes off in a commercial centre. The role of terrorism in the overall balance of the narrative cannot fail to appear ambiguous. On the one hand it may serve the purpose of anchoring the story into an easily recognisable socio-political context (Europe in the 1970s), thus implicitly criticising the male protagonist's individualistic, bourgeois fixation; on the other hand, however, it would seem to externalise the deadlock of sexual difference onto the social sphere. The explosion that ends the film, for instance, is linked logically to the two characters' inability to find an answer to their unending struggle, as it takes place immediately after Conchita's defiant gesture of refusal when Mathieu hints at the possibility of their marriage. There is no solution, the Real of sexual difference, just as that of class difference, is presented by Buñuel as substantive and inerasable.

The same question also has a strong impact on *The Discreet Charm of the Bourgeoisie* (Le charme discret de la bourgeoisie, 1972) where sublimation is, again, Buñuel's best ally. The three bourgeois women embody, like Marcello's three women in *La dolce vita*, a selection of sublimations of Woman that might please or appease the masculine gaze. Simone Thevenot (Delphine Seyrig) plays the intelligent, cynical, modern wife who, of course, does not have any qualms when it comes to betraying her older and self-complacent husband; her sister Florence (Bulle Ogier) – excessive, impertinent, clumsy – is her explicitly transgressive double, her constitutive exception; finally Alice Sénéchal (Stéphane Audran) personifies the fantasy of woman as man-eater, eternally craving sexual pleasure. There is also a fourth model of woman in this film, represented by the revolutionary girl from the obscure Republic of Miranda. That she is too the product of masculine fantasy becomes apparent in the wonderfully crafted sequence of her confrontation with Don Rafael (Fernando Rey) in his apartment. Far from incarnating any real revolutionary potential, this feminine character stands for a caricaturised object of amusement and diversion created by Don Rafael for his own momentary titillations. He mocks her, enjoys trying to seduce her, and eventually, when he has had enough, easily disposes of her. Once again we are totally locked within the polymorphous universe of masculine fantasy.

Through a constant shifting of fantasmatic objectifications of woman, the film thus attempts to gentrify the central deadlock of sexual difference, which nevertheless remains strongly at its heart. While there is no sexual relationship between Simone and her smug husband (they even sleep in different beds), it is left to Alice to bring to the fore the *constitutive* impossibility of the relationship. I am referring to what is perhaps the most enlightening theme in Buñuel's cinema, that of 'the impossibility of satisfying a simple desire' (Buñuel 1985: 240). While this theme explodes hilariously as the main characters experience the impossibility to have dinner together, and is further depicted in their endless walk on a country road, it also emerges at the start, when the couple struggles to complete a sexual rapport. Here the narrative solution is particularly intriguing. Having invited some friends over for lunch, the Sénéchals are nevertheless busy upstairs, in their bedroom, trying to have sex. As the maid alerts them on the guests' arrival, they decide to escape furtively by climbing down the window and continue their lovemaking in the garden, behind some bushes. What is laid bare here is the motif of the "third": rather than representing an obstacle to their sexual arousal, the presence of the invitees, of their potentially intrusive gaze, works as *the necessary fantasy support to the sexual rapport*. In other words, it is only insofar as they "might be seen" that the Sénéchals manage to get aroused. The obstacle turns again into the very cause of desire.

1.2   From voyeurism to pornography, and back

In Fellini's *Amarcord* (1973), the beginning of Spring is marked by a curious ritual: a group of kids spy upon the village women as they set out on their bicycles for a day's work in the countryside. What they stare at, enraptured, are these women's generous posteriors as they accommodate themselves on the bicycle seats. In François Truffaut's first work, the short film *Les Mistons* (1958), some young boys follow the woman of their dreams, ending up sniffing adoringly the seat of her bicycle. In Fellini and Truffaut sublimation often overlaps with voyeurism, the object of fantasy coming close to serving as the proverbial fetish. To what extent are we dealing with perversion here? Let us first acknowledge that these women inhabit the same fantasy universe: they are stuck in the medieval court.

Sustainable *ménages à trois*?

The above assertion has often been contested with regard to a specific work by Truffaut, *Jules et Jim* (1962), whose enigmatic heroine, Catherine (Jeanne Moreau), has regularly been interpreted as a symbol of the gender-specific freedom that man is unable to understand or equal (see for example Insdorf 1981, 112–13). If this reading undoubtedly reflects Truffaut's own characterisation of Catherine very closely, it shares with it the fundamental illusion at the heart of courtly love: the perception of Woman as an elusive entity whose uniqueness is rooted in her imperviousness to classification, her determination not to be defined by the masculine gaze. However, Lacan's courtly love opens our eyes to the fact that this classic conceptualisation of the "eternal feminine" *is* the ultimate masculine cliché about woman, the perfect illustration of how man relates to woman by sublimating her into an almost supernatural creature. *Jules et Jim*, like most of Truffaut's films, is caught in the loop of masculine desire, which is *the desire to keep desiring woman*. This is why nothing would satisfy Truffaut except the heroine's final suicide by water – already attempted when she jumps into the Seine – for such a "beautiful death" ratifies her inviolability, securing her place into a Kantian universe where the only chance we have to connect with the Absolute, the Thing-as-such, is via the sublime. As a formidable force of nature, Catherine epitomises the transcendental lure embedded in the Kantian sublime.

At the core of Truffaut's ambition with *Jules et Jim* there is an intriguing hypothesis which in many ways anticipates some of the concerns raised by the soon to come sexual liberation movement. As Truffaut himself explicitly stated (see Gillain 2005: 82; Ingram and Duncan 2004: 64), the premise to his film regards the potential redefinition of love ethics on the basis of an understanding of the relationship that might be liberated from possessiveness and jealousy. As Jim (Henri Serre) tells Catherine, 'you want to invent love from the beginning' – which essentially implies contemplating the sustainability of a *ménage à trois*. However, it seems to me that *Jules et Jim* is less about experimenting with the possibility of alternative love ethics than the refusal to confront the intrinsic impossibility for the couple to attain full autonomy. What if the true trauma voiced by the film does *not* concern the failure of the experiment as such (a love triangle where two friends end up sharing the same woman *and* remain best friends) but rather the disavowed awareness that $1 + 1 = 3$? This is precisely what Žižek claims apropos the lovemaking scene in Orson Welles' *The Immortal Story* (1968), where the rich and old merchant Charles Clay, played by Welles himself, sets up a love encounter between his wife Virginie (Jeanne Moreau) and Paul (Norman Eshley), a young Danish sailor, and then eavesdrops on them in the dark:

> here we have the Third Gaze as the ultimate guarantee of the sexual relationship. That is to say, it is the very presence of the silent witness

who listens to the couple making love that transubstantiates what is ultimately an encounter between a paid sailor and an aged prostitute into a mythic event that transcends its material conditions. [...] The silent witness, far from intruding in an intimate situation and spoiling it, is its key constituent. (Žižek 2000a: 287)

A consideration that follows naturally from this example concerns pornography. Could we not argue that pornography is based on the real-isation of the *myth* of the accomplished sexual relationship insofar the sexual act is *explicitly* sustained by a third gaze (the spectator's)? The key aspect of pornography can be grasped by turning around the standard interpretation of voyeurism: it is not so much that two (or more) are mak-ing love and, *in addition to that*, a pervert looks at them from an external position; rather, the gaze of the pervert is always-already included in the picture, to the extent that without it there would not be any sex at all:

The illusion, of course, is that without this intruder one would obtain 'full sex' [...]. The true enigma of pornographic sexuality lies in the fact that the camera not only does not spoil *jouissance*, but enables it: the very elementary structure of sexuality has to comprise a kind of opening towards the intruding Third, towards an empty place which can be filled in by the gaze of the spectator (or camera) witnessing the act. (Žižek 1997: 178)

With regard to *Jules et Jim*, what prevents it from becoming a porno-graphic film is precisely Truffaut's attempt to conceal the fact that the third is the necessary supplement that sustains the "healthy" functioning of the couple. Nevertheless, I can hardly resist the temptation to claim that it remains potentially formidable porn material: with only a few touches, any screenwriter could easily turn it into a pornographic film. The basic problem with *Jules et Jim*, then, is that it ignores the intrinsic lesson of pornography in the name of an idealistic and ultimately con-trived attempt to celebrate – albeit nostalgically, as a failed attempt – the freedom of the human spirit. The poetic élan of the film is the director's worst enemy. Truffaut's portrayal of Jules's (Oskar Werner) placid accept-ance of Jim's relationship with his wife Catherine, fails to highlight the necessity for the voyeuristic position of the third (Jim, but also the rest of Catherine's lovers) as that which lends the couple at least a semblance of compatibility. In short, what Truffaut fails to say (just like Henri-Pierre Roché, from whose novel the film was adapted) is that in real life Jules would be a pervert.

The finale, with Catherine driving to her death with Jim, cannot but appear highly suspicious. Is not the suicide of this sublime and amoral *femme fatale* a convenient solution aimed at nourishing the masculine cliché about the unfathomable nature of femininity (and, at the same time, the equally worn-out stereotype about the mysterious correspondence between femininity and art, since Catherine is repeatedly likened to a Greek statue)?[3] If we apply Lacan's lesson, we should realise how Truffaut's fascination with the "eternal feminine" is often at risk of tipping over into masculine patriarchal ideology. Despite the focus on the Jeanne Moreau character, in fact, it is the representation of the two males' camaraderie and the inconsequential uncovering of the space occupied by fantasy (Jim *qua* third) that achieves centre-stage in the narrative. From this angle, it is evident that the theme of the three characters' project of "love in friendship" works as a way to obfuscate the disturbing awareness that, deep down, we always "do it" for the Other, for a disavowed third gaze.

One of the most entertaining illustrations of the centrality of fantasy in cinema can be found in a scene from Lina Wertmüller's Holocaust tragicomedy *Seven Beauties* (Pasqualino settebellezze, 1975). Towards the end of the film, Pasqualino, a small time Neapolitan crook, convinces himself that his survival in the concentration camp depends on his ability to seduce the sadistic and repulsive Nazi officer in charge of the camp. The problem is that she takes him on: she will spare his life only if he manages to have sex with her. After a first, embarrassingly failed, attempt, he instinctively realises that to succeed in the ordeal he needs to close his eyes tight and reminisce scenes of seduction and arousal from his past. Overall, his strategic recourse to fantasy works, except for those comical and yet traumatic instances when the huge woman pulls up Pasqualino's eyelids by force, informing him that, as a real lover, she wants to look him straight in the eyes. Here, very explicitly, the rapport *needs* fantasy.

Amongst his various examples on this subject, Žižek often refers to a paradox concerning masturbation: if masturbation is fantasy about real sex, real sex is nothing but masturbation with a partner. The paradox is meant to demonstrate that fantasy is consubstantial with sex, i.e. that *there is no sex without fantasy*, since it is the insubstantial screen of fantasy that makes real sex possible. Thus, what is normally regarded as the most authentic and spontaneous experience through which human beings can feel as One, is exposed as a divisive dimension that relies on a "third" immaterial intruder: 'any sexual pleasure that we find in touching *another* human being, is not something evident but inherently traumatic, and can be sustained only in so far as this other enters the subject's fantasy-frame' (Žižek 1997: 65). Lovers, in other words, are never alone; they always hang on to a minimum of fantasmatic narrative. It is difficult here to resist mentioning Žižek's fairly tasteless but accurate joke about the peasant and Cindy Crawford. Following a shipwreck, a poor peasant finds himself stranded on a desert island with Cindy Crawford. After having sex with her he tells her that his satisfaction would be complete if only she could do one last thing for him – could she dress up as his best male friend, even drawing a nice moustache on her face? Despite fearing that the poor peasant is a hidden pervert, Cindy Crawford decides to comply with his request. So after she has dressed herself up as a man, the peasant approaches her, elbows her lightly in the ribs and tells her, with an obscene smile of male complicity: "You know what just happened to me? I had sex with Cindy Crawford!" Since in psychoanalysis truth resides in exaggerations, the joke tells us that this imaginary friend is the necessary intruder that makes the relationship possible, a fantasmatic gaze which also 'belies the ideal of hedonism – that is, it introduces the moment of reflexivity on account of which unspoilt innocent private pleasure is never possible: sex is always minimally "exhibitionist", it relies on the gaze of an Other' (Žižek 1997: 179).

The status of this Other comes explicitly to the fore in the most intriguing sequences of Truffaut's *The Man Who Loved Women* (L'homme qui aimait les femmes, 1977), namely the ones concerning Delphine (Nelly Borgeaud). A married woman and by far the most hysterical of Bertrand Morane's (Charles Denner) numerous lovers, Delphine insists on having sex in "dangerous" places where the couple are potentially exposed to other people's gazes (in shops, at work, etc.). Belying the romantic myth of the loving couple's enclosed and self-sufficient universe, this passage suggests that the status of the couple is always implicitly "perverse". This idea is indeed confirmed later on when Delphine, having been released from prison after attempting to kill her husband, pays a secret visit to Bertrand whilst he is in bed with Bernadette. Instead of exploding in a violent fit of jealousy (which, given the character's passionate nature, the spectator expects) Delphine takes the opportunity to invite herself to a *ménage à trois*. Truffaut suggests that in prison Delphine has matured ('I changed a lot in prison [...] When you are locked up all day, then you know what is important and what isn't. [...] It's wonderful not to be jealous anymore'), and yet such a transformation tells us less about the director's new sensitivity towards independent women than about his strategy regarding sexual difference. The impromptu *ménage à trois*, an apparently light-hearted and inconsequential narrative solution, works as a symptomatic knot exposing the truth about *Jules et Jim*: what we have here is effectively an allusion to a classic pornographic situation.

Love can only be staged...

The ending of *Pocket-Money* (L'argent de poche, 1976), probably Truffaut's most overt celebration of childhood, emphatically confirms the above point whilst encouraging further analysis. I am referring to the first innocent kiss exchanged by young Patrick and Martine, which optimistically signals the beginning of their relationship. The extraordinary construction of this apparently simple sequence is worth some attention. Patrick, one of the young protagonists, meets his peer Martine during a summer camp. The two kids develop a mutual attraction but, due to their shyness, do not find the courage to confront it, until something precipitates the events. One day all the children are grouped together in the refectory, girls on one side and males on the other. When Martine leaves the room to go to the toilet her girlfriends decide to play a prank on her and hasten to tell Patrick that she is waiting for him outside so that they can kiss undisturbed. At first Patrick ignores the advice but soon after he leaves the room. Once outside, however, the two kids miss each other and Martine returns to the refectory alone. At this point Patrick's male friends play the same trick on her, alerting her that Patrick is waiting outside for a kiss. This time the stratagem works: the two young lovers finally meet, kiss each other, and timidly return to the room together, welcomed by general cheering and a thunderous applause.

The theme of the artificial "staging" of love encounters, with the added bonus of the "stolen kiss", is indeed one of the most recurrent and significant *topoi* of Truffaut's cinema. It tells us that Truffaut refuses to represent the relationship as a spontaneous encounter between two individuals. Instead, this encounter is referred to as *artificial*, as the consequence of a certain *explicit* manipulation of the normal course of events introduced by the narrative. Something similar happens half way through Aki Kaurismäki's *The Man Without a Past* (Mies vailla menneisyyttä, 2002), when M (Markku Peltola) "steals a kiss" (on the cheek) from Irma (Kati Outinen) by way of the "you have something in your eye" expedient.[4] As with Truffaut, the aim here is to introduce a deception that gentrifies the Real dimension at work in sexual difference. Another example of this logic can be found in the passage of *Mississippi Mermaid* (La Sirène du Mississippi, 1969) where Marion (Catherine Deneuve) records her love message to Louis (Jean-Paul Belmondo); the disc, however, is never delivered as it slips from her hands and is shattered under the wheels of a passing car when Marion leaves the recording studio. This disc also reminds us of Truffaut's fondness of pop music. In *The Woman Next Door* (La femme d'à côté, 1981), for example, he has the broken-hearted Mathilde (Fanny Ardant) claim that 'songs tell the truth... the sillier, the truer they are', which in turn brings us to the most unequivocal cinematic illustration of this point, Alain Resnais' *Same Old Song* (On connaît la chanson, 1997). In a way reminiscent of Jacques Demy's *The Young Girls of Rochefort* (Les demoiselles de Rochefort, 1967), the characters in Resnais' film suddenly burst into singing lines of well-known French popular songs to convey their deepest emotions with regard to their troubles with the other sex. The non-existence of the sexual relationship, in other words, is magically sublimated into music. In what is perhaps the most significant of these musical breaks, Claude (Pierre Arditi) rehearses Serge Gainsbourg's classic 'Je Suis Venu Te Dire Que Je M'en Vais', determined as he is to leave his wife Odile (Sabine Azéma). However, as he is about to sing his message to his wife, she starts sobbing in relation to another incident, and Claude can do nothing but reassure her, suddenly realising that he still loves her. The charm of this passage resides in the fact that music for once *fails* to neutralise the sexual deadlock, while love, the "miracle of love" (see sub-chapter 3.7) intended as the unexpected encounter between two frail and deeply wounded human beings, *triumphs*.

The lesson to learn from all this is that for Truffaut, as for most great European directors, cinematic fiction *is not enough*. Instead of moving in the direction of naturalism, however, Truffaut raises the stakes, *increasing his investment in fiction*. First we have the invisible artificiality of cinema, which creates a seamless realism eliciting audience identification; then this realism is broken by a second, overt reference to staging, whose purpose, however, is not to denounce the intrinsic artificiality of the cinematic act, but rather to elevate the fictional dimension to a higher, loftier ground where "love happens". Like "woman", "love" is treated by Truffaut as a supremely sublime event that *can only be staged*, immortalised in the big Other of fiction. In *Pocket Money*, Patrick and Martine desperately need the intervention of the big Other (their friends' stratagem) to fulfil their mutual attraction. If it is clear that this external agency is actually Truffaut himself, here celebrating his own childish creativity, we should not overlook the impact of this reference to the third *qua* external gaze. As Lacan would have it, the ultimate fantasy does not lie in fictional representation, but in the gaze itself. The unconscious lesson of the film is that this gaze (the children, the director, the child-director) *in itself does not exist*, it is simply an imaginary point of view fantasised about by the couple in their effort to achieve a degree of consistency and self-awareness. When Žižek claims that every relationship is always minimally exhibitionist, he means precisely that it relies on a gaze that exists only insofar as we secretly desire to submit ourselves to its scrutiny. In this respect, if every fictional couple has its real director, the opposite is also true: *every real couple has its fictional director.*

1.3 Burning fictions

Truffaut's insistence on the conflation of love and artifice provides the measure of his understanding of the couple. Every time in his films two characters attempt to establish a relationship, they either fail miserably or depend on the mediation of a third denominator, which, ultimately, is nothing but fiction itself, the domain of self-relating artificiality. This is perhaps nowhere more evident than in the final sequence of *Fahrenheit 451* (1966), when hero Montag (Oskar Werner) and heroine Clarisse (Julie Christie) establish a new relationship in the outlaw community of book-people (people who have "become books", i.e. have memorised entire books and named each other after their titles to dodge the ban on literature decreed by the central government of a futuristic totalitarian society). As with all great directors, this reference to artifice remains truly ambiguous: if it may be said to voice Truffaut's own fear of confronting sexual difference, it also stands for his intuition that life itself is structured around a fictional core. This, as anticipated, is particularly true of Truffaut's views on women and love. In *The Man Who Loved Women*, for example, Bertrand writes a book about the countless women he has conquered, thus sublimating the impossibility of the relationship into a narrative act – which is precisely what Truffaut does with his cinema.[5] The ultimate cinephile, he tells us that love is so intense and magical an experience that it can only be referred to as fiction – but a fiction that, in the flickering glimmer of its illusion, can be *more real than ordinary reality*. The gap separating life from film already belongs to life itself, and cinema has a chance to evoke it as life's sublime core. When we say that Truffaut really believed in the magic of cinema, we need to add that he believed in cinema's potential *to elicit the truth of fiction*. His representation of love as sheer, luminous artifice would seem to confirm Jean Epstein's famous quip that love on the screen 'contains what no love had contained till now: its fair share of ultra-violet' (in Abel 1988: 242).

Let us take as another case in point *Confidentially Yours* (Vivement dimanche!, 1983), Truffaut's last film. The key to this underrated work, a Hitchcockian love story camouflaged as noir, is the "oddness" of the relationship between the Jean-Louis Trintignant character (Julien) and his secretary (Barbara), played by Fanny Ardant. As Julien, an estate agent, is suspected of killing his unfaithful wife and her lover (the spectators themselves are tricked into believing Julien to be guilty by the way Truffaut edits the initial murder sequence), Barbara, the secretary he has just sacked, inexplicably decides to take upon herself the onus of the investigation into the murders. Repeatedly putting her life at risk, she uncovers Julien's dead wife's double identity as well as the hidden existence of a prostitution racket linked to her name. Eventually the heroine unmasks the real murderer in the figure of Julien's lawyer, and the film ends with her happily marrying her former boss. The major displacement onto which the film is grafted, in a move which is largely typical of film noir, is the fact that the richness and complexity of the narrative (this is Truffaut's only true action film) clearly hinges on the constant postponement of the two characters' sexual relationship. Put differently, this breathtakingly adventurous crime story functions as the sublimated libidinal substance of the mutual attraction Julien and Barbara convincingly repress throughout the film, until the mystery is solved – only then are they entitled to have sex. Similarly to what Žižek argues apropos the TV series *The X Files*, the point is that everything happens "out there" because nothing happens between the two main characters (see Žižek 2000a: 367–8). The burning question of sexual difference is here happily displaced onto a furiously paced narrative crammed with exquisite twists – and the point is that 'there is signification precisely because there is an excessive, nonsignifiable, erotic fascination and attachment: the condition of possibility of signification is its condition of impossibility' (Žižek 2004: 97).

The same strategy is at work in Truffaut's second film, *Shoot the Piano Player* (Tirez sur le pianiste, 1960), another narrative reflecting on the impossibility of sexual relations whilst camouflaging this central preoccupation through an overt reference to genre, Hollywood gangster movies. This is why the charm of the film is in its details (its symptoms), those dialogues and brief passages which cannot fail to appear redundant in terms of plot development and, simultaneously, betray the director's true enjoyment. An example of this is the memorable song "Avanie et Framboise" – sang in the film by Boby Lapointe, a real-life Parisian pop singer – which refers cheekily to a woman's breasts. Or, arguably the film's best dialogue, the sexist conversation between the two gangsters in the car, after they abduct Charlie (Charles Aznavour) and Lena (Marie Dubois): 'Watch the road instead of looking at girls!', 'If I kill someone I'll avenge my father, who was run over when, whilst crossing the street, he was looking at girls', 'Your father was a dirty old man!', 'I'm proud of him. I always manage to look at girls when the wind blows, lifting their skirts... Women, they all want it. I'm not against women, I love them for what they are. Trouble is, you have to talk to them beforehand, and especially afterwards, when you want to leave'. At this point Charlie ends the conversation with the following afterthought: 'If I'm allowed, my father used to say about women that when you've seen one, you've seen the lot'.

The significance of these vulgar remarks is more subtle than we might assume. What if, instead of merely voicing Truffaut's ironic representation of macho gangsters, they actually aim (unconsciously) to connect with the disavowed surplus of the masculine position *tout court*, the fact that man's relationship to woman necessarily relies on a minimal degree of objectification? And, following Žižek's argument against today's ideological attitude of Political Correctedness, what if it is only a daring (and yet humorous) mobilisation of the stupid masculine clichés about woman that may lead to a meaningful connection between the sexes? Truffaut seems to be aware of this logic, for as soon as Charlie makes the final remark, the four inside the car, including the woman (Léna, Charlie's fiancée), burst out laughing, as if acknowledging the worthlessness and stupidity of the sexist fantasy they have just tapped into. As Žižek claims, the same strategy of directly confronting the disavowed, obscene fantasy may also function as the best antidote against racism. The problem with today's PC attitude towards sexually or racially charged expressions is that instead of eliminating the offensive effect it actually enhances it by transferring it on to a disavowed fantasmatic plane. By trying to purge certain words from their surplus of aggressivity, the PC attitude forces us to amass aggressivity at the level of obscene fantasy, which then is bound to return, or explode, in the Real of psychotic racist/sexist behaviour. One of the ways out of this double-bind predicament is to risk the direct confrontation with the repressed fantasy.

Back to *Confidentially Yours*. As with *Shoot the Piano Player*, the film's merit, and a measure of Truffaut's genius, is to be sought in those apparently secondary passages where the Real of the relationship surreptitiously breaks through the narrative. If the final marriage is an intrinsically false but necessary addendum that offers the key to understanding the disavowed significance of the noir narrative, the crucial moment is perhaps the sequence, half-way through the film, where the two protagonists for the first time suddenly embrace and kiss. What makes this "stolen kiss" so unmistakably Truffautian is, again, its ostensible artificiality, since it is not directly dictated by romance but serves the purpose of protecting the couple's identities (especially Julien's) whilst in a situation of sudden danger (their kissing allows them to elude the police – an expedient also deployed at the beginning of *Jules et Jim*). Again, we should risk reading this self-referential passage against the postmodern grain. What if instead of merely working as a narrative expedient, it relates to an impossible/Real moment of love that can only materialise insofar as it is anchored in a third, decentred dimension? This interpretation would reverse the standard reading: the explicit inauthenticity of the kiss, its non-spontaneous, even opportunistic scope, actually stands for a symptomatic concretion of authentic *jouissance* necessarily sustained by the gaze of a fantasmatic Other. From this viewpoint, the complex narrative is itself the fantasy scenario that the couple rely on to sustain their relationship. That is to say, once again, $1 + 1 = 3$. These observations provide an insight into Truffaut's proverbial reluctance to show sex scenes. Lovemaking is practically absent from his vast filmography, and in this sense *Confidentially Yours* confirms the rule. When, once the mystery is about to be solved, passion between Julien and Barbara explodes, their lovemaking is only alluded to as the final shot is suddenly dissolved. The couple's marriage provides a happy ending also in obscuring the Real of sexuality.

Truffaut's tendency to displace (and thus neutralise) the sexual deadlock onto a fantasy screen that explicitly exposes its own artificiality is evident in the majority of his films. If *Day for Night* (La nuit américaine, 1973), a prototypical film about filmmaking, constantly mixes life and fiction, with the problematic love stories off screen effectively reflecting the narrativised ones, perhaps the most obvious illustration of this metacinematic inclination comes from the final sequence of *The Last Metro* (Le dernier métro, 1980). A film on a French theatre company during Nazi occupation, *The Last Metro* focuses on yet another love triangle between Marion Steiner (Catherine Deneuve), the actress who manages the theatre; her Jewish husband Lucas Steiner (Heinz Bennent), who is said to have fled to South America but in fact directs the play from the theatre cellar where he hides; and Bernard Granger (Gérard Depardieu), an actor whom Marion falls in love with and who decides to join the French Resistance. The despairing love lines recited by Marion at the end of the film, after the Liberation, first appear to be addressed to Bernard, who by then has returned to Paris and re-joined the company. However, the slow backing movement of the camera reveals that she is actually on stage, acting, addressing *a character* played by Bernard. Despite the distancing, alienating effect, the result is nevertheless ambiguous, since her words appear painstakingly real, referring us back to the impracticability of her relationship with Bernard.[6]

1.4   Beyond *amour fou*

In Truffaut, one of the most interesting cases of displacement can be found in *The Story of Adèle H.* (L'Histoire d'Adèle H., 1975). Here for once the standard situation is reversed: it is woman who desires and idealises man, elevating him into Φ, the Lacanian mathem symbolising phallic authority. The first thing to note is, again, Truffaut's explicit reliance on the "third" of fiction. From the start he tells us that the film's source is the really existing diary written by Adèle Hugo, Victor Hugo's daughter; however, the ultimate evidence for the story's truthfulness (as well as its "histories", as in the French title) works simultaneously as an indicator of its fictionality, for the film's most explicit feature is the artificial character of Adèle's (Isabelle Adjani) world – since from her point of view everything is distorted by her obsession with Lieutenant Pinson (Bruce Robinson), the British officer she is besotted with. Adèle follows Pinson from France to Halifax, in Nova Scotia, and then to Barbados, ignoring the fact that her love is unrequited and consequently a humiliating affair. During her travels, Adèle progressively contracts into her private, solipsistic universe, writing memoirs as well as a number of letters packed with lies to her parents in France. The status of this reflexive gesture (writing) is of the utmost importance if we are to penetrate the real purpose of Adèle's obsession, for it displays a deeply narcissistic character. Her fixation with Pinson, in other words, is synonymous with a desperate attempt to cover up the true trauma of her life, which concerns her relationship to her father, at that time regarded as the greatest writer in the world. Annette Insdorf (1981: 132) has rightly emphasised how '[t]hrough her feverish transmutation of life into literature, increasingly less connected to reality, she finally lives only to write'. And later:

> we should realize that Pinson is merely a pretext for Adèle's story. Her relationship to her father, on the other hand, is more complex and emotionally troubling. In refusing his repeated offers of love, for which she hungered when she was younger, she asserts her freedom from his powerful presence and her own need for it. (Insdorf 1981: 138)

The role of literature is therefore eminently ambiguous: on the one hand it inscribes a protective distance between the heroine and her object of desire; on the other hand, it points to the deepest, unconscious kernel of enjoyment that defines Adèle, i.e. her attachment to her father. By falling in love with Pinson and reporting the fictional story of her idyllic relationship with him to her father, she aims to gain a distance from her unshakeable fascination with the father himself. Ultimately, the heroine's aim is to become Adèle H., where the famous surname is eclipsed, reduced to the initial. Truffaut acknowledges that "liberation hurts": Adèle achieves freedom from what she is most attached to through an act that implies a psychotic "passage through madness". The fact that, in "real life", she never recovered from this madness (she spent the last 40 years of her life in an asylum) should be taken as testament to the terrible risk implied in "choosing freedom".

The theme of feminine self-destructiveness returns powerfully in Truffaut's *The Bride Wore Black* (La mariée était en noir, 1968), where the murder mystery is simply a pretext to conceal the non-existence of the sexual relationship. The sublimation at work here is double: first we have Julie Kohler's (Jeanne Moreau) idealisation of David, the man of her life since childhood, which leads to their marriage; then, after the husband's accidental death on the day of their wedding, the bride morphs into five different forms of *objet a* so as to break into the private lives of the five men who caused David's death. The result is that by playing on her ability *to read the other's desire* she is able to coldly eliminate these men one by one, thus avenging her husband. The exploration of woman's ability to "bank" on her own sublimation in order to achieve what is, ultimately, her self-destructive aim (for she cannot live without David) is the film's most intriguing motif. Julie's masquerading provides excellent examples not only of man's idiotic dependence on *objet a*, but also, more crucially, of woman's strategic investment in the seduction game, which, at a fundamental level, allows her to mobilise that self-relating negativity which *drives* her to shun the human laws. This is no minor consequence, for it turns her into a *vraie femme*, a woman who, motivated by her drive, achieves the suspension of the law.

What strikes us about the Moreau character, in a much more compelling way than apropos her role in *Jules et Jim*, is her barbaric embracing of what we might risk calling divine violence. She is indeed "beyond the good" – beyond, that is, the economy of goods sustaining the pleasure principle. Her being borders dangerously on the barrier that separates the subject from the Thing, a barrier Lacan calls 'beauty':

> The true barrier that holds the subject back in front of the unspeakable field of radical desire that is the field of absolute destruction, of destruction beyond putrefaction, is properly speaking the aesthetic phenomenon where it is identified with the experience of beauty – beauty in all its shining radiance, beauty that has been called the

splendor of truth. It is obviously because truth is not pretty to look at that beauty is, if not its splendor, then at least its envelope. (Lacan 1999: 216–17)

Truffaut, as always, employs all his resources to disguise the uncomfortable content of his "comedy". Nevertheless, there is little doubt that Julie epitomises *something different from use value*, something thoroughly unserviceable which, ultimately, coincides with *jouissance* and occupies that 'position of criminal good' that Lacan assigns to Antigone (Lacan 1999: 240). Julie's indifference to the human laws signals that she has died to herself, and therefore entered that psychotic space where nothing matters (she has nothing to lose) except the execution of the plan.[7] It is this strange coincidence of action and passivity *qua* blind subjection to drive that allows her to accomplish a real act – the act as a result of which the masculine economy of desire appears suspended, suddenly rendered ineffectual. Displaying the same stubborn inscrutability we admire on Isabelle Adjani's face in *The Story of Adèle H.*, Julie Kohler is able to wear so many interchangeable masks because she has relinquished her attachment to the self. Her fantasy – and consequently her identity – concerns her bridal status; once her husband dies she undergoes subjective destitution ('I died the day David died'), first attempting suicide and then turning her rage against the five men indirectly responsible for her downfall. We should not overlook that Truffaut describes these five bachelors as 'only interested in hunting and women'. The point not to miss is that Julie's murderous fury is not merely directed at these men *qua* careless hunters, negligent users of rifles, but rather to men *qua* hunters of women. The film's central metaphor, hunting, tells us that Julie's target is masculine fantasy *tout court*, the male's gender-specific way of organising the sexual relationship. Only through this reading are we able to access the unconscious rationale behind Julie's act, for what she aims at disturbing through her homicidal rage is, in the final analysis, the repressed knowledge that David himself, the incarnation of Prince Charming in her fantasy framework, was also a man.

Contrary to what the explicit narrative line leads us to believe, then, Julie's revenge is not an over-sentimental case of *amour fou*, but an act of over-identification with the Real impossibility of the sexual relationship. By eliminating the five men, in other words, Julie unconsciously liquidates her attachment to David, implicitly conceding that her own idealised relationship *would also have been fraught with the burden of sexual difference*. Julie's drive enables her to fully accomplish the work of mourning; it is not simply that after killing the last man she has avenged her lover, but that at that point she is relieved of the pressure exercised by the fantasy of the idealised husband.

As far as the hunting metaphor is concerned, we should consider the film's most captivating episode, the one involving Fergus, the painter. Clearly functioning as Truffaut's alter-ego, Fergus is played by Charles Denner, the same actor who stars in *The Man Who Loved Women*; like him, he is an unrepentant womaniser. When he tells Julie about his habits and tastes on the subject of women, he immediately adds that he fancies them all *apart from her*, the one woman he had always dreamt of painting ('Now you know I'm a skirt-chaser. But don't worry, you're in no danger. You're not my type'). In fact, he had already "seen" her, as he demonstrates by producing her portrait and quoting Oscar Wilde's motto that 'nature imitates art'.[8]

What is explicitly at stake in the "Fergus episode" is Truffaut's ambivalent take on sublimation. To be sure, the fact that Julie already existed in Fergus' imagination testifies to the logic of courtly love, i.e. masculine sublimation of woman through art (as he is painting Julie's portrait, Fergus tellingly comments: 'Your nose is remarkable. And your mouth… If I were a writer, I'd write a novel about it'). Painting functions here as the typically Truffautian reference to art through which the male character postpones the encounter with the threatening (indeed, lethal) Thing (he even paints her on the wall next to his bed). As we often find in Truffaut, however, the very *image* of woman also tends towards the Real object. Precisely because Julie is defined by her drive – her fixation on bringing the plan to completion – her status can only be rendered as fictional, illusory. Or, differently put: insofar as she inhabits the Lacanian "space between the two deaths" – i.e. she has already "died to herself", she wanders through the scenes like a ghost – she can only be caught as a fleeting image. Thus, the void effectively embodied by Julie's psychotic fixation can only be rendered as the vacant expression of her *painted* face, the same face we see at the beginning of the film, in the credits sequence, *printed* on the newspapers used by the police to identify her. Identification works through fiction, literally. In Lacan, the deepest dimension of the subject (the unconscious) corresponds to the most superficial one, *her image*. Ultimately, this is why Fergus had already painted Julie's portrait: the image of substanceless subjectivity she stands for precedes identity *qua* process of subjectivation.

An example of a Truffaut film where, on the other hand, feminine enjoyment remains foreclosed is the previously mentioned *Shoot the Piano Player*. Here the male in question, Charlie, embodies to perfection the logic of courtly love and the falsely nostalgic or melancholic tone that accompanies it. Everything about him is narcissistic, from his timidity to his piano playing. The central reference to music, which works in the same way as Truffaut's usual allusions to literature or painting – i.e. as a smokescreen protecting the character from getting too close to the loved object – is indeed equivalent to the use of lyrical poetry in the medieval court: it turns woman into an impossible object of desire so as to avoid the shock of the encounter with her. Although Truffaut wants us to identify with his hero's unfortunate fate, Charlie's failures in love are actually part of a narcissistic strategy through which he can continue playing the piano and desiring women – let us remember that the film ends with Charlie back at the bar, sitting at his piano, with a new waitress introduced to him.

We need therefore to acknowledge the role played by Charlie's unconscious. If the emotional focus is the tragedy of a man who indirectly causes the deaths of his female lovers – first Theresa and then Lena – we can only reconstruct the whole story by adding that Charlie *unconsciously wants these women to die*. Charlie's problem is not fate, but the over-proximity of the other *qua* woman he loves. Romanticism here deflects our attention from the quandary of the sexual deadlock. What the hero is unable to face is the loved woman's *jouissance*, which is also why the only unproblematic sexual relationship he has is with a prostitute. Incidentally, Truffaut's tongue-in-cheek reference to censorship in the scene where Charlie is in bed with the prostitute (her breasts are shown and immediately covered up by Charlie who claims "this is what they do in the cinema") goes much deeper than we might think. The real aim of Charlie's gesture is once again to conceal *objet a*'s true core, re-inscribing the object into a logic of desire that might still fool us into believing that it hides *something* instead of *nothing*. Truffaut is a master in concealing the inconsistency of *objet a*.

1.5   Les femmes sont magiques...

'Women are magical' is what the murderer poetically claims at the end of *Confidentially Yours*, after the Fanny Ardant character, Barbara, brilliantly uncovers his plot. Given the strength of the feminist movement in the 1970s, Truffaut's compulsion to represent femininity as object of the male gaze inevitably attracted criticism. However, in *Confidentially Yours*, Truffaut's last film, the Fanny Ardant character cannot fail to appear as a very modern *femme fatale*, one which would seem to have read at least a few pages of Kristeva, Cixous and Irigaray. Her emancipated status is confirmed by the active role she plays in the narrative, a situation echoed very closely by the Deneuve character in *The Last Metro*. These two films may be said to be emblematic of a change in Truffaut's representation of femininity, for woman in them is not only emancipated but also the driving force in the narrative, whilst her male companion is relegated to a passive if not static function. Just as Julien in *Confidentially Yours* remains hidden in the backroom of his office for the entire duration of the film, so is Lucas, in *The Last Metro*, confined to the dark refuge underneath the theatre where Marion plays her fictional roles. Whilst this can to an extent be seen as a sign of Truffaut's adjustment to the expectations of contemporary audiences (he was always extremely sensitive to his public's reactions), I claim that ultimately such reversals of roles do not modify but confirm his overall view of femininity – the one, say, that emerges in as early films as *Jules et Jim* (1962) and *The Soft Skin* (La peau douce, 1964).

The first observation to make is that the figure of the autonomous woman who refuses to submit herself to masculine scrutiny was already present in his first works. Let us recall Franca Lachenay (Nelly Benedetti) unleashing her murderous fury against her unfaithful husband at the end of *The Soft Skin*; or Catherine's superior awareness and command of the narrative situation in *Jules et Jim*. Secondly, what goes missing in the argument according to which Truffaut responds positively to the changing role of women in contemporary society is that despite being presented as more autonomous individuals, his "liberated" women do not manage to sever their link to *objet a*. This is proved by a simple observation about *Confidentially Yours* and *The Last Metro*: both Julien and Lucas, in their respective masculine roles, occupy the classic position of the voyeur. Despite their passivity, they effectively provide the point of view with whom the audience is encouraged to identify. The paradox is that even if Truffaut's females are depicted as strong, active, even dominant, their activity fulfils a single purpose: to fascinate the masculine gaze. Put differently, *they remain magical creatures*.

If there is an exception to Truffaut's obsessive treatment of femininity as embodiment of *objet a*, perhaps we find it in the character of Geneviève Bigey (Brigitte Fossey), the editor from *The Man Who Loved Women* who decides to accept Bertrand's autobiographical manuscript for publication. Annette Insdorf (1981: 143) argues that

> she is a professional and, therefore, liberated woman, [...] she articulates the liberated vision of relationships between the sexes. While sharing Bertrand's appreciation of the game that is part of love, she is aware that 'the rules of the game' are in the process of changing: 'And

what will disappear first is force. The game will always be played, but equally'. [...] She fulfils her theory by her action, which is to 'play' tenderly with Bertrand.

Two questions arise here: (1) the debate concerning the extent to which the ultimate aim of the feminist struggle for emancipation effectively means adjusting to the masculine vision of social relations and competing with man for power; (2) the extent to which Geneviève actually differs from other Truffautian women. While Truffaut's homage to the feminist movement seems confined to what today we would call the struggle for equal opportunities – i.e. a struggle that does not challenge the masculine foundations of the social order as such but strives to adapt to it – on second thoughts this strategy cannot but appear suspicious if we look at it from the Lacanian perspective on sexual relations. What if Truffaut's emphasis on the degree of control exercised by Geneviève in her relationship with the fickle womaniser is nothing but a way to elude once again the question of the sexual deadlock? My point is that conceiving the relationship as a "play" between emancipated, enlightened individuals (Geneviève's position) is aimed at concealing the critical imbalance between the sexes, the fact that every relationship emerges within a regime of power relations. In Lacan, this imbalance is inerasable, for the simple reason that 'to be human means precisely to be differentiated along the lines of sexual difference':

> The Lacanian thesis is that while sexual difference, in the specifically human sense, cannot be understood in biological terms, neither can it be understood as a simple symbolic difference – as in John Gray's book *Men are from Mars, Women are from Venus* (i.e. from different symbolic universes). The point is that sexual difference is something that is co-substantial with universal humanity. There is no neutral definition of the human being without a reference to sexual difference. What defines humanity is this difference as such. (Žižek and Daly 2004: 81)

The act of repression that neutralises sexual difference clearly foregrounds a film like *Claire's Knee* (Le Genou de Claire, 1970), by Truffaut's contemporary Eric Rohmer, where the sophisticated friendship between womaniser Jérôme (Jean-Claude Brialy) and female writer Aurora (Aurora Cornu) is represented as a transparent, honest intellectual exchange devoid of sexual complications. What one should highlight is that the very unfolding of the storyline, which centres on Jérôme's attraction to teenage girl Claire, depends on the foreclosure of the liaison between

Jérôme and Aurora. In other words, what is missing is the crucial twist at the heart of Stephen Frears' *Dangerous Liaisons* (1988), where the refined "alliance" between Vicomte de Valmont (John Malkovich) and Marquise de Merteuil (Glenn Close), both members of the French aristocracy in the *ancien régime*, *does* turn into the nightmare of a vicious power struggle between the sexes. As for Truffaut, then, we may suggest that in celebrating the magic of women he often *fails to go all the way down the road of magic*, thus falling prey to the typically masculine stereotype about femininity that Lacan consigns to the tradition of courtly love. This reticence has importance consequences.

1.6   Virgin or whore? Yes, please!

In *The Bride Wore Black*, David (Serge Rousseau), one of Fergus' friends, warns him thus: 'Remember what the Italians say: all women are whores, except the mother, who's a saint'. Despite their attempts at avoiding the deadlock of sexual difference, directors such as Fellini, Buñuel and Truffaut as a rule fail to provide a representation of woman that might challenge the standard masculine fantasy. The most evident proof for this failure is their recurrent recourse to the splitting of woman into virgin and whore, generally regarded as a central feature of Latin masculinity. Beyond the stereotype, this splitting is to be regarded as part and parcel of the strategy previously highlighted concerning the necessity of the "third". The reference to whore *qua* third is what allows the male hero to sustain his relationship to the virginal wife, to woman insofar as she has been made unavailable to others, withdrawn from socio-symbolic circulation.

   In Fellini's *I vitelloni* (1953), for instance, Fausto (Franco Fabrizi) marries the innocent and naïve Sandra (Leonora Ruffo) but is unable to give up his old philandering ways. Especially memorable is the sequence where he attempts to seduce a *femme fatale* type in a cinema while seated between her and his wife, who in the meantime remains glued to the screen and completely unaware of her husband's impromptu performance. This provides a concise visual exemplification of Fellini's splitting of woman into the faithful wife and the promiscuous lady, a strategy which is perhaps at its clearest in Buñuel's Mexican film of the same period, *Ascent to Heaven* (Subida al cielo, 1952). Here the hero, young newly-wed Oliverio (Esteban Màrquez), is forced to interrupt his wedding night to embark on a perilous bus journey to meet a lawyer who may notarise his dying mother's will. Amongst the many dangers encountered during the journey, the most worrying for the hero is embodied by

Raquel (Lilia Prado), a predacious (and surprisingly modern) young woman who is determined to "get what she wants", i.e. to sleep with Oliverio. Despite his laudable, uncompromising rejection of his seductress, whom he genuinely seems to find irritating, Oliverio eventually succumbs to her licentious charm and betrays his wife.

As anticipated, this surreal and playful parable on the helplessness of male sexuality when faced by the feminine temptation is completed by the presence of the hero's dying but authoritative mother. In a decisive passage, she appears to her son in a dream, *approving of his infidelity*, as if to confirm her role as *the* woman in his life. The measure of Buñuel's genius is that he does not hesitate to add mother to the series whore-virgin, thus drawing the Oedipal question into the equation. The masculine splitting of woman into virgin (wife) and whore (lover), he tells us, is sustained by the figure of the mother, whose pervasive allure in the subject's fantasy functions as an obstacle to his achievement of a successful relationship, whilst simultaneously asserting the Oedipus myth as a safety net, a reassuring illusion that *he is being loved*.

Pasolini's *Mamma Roma* (1962) goes a step further in this direction by problematising the Oedipus myth, or else by bringing it to full fruition. In Pasolini's second film the central female character, nicknamed Mamma Roma (Anna Magnani), is both a protective mother and a prostitute: she is indeed a mother who also embodies an idea of promiscuity which eventually proves too much for Ettore (Ettore Garofolo), the son. A typically Pasolinian Roman sub-proletarian youth, Ettore develops an illness and eventually dies (in prison) after discovering that his mother is not quite the respectable working-class woman she strives to be, but a prostitute. The knowledge about the mother's real occupation, that is to say about her (obscene) enjoyment, proves to be lethal for the son, whose symbolic world suddenly crumbles (disease and death are Pasolini's usual ciphers for loss of symbolic consistency as well as moral corruption). The film's merit lies in the way it exposes the basic repression that sustains the masculine illusion of a "normal" relationship with the other sex: a man conceives all other women as sexually available (at least in principle) only on condition that one of them remains excluded, unavailable, off-limits. This woman is of course the mother (with the additional bonus of the sister), and we need to add that it is alongside her example that the type of the "virginal wife" emerges.

Problems therefore arise once the mother is perceived as sexually promiscuous, or even simply "active", for at that point the son comes face to face with the nucleus of illicit enjoyment that allows him to acquire and retain a sexual identity *only insofar as it remains foreclosed*.

As in Ettore's paradigmatic case, the knowledge of the mother's enjoy-ment has catastrophic consequences on the son's sexual balance. Despite the explicit socio-political content of *Mamma Roma*, centred on Pasolini's customary denunciation of social mobility (the sub-proletariat being pro-gressively co-opted by petit-bourgeois, consumerist ideology), what is perhaps more interesting to discuss is the *jouissance* the film manages to disturb through its Oedipal subtext. *Mamma Roma* powerfully sug-gests that the son's discovery of the mother's *jouissance* corresponds to his identification of 'incest as the fundamental desire', the desire which 'structures man's unconscious' (Lacan 1999: 68).

Going back to *Ascent to Heaven*, the first thing to do, as with *That Obscure Object of Desire*, is to recall that the splitting of woman into vir-gin and whore (in her unabashed promiscuity Raquel reminds us of the Conchita character played by Angela Molina in Buñuel's last film), is nothing but the product of male sublimation, insofar as through fantasy man compensates for the non-symbolisable status of the other's desire. As Žižek (1997: 31) succinctly puts it, 'fantasy is the screen by means of which the subject avoids the radical opening of the enigma of the Other's desire'. We may add that there is something both tragic and unavoidable about masculine vulnerability vis-à-vis woman. Fellini and Buñuel seem to be aware of it, for characters such as Fausto and Oliverio, in their fun-damental *frankness*, suggest that there is no easily available alternative to phallic *jouissance*: they are condemned to relate to woman by missing her, i.e. by producing fantasmatic distortions of femininity. The same dis-tortions make up the core of Truffaut's cinema, as is confirmed by another case of Hitchcockian doubling, this time concerning the Deneuve char-acter in *Mississippi Mermaid*. Here the heroine is suspended between an atemporal ideal of purity and the raw image of a female dominated by base and undignified instincts. The fantasy of Louis Mahé (Jean-Paul Belmondo) reflects to perfection Truffaut's desperate attempt to come to terms with Woman. First he constructs an entirely fictional image of his ideal bride (Julie Roussel) through the letters and photos he exchanges with her; then he falls for Marion Vergano, a cold-blooded prostitute who, with a male accomplice, had eliminated Julie before Louis could meet her, taken her place as his bride, and drained his bank account. What we should note is that Julie and Marion, despite their opposite roles, are both paradigmatic fantasy images of woman, whose main func-tion is to protect the masculine identity from encroaching upon the traumatic core of feminine desire. Thus, Mathieu's double vision in *That Obscure Object of Desire* and Louis' inability to distinguish between two different women in *Mississippi Mermaid* are one and the same thing.

Those critics, especially feminist ones, who detect in Fellini, Buñuel and Truffaut a "phallocentric" vision of the world are therefore by and large right. Despite their efforts to convince us otherwise, these directors remain largely dependent on the understanding of woman as *objet a*. What (feminist) critics as a rule do not acknowledge, however, is that this view of femininity ultimately reflects the tragic awareness that the sexual deadlock is inerasable. Far from simply amounting to an unreflected sexist position, it testifies to the encounter with the trauma of sexual difference.

One of the European films that most movingly and understatedly sanctions this logic is Fellini's *Ginger and Fred* (Ginger e Fred, 1986), where Amelia (Giulietta Masina) and Pippo (Marcello Mastroianni), two elderly tap dancers, resoundingly demonstrate how the impossibility of sexual relations accompanies the couple through their physical decay, until the very end of life. Typically, Fellini's melancholic gaze mitigates the traumatic impact of this awareness. The dimension of social critique here (Fellini's rage against the wild proliferation of private TVs in 1980s Italy, peppered with a thinly-disguised reference to TV-tycoon Silvio Berlusconi) functions more than ever as an external mechanism aimed at partly neutralising the explosive fact of sexual difference. The most appealing aspect of the film is that these two ex-dancing-partners and ex-lovers, now reunited to take part in a TV variety show, manage to confess their mutual love – and therefore briefly affirm the viability of the relationship – only on the dance-floor, i.e. during the actual performance of their "Ginger and Fred" act in front of TV cameras. Here we have again the Lacanian view that the Real (of the sexual relationship) can only emerge, fleetingly, in fiction, for it belongs to the symbolic/imaginary order rather than to what would be a truly deceptive "Real beyond fiction". One of the meanings of Lacan's 'les non-dupes errant' is precisely that the Real is consubstantial with the illusionary realm of fictions, and that the truly foolish thing to do is to behave as if we are not being fooled, to believe that we are not going to be "duped".

In Fellini's film the couple's participation in the TV show retains a complex significance, for their performance is initially brought to a halt by a sudden black-out which plunges them into complete darkness. It is exactly in the darkness of the TV studio, when the artificiality of its "apparatus" is momentarily suspended, that they find the courage to talk about love. It seems to me that the sudden interruption of the show is not to be read as the inscription of an autonomous space "beyond the plague of fictions", where the characters are able to freely articulate their feelings; rather, it points to the radical alienation of fiction itself, the "dark core" of appearances where reality dissolves into the Real. Perhaps the film's main weakness is that it does not show any true awareness of the regenerating potential carried by this traumatic "moment of truth": after the show, the two characters re-inscribe a distance between each other, relegating once more their mutual affection to the realm of fantasy. This would seem to confirm that melancholy, in Fellini, prevails over the acknowledgment that *loss* is *lack* (that the object is always-already lacking). What matters to the director is the melancholic fantasy that provides the attachment to the primordially lost/impossible object – in this case, the other as partner in a "successful" relationship.

In *Ginger and Fred* the comforting function of fantasy is wittily epitomised by Pippo's relentless attempts to fashion vulgar rhymes expressing, in his own words, 'the rapport between masculine desire and the feminine object' – such as, for example, 'chiappa rotonda, fava gioconda' (round cheeks, happy dick). The truth-content of these attempts at symbolising lack materialises in the film's musical theme, which, in its compulsive repetitiveness, cannot but remind us of one of Robert Bresson's key stylistic features (let us only recall the obsessive whining of horses in *Lancelot du Lac*, 1974). The sinister, nightmarish ring of this musical motif reveals the immense fragility of Fellini's fantasy-universe, piercing through its delicate balance and leading us directly to its repressed frightening core.

Another important aspect of Fellini's "phallocentrism" that may be used to its defence is that it involves a desperate attempt to erase its point of inscription, the very masculine compulsion to reduce woman to an object of fantasy. This retroactive effort is particularly striking in *Fellini's Casanova* (Il Casanova di Federico Fellini, 1976), a film that more than any other reflects the director's awareness of the catastrophic impasse in which masculine sexuality is caught. Despite the habitual moments of humour, the series of erotic adventures of the Venetian philanderer, played by Donald Sutherland, assume a deeply morose tone verging on the tragic. The main theme is *the repetition of drive*, a Sadean-like compulsion to reiterate endlessly the mechanical gesture of lovemaking, a gesture that does not imply any intimate exchange or meaningful contact between man and woman, but proves man's tragic failure to overcome his solitude. This point is confirmed by the voyeuristic dimension in which Casanova's lovemaking is often immersed. When making love with Maddalena (Margareth Clementi), the French ambassador's mistress dressed as a nun, or the Marquise d'Ufré (Cicely Brown) – or, even more blatantly, when he engages in a lovemaking contest in Rome – Casanova is deliberately performing a show for a third gaze, which (as in the case of Ginger and Fred dancing for the TV cameras) confirms that "there is no such thing as a sexual relationship".

The terrible sadness of the film has to do with this profound awareness, which emerges indisputably and yet delicately in the wonderful final sequence. By now old and working as a librarian in Bohemia, Casanova has a dream of his native Venice where some women appear and then quickly vanish. The only one left on the frozen lagoon is Rosalba (Leda Lojodice), the mechanical doll he had met (and seduced) years earlier. He approaches her and they start rotating slowly, rigidly, until the end of the film. The brief dance with the doll works well as an intimation of Casanova's own death, whilst also reminding us of the central motif of sexual difference. The director's awareness is also his character's awareness, insofar as Fellini's Casanova knows that he can only seduce *shadows of women*, not woman. The mechanical doll provides a perfect correlative for this knowledge: woman for Casanova exists only if reduced to an object (*a*). And yet, perhaps it is precisely as *objet a*, as a soulless, thing-like doll, that the standard masculine objectification of woman may miraculously turn into something else, something paradoxically closer to the core of the subject vindicated by femininity. What if, instead of working as a misogynist stultification of woman's human potential, the image of the mechanical doll clarifies the controversial Lacanian insight into the non-existence of Woman – the notion that it is woman, and not man, who has a chance to evoke the deepest, empty core of the subject as such, against the humanist belief that "deep down" there is something uniquely affirmative about each of us? Fellini did not make a mystery of his dislike for Casanova, and as many critics have advised it is sensible to read in this aversion for the unrepentant womaniser a degree of pent-up anger against himself – or, rather, against his inability to conceive of woman in terms which might disprove the standard masculine perspective. In this case, if behind the mask of Casanova there lurks Fellini himself, the difference between anger and affection could be seen as negligible, just as the reduction of woman to *objet a* might lead us to an unconscious recess of Fellini's mind where the way to the other's emptiness, negativity, or *jouissance*, is also a (traumatic) way to freedom.

1.7   The other as voice and gaze

As we have seen, the cinemas of Truffaut and Fellini (amongst others) epitomise to perfection the paradox of the detour at the heart of courtly love. The cinematic *inventio* is itself founded on a formal instance of sublimation, which in many European directors makes itself available through their compulsive framing of woman as object of desire. The authority, or muse, these directors pay homage to is *objet a* in its supreme ambiguity, for *objet a* gives body to varying degrees of sublimation, different ways of concealing the traumatic emptiness that sustains desire: 'The place of the Lady-Thing is originally empty: she functions as a kind of "black hole" around which the subject's desire is structured' (Žižek 1994: 94). What unites a surprisingly high number of classic European films is, effectively, a mechanism akin to the Freudian "Fort Da": a continuous movement *towards* and *away from* woman as *objet a*, a movement comparable to the oscillations of a pendulum. Let us take Antoine Doinel in Truffaut's *Stolen Kisses* (Baisers Volés, 1968). Paradoxically, he can only relate to Christine (Claude Jade) and especially Fabienne (Delphine Seyrig) by moving away from them, by hiding behind love letters and phone calls; when alone with them, on the contrary, he freezes, runs away, or proves himself awkwardly inarticulate. The point is that, like the hero of Balzac's *Le Lys dans la vallée*, with whom he associates at the beginning of the film, Antoine is narcissistically attached to the idealised impossibility of the relationship, thus failing to experience it as Real. The repressed truth of his cynicism returns in two different aspects of his life: first, it effectively allows him to fantasise about "the woman of his dreams" (Fabienne), and second, it opens up the space for unproblematic sex with prostitutes.

The trap to avoid, then, is once again the Romantic myth of courtly love. Instead, we need to recognise the unconscious desire that inhabits the gaps separating the explicit text from its metaphorical meaning: in truth, there is nothing Antoine fears more than a Lady who might yield generously to his desire, which means that he desires neither Christine nor Fabienne, but desire itself – or, put differently, he aims to steer clear of the other's *jouissance*.

If in Truffaut's narratives we tend to move away from woman in order to be able to fantasise about her, there are rare but highly significant moments in Fellini's cinema where sublimation explicitly fails to deliver the goods: the idealised object, as it were, implodes, unmasking the masculine ploy in its hyperbolic impotence. Perhaps none of these examples is more appropriate than that of the midget nun in *Amarcord*, who embodies *objet a* in all its inconsistency, devoid of its fantasmatic support. I am referring to the passage where uncle Teo (Ciccio Ingrassia) climbs up a huge tree and shouts his irresistible, disconcerting 'Voglio una donna!' ('I want a woman'!). Although we are aware that uncle Teo is insane, what resonates in his desire is a question that has to do with the essence of Fellini's cinema. After many failed attempts from members of his family to get him down the tree, it is left to none other than a midget nun, whose face we never see, to successfully accomplish the task. The obvious question is: why does *she* succeed? Why does uncle Teo tamely and willingly obey *her*? Here, the standard explanation does not suffice, since the purpose of the sequence is not merely to indict the repressive power of the Catholic Church, symbolised by the miniaturised nun. Rather, the passage uncannily tells us how Fellini's obsession with femininity is sustained by a reference to a traumatic kernel of foreclosed knowledge operating as an irresistible injunction. More precisely, uncle Teo's docile behaviour vis-à-vis the nun shamelessly reveals that woman *qua* object-cause of desire is – once stripped of all the fantasy invested in her – a cruel, soulless Lady-Thing.

Particularly enlightening here are two details: first, the nun's face is completely hidden under her hat, and second, her voice is strangely derealised, fast-forwarded into a noise (Fellini's regional dialect) we can hardly understand. In short, her physical presence is reduced to a voice that acquires a nearly autonomous status, independent of the body it originates from. In fact, it is not so much the content of the nun's words, but the *sound* of this voice that functions as a partial object for uncle Teo. To Fellini's credit, the sequence provides another example of the extent to which he was aware that woman as object-cause of desire is homologous to a dehumanised injunction.

Let us briefly consider three more examples of Fellini's use of voice as love object. For the first, we need to go back to another key sequence of *La dolce vita*, where Maddalena speaks to Marcello in an echo chamber of the aristocratic palace in Bassano di Sutri. The effect is truly uncanny, as Marcello, unable to locate Maddalena, is kept in check by her voice, aroused by its disembodied, incorporeal quality. The second is often referred to as the "orgasm sequence" from *The City of Women*, when Snaporaz wanders into the villa of Dr Katzone (Ettore Manni), a name that translates roughly as "Big Cock" (*cazzone* in non-Germanicised Italian). Here he walks along a corridor surrounded by screen images of all the women his counterpart Katzone has conquered. As he switches the TV sets on, photographs of these women appear, each supplemented by recordings of their sighs of pleasure the moment they were seduced. At the end of the arcade, however, he finds none other than his wife Elena who, spitefully, presses a button which turns on all the devices at once, filling the room with innumerable voices of sexually aroused women. Unlike the episode in *La dolce vita*, where voice is used as an expedient to arouse desire, here the final "overlapping effect" captures nicely the shift from desire to the excess of *jouissance* mobilised by drive, as enjoyment effectively turns into an unpleasant experience for the hero. As a third example, there is the central reference to voice in *And the Ship Sails On...* (*E la nave va...*, 1983). The entire film is structured around the missing figure of Edmea Tetua, the "greatest opera singer of all times", whose death is commemorated by a number of celebrities who board a luxury liner to reach the island of Erimo and there disperse her ashes. A supreme case of sublimation, Edmea's voice sums up Fellini's relationship to woman in all its ambiguity, as is made explicit during the funeral rite, when Sir Reginald (Peter Cellier) recollects what the singer had once told him:

> You always talk about my voice, but at times I'm almost certain it's not my voice at all. I'm pure voice, a diaphragm, a breath, and I don't know where the voice comes from. I'm only an instrument, a mere girl who's even afraid of this voice, which for all my life it has forced me to do what it wanted me to.

It is here that we encounter the autonomous status of the voice as a traumatic partial object, something which is *in me more than myself*. Implicitly traumatic is the fact that voice as object of desire brings about the subject *qua* Real of *jouissance*, unmasking us for what we truly are, knots of excessive, non-symbolisable enjoyment. The whole of Fellini's film is constructed around this hard kernel of *jouissance*.

Apropos the unmasking of enjoyment, one is reminded of the beginning of the first vignette in Max Ophuls' *Le plaisir* (1952), when a young dancer collapses to the floor after a series of wild acrobatics at a party. As he examines him, the doctor realises he is wearing a plastic mask, behind which the face of a decrepit old man is revealed. What is unmasked here is precisely the subject of drive, the very *jouissance* that ultimately coincides with the mask itself: the old man *is* the mask he wears.[9] Like Fellini and Truffaut, Ophuls constantly sets up hindrances between his cinematic gaze and woman. The correlation between his camera and *objet a* is best described by the stylistic cipher of his cinema, the tracking shot. One example above all: the wonderful depiction of the brothel in *Le plaisir*'s second vignette, all shot from outside, with the camera gliding elegantly yet compulsively from window to window, attempting to get a glimpse of a sight that could not be endured for too long. The voyeurism involved here is without a doubt the voyeurism of the mechanical eye of the camera, which signifies that we are beyond the human, beyond the condition of sexual excitement pure and simple; rather, what is invoked is, again, the dimension of drive (more precisely, scopic drive), Freud's *konstante Kraft* (constant force), which Lacan refers to in *Seminar XI* (see Lacan 1998a: 164 and 181). Significantly, when the brothel reopens after a brief period of closure, the village literally comes back to life. Again, Ophuls' camera is outside, excluded and yet buzzing like a bee around the brothel *qua* sublime concentrate of *jouissance*.

2
Ethics of Drive: Beauty and its Enjoyment from Rohmer to Pasolini

Insofar as it is has a chance to articulate the dynamics of drive within the sexual relationship, cinema provides evidence for Lacan's argument that the domain of ethics is defined by the endorsement of "headless" enjoyment, that terrifying frontier where all is decided. In the seven sections of this chapter I identify filmic narratives exploring the connection between drive and jouissance. *Drive is not only unravelled as a direct endorsement of explosive enjoyment, but also as a formal gesture which is both imperceptible and absolutely decisive for the symbolic reconfiguration of the filmic text.*

2.1   Terrifying beauty

The burden carried by male fantasy is engraved in the title of one of Eric Rohmer's masterpieces, *La collectionneuse* (1967), the third from his six "Moral Tales". The woman at the heart of the drama is Haydée (Haydée Politoff), one of the purest, most refined products of male fantasy in European cinema. What is unmistakable in Rohmer's first colour film is the unbearable libidinal energy generated by the sheer presence of this bikini-clad, bronzed, apparently ordinary girl, who every night sleeps with a different man without any specific reason, simply following her inclination. The film opens with a silent sequence of the protagonist walking alone on a beach, seemingly self-absorbed. The camera pays homage to its muse, lingering on the girl's tanned body, on her face partly covered by her brown hair. Contrary to the typical female in Rohmer's talkie films, Haydée is almost inarticulate. Rohmer's decision to render her as a self-confined, elusive, and yet self-sufficient being cannot but strike us as unusual. Haydée looks through things, in a way that reminds us of some memorable lines from Rilke's eighth Duino elegy:

> The creature gazes into openness with all
> its eyes. But our eyes are
> as if they were reversed, and surround it,
> everywhere, like barriers against its free passage.
> [...]
> We never have pure space in front of us,
> not for a single day, such as flowers open
> endlessly into. Always there is world,
> and never the Nowhere without the Not: the pure,
> unwatched-over, that one breathes and
> endlessly knows, without craving. As a child
> loses itself sometimes, one with the stillness, and
> is jolted back. Or someone dies and is it.
> Since near to death one no longer sees death,
> and stares ahead, perhaps with the large gaze of the creature.
> Lovers are close to it, in wonder, if
> the other were not always there closing off the view...
> As if through an oversight it opens out
> behind the other...But there is no
> way past it, and it turns to world again.
> [...]
> But its own being
> is boundless, unfathomable, and without a view
> of its condition, pure as its outward gaze.
> And where we see future it sees everything,
> and itself in everything, and is healed for ever.

In Haydée's vacant gaze we find this 'Nowhere without the Not', an absence, an apathetic promiscuity, always threatening to turn into enjoyment. As with Rilke's creature, there is no real craving in her, only the outward gaze of unreflected life. Along these lines, Adorno wrote that 'the expression called human is precisely that of the eyes closest to those of the animal, the creaturely ones, remote from the reflection of the self', referring to those types of women for whom Oscar Wilde coined the idiom 'unenigmatic Sphinxes' (Adorno 2005: 169–70). Although her male counterpart sees her as an active seductress, a cynical collector of lovers (or a whore), what truly bothers him is her unenigmatic and yet inexplicable passivity, her mute giving in to fate.

The narrative emphasis is placed on the male character's moral dilemma. Adrien (Patrick Bauchau) is a solemn intellectual who, as the standard Rohmerian situation has it (at least in the Moral Tales), is torn between temptation and moral obligation. When he accepts to share the St Tropez villa with the unknown temptress, his vow is that he will remain faithful to Mijanou (Mijanou Bardot), his girlfriend, who is spending the summer in London. Adrien's problem is how to come to terms with Haydée's *jouissance*. His solution is, typically, sublimation: he places a series of hindrances between himself and the girl in order to gentrify the enigma of her desire. For example, he wilfully accepts being reduced to the humiliating position of the voyeur rather than confront the consequences of his own desire, as when he convinces Haydée to spend the night with an art collector, a wealthy friend of his. As made explicit in his freind's Daniel's following monologue, these desperate tactics are truly symptomatic of the masculine fear of Woman, of the trace of void encapsulated in her *jouissance*:

> What fascinated me was your insignificance. I don't even think you're ugly. What attracted me to you was a certain trace of ugliness in your face, in your gaze. There you can be moving. But when you're pretty, or lovely, then let me laugh! You represent the lowest, most degraded and absent stage of beauty.

This passage betrays the true stakes of masculine desire, insofar as the Lacanian object-cause of desire is, in its deepest connotation, an objectively insignificant feature that suddenly starts bothering us. What attracts us in the other is precisely the disturbing presence of an uncanny detail (a tic, a facial expression, the sound of one's laughter, etc.) which stands for the other's *jouissance*, the specific way in which she structures her enjoyment. To describe Adrien's predicament we could call into question the 'strange malaise' defined by Lacan with the German word *Lebensneid*:

> *Lebensneid* is not ordinary jealousy, it is the jealousy born in a subject in his relation to an other, insofar as this other is held to enjoy a certain form of *jouissance* or superabundant vitality, that the subject perceives as something that he cannot apprehend by means of even the most elementary of affective movements. Isn't it strange, very odd, that a being admits to being jealous of something in the other to the point of hatred and the need to destroy, jealous of something that he is incapable of apprehending in any way, by any intuitive path?

[...] Now we have reached the frontier. What will enable us to cross it? (Lacan 1999: 237)

If this is the frontier of *jouissance* brought about by drive, Adrien's fate depends on how he decides to position himself towards this surplus of enjoyment which he is increasingly drawn towards despite consciously despising it as a case of moral corruption. The conclusion to this dilemma is revealing. As he is driving back to the villa with Haydée, he finally admits to himself (in voiceover) his attraction for the girl, and even plans to spend with her the final week of his holiday. However, on the way they meet two friends of Haydée's who invite her to join them for a trip to Italy. She gets out of the car and hesitates, whilst Adrien lights a cigarette. There we have the turning point: as he is moving his car forward to let another vehicle pass through, he simply continues driving, without the girl. His words are emblematic of the Kantian imperative at the heart of Rohmer's moral universe: 'for the first time I felt I was making a real decision... I was asserting my freedom. I enjoyed my victory, which I ascribed to myself alone and not chance or merit. I felt overwhelmed by a wonderful feeling of independence and total self-determination'. And yet, as soon as he enters the big villa, now empty, he is overcome by anguish, cannot sleep, and eventually phones the airport to book a flight to London, where he will join his girlfriend.

This finale is ambiguous. Is Adrien's decision equivalent to a moral choice that, despite initially causing him distress, effectively affirms his self-determination and integrity? It seems to me that behind Adrien's sudden gesture, by which he chooses "to lose" Haydée, there is simply the need to safeguard the balance of the pleasure principle. When he drives away, we realise that he is truly terrified at the prospect of confronting directly the object-cause of desire. What scares him is that he has, as it were, run out of obstacles, of detours. It is not so much that the hero is afraid of falling in love and losing his self-control; what truly concerns Adrien is the prospect of *not finding anything* behind Haydée's enigmatic persona, nothing but the lack that sustains his desire for her insofar as it is determined by the enigma of her desire. And yet, this is the closest Rohmer has ever got to evoking Kant's moral law, provided we read the latter with Lacan, i.e. as an instance of excessive enjoyment.

If the story of *La collectionneuse* had continued, we would have probably found ourselves in Rohmer's next and more famous work, *My Night at Maud's* (Ma nuit chez Maud, 1969, the fourth moral tale), where in the famous final sequence by the beach Jean-Louis (Jean-Louis Trintignant), by then a few years into his marriage with the blonde, Catholic Françoise (Marie-Christine Barrault), again meets Maud (Françoise Fabian), the effervescent (non-practising) Protestant brunette with whom he had had an unconsummated fling at the time of his first encounter with his future wife. As he bumps into Maud, Jean-Louis's sudden bafflement – which alone infuses the entire film with meaning – appears more than legitimate, for he realises what he did not consciously know: that his decision to marry Françoise was nothing but a stratagem to avoid Maud (the Lady) – or, in other words, a way to keep Maud alive in his fantasy as the real object-cause of desire. Maud, like Haydée and many other Rohmerian heroines, is a *spectre* that exists only insofar as she is kept at arm's length by the male hero. If she came too close, she would vanish, or turn into an unpleasant sight. The distance she relies on in order to be seen is explicitly affirmed in the very intimacy Jean-Louis and Maud share in the key sequence of the film, the one of the winter night they spend in Maud's flat. Indeed, they come so close to each other as to share the same bed, and yet there is only distance between them. It is here that we understand the significance of Rohmer's idiosyncratic recourse to dialogue. Words – Jean-Louis' endless panegyric about Catholicism when in bed with Maud – are Rohmer's favourite way of rendering the necessity of procrastination: the hero talks incessantly, in neurotic fashion, betraying the fact that he wants to keep the Lady at a safe distance.

The final of the six moral tales, *Chloe in the Afternoon* (L'amour l'après-midi, 1972), is still secretly centred on Rohmer's sublimation of woman. Again, it works as a perfect follow up to *My Night at Maud's*, for at the start of the film Frederic (Bernard Varley), the hero, is already married. His ordinary life in Paris is regulated by rituals which revolve entirely around family and work. He spends his time between his office, where he works as a lawyer, and his home, which he shares quietly but warmly with his virginal wife Hélène (Françoise Varley), an English teacher, and their baby daughter. Rohmer focuses at once on the key element that allows for such a balanced existence: Frederic's fantasy. When on a train or in a crowd, Frederic confesses, in the usual Rohmerian voiceover, that marriage "closes him in", and that he often feels the need to escape. This is why he cannot stop fantasising, to the extent that he daydreams of possessing an amulet that gives him full control over women in the street, whom in his imagination he takes advantage of. What needs to be remarked is that it is through these "transgressions in fantasy", these habitual and well-planned frissons, that he is able to endure the fundamental boredom of his life. Far from providing a true form of escape, fantasy is what keeps the hero within the limits of the world he would like to flee. By making that world minimally bearable, fantasy is the invisible bolt that "closes us in", making true change a chimera.

Until Chloe (Zouzou), the Lady, re-enters Frederic's world, we can safely say that there is a perfect correspondence between the hero's marriage and his half-hearted fantasies of promiscuity. Until, that is, Chloe, an old friend, walks into Frederic's office, upsetting the delicate balance between duty and fantasy (see the two secretaries in their miniskirts) which makes work bearable. Chloe's first address to Frederic is exemplary: 'You look at me as if I were a ghost. Did you think I was dead?' As the film progresses, we realise (once again) that the female protagonist – this free-spirited, fully emancipated and decidedly promiscuous young woman – is indeed nothing but a ghost, an apparition whose aim is to *increase Frederic's investment in fantasy*. Despite the hint at women's lib through the independent and assertive character of Chloe, the film is unmistakably drenched in male fantasy. At one point during their regular afternoon rendezvous, Chloe, who is determined to seduce Frederic, tells him: 'since you're a bourgeois, act like one: stay married and cheat on your wife. It's a safety valve. It would be good for you, if taken in moderation'. What such an exemplary statement does not account for, however, is the fact that, in a way, Frederic *is already cheating on his wife* (in moderation), for the healthiness of his marriage is strictly dependent on his private fantasies of betrayal, which normally take place in the afternoon, every day, at around 1.30.

As in the previous "moral tales", at this stage the main narrative twist consists in progressively reducing the space between the male subject and the fantasised female, so as to prepare the intervention of a moral choice. In other words, Chloe slowly acquires the status of a Real object, fully immersed in enjoyment. As with Adrien in *La collectionneuse*, Frederic is more and more attracted to the Lady, to the extent that eventually he kisses her. Then, in the final scene, Chloe is naked in front of Frederic, her perfectly shaped body at his complete disposal. He seems to give in, even starts to undress, when, catching a glimpse of his face in the mirror as the jumper is about to come off (something that had happened to him earlier in the presence of his wife) he suddenly decides, following in the footsteps of his predecessor Adrien, to run away, back to his wife, at home. Once reunited, wife and husband cry, kiss, and eventually move to the bedroom to make love (for the first time in the film). As with *La collectionneuse*, there would seem to be two ways of reading this finale. Either their lovemaking ratifies the triumph of the moral law (marriage, family, etc.) over pathological impulses, reminding us of Kant's categorical imperative; or, in what is perhaps a more productive interpretation, they make love in a desperate attempt to shut off the frightening underworld of fantasies that threatens to escalate in destructive *jouissance*. What is moving in this extraordinarily subtle finale is the authentic dread seizing the two characters, when for the whole film they had seemed a perfectly responsible and mature couple, trustworthy and never doubting each other's words or thoughts. Now the repressed truth of this balanced situation emerges. Particularly compelling is the wonderfully suspended, unexplained expression of panic on Hélène's normally serene face. This veritable dread is meant to reveal not merely her untold suspicions regarding her husband's fidelity, but, much more insightfully, the existence of *a fantasy scenario of her own*, a wealth of secret desires that need to be kept under strict surveillance if she is to prolong her successful conjugal relationship. Similarly to what is disclosed at the end of Stanley Kubrick's *Eyes Wide Shut* (1999), sex works here as an intrinsically desperate strategy to keep illicit enjoyment at bay.

Through the character of Chloe, then, we understand the meaning of Lacan's words in *Seminar VII*: 'when one aims for the center of moral experience, the beautiful is closer to evil than to the good' (Lacan 1999: 217). Despite Rohmer's attempt to convince us that at the centre of the moral experience lies our decision to renounce the object – i.e. renouncing the madness of drive, the destructive fury of *jouissance* – his film reveals a slightly more complex intention, the same one addressed by Rilke at the start of his first Duino elegy:

> For beauty is nothing but the beginning of terror, which we are
> still just able to endure,
> And we are so awed because it serenely disdains to annihilate us.
> Every angel is terrifying.
> […]
> Perhaps there remains for us some tree on a hillside, which
> everyday we can take into our vision;
> […]
> Is it any less difficult for lovers?
> But they keep on using each others to hide their fate.

These lines bring us to what is perhaps Krzysztof Kieślowski's most enigmatic and compelling work, *The Double Life of Veronique* (La double vie de Véronique, 1991), and specifically its finale, when, after the sexual rendezvous with the puppeteer, the heroine runs away and returns to her father – yet another case of turning one's back on enjoyment; or, as Lacan famously put it, *le père, ou pire* (the father, or worse). The key figure is undoubtedly the puppeteer who, in one of the crucial passages, stages for Véronique what Žižek (2001c: 151) calls the scene of 'her ultimate unbearable freedom':

> In other words, what is so traumatic for her in the puppeteer's performance is not that she sees herself reduced to a puppet whose strings are pulled by the hidden hand of destiny, but that she is confronted with what F.W.J. Schelling called the primordial decision-differentiation (*Ent-Scheidung*), the unconscious atemporal deed by means of which the subject 'chooses' his/her eternal character which, afterwards, within his/her conscious-temporal life, s/he experiences as the inexorable necessity, as 'the way s/he always was'.

Kieślowski here plays with one of his favourite themes, the subject's mixture of attraction and dread when faced by the possibility of his or her freedom. Véronique's attraction to the mysterious puppeteer reflects her desire to know more about the feeling of, as she puts it, 'not being alone'. However, Žižek is right when he warns us that 'the mystique of being spiritually connected with another being is thoroughly misplaced' (83) in this film, which is therefore definitely not to be read as a fairy-tale. He claims rather that '[w]hat interests Kieślowski in the motif of alternative histories is the notion of *ethical choice*, ultimately the choice between "calm life" and "mission"' (Žižek 2001c: 79). This, incidentally, allows us to locate the problem with Wim Wenders' *Wings of Desire* (Der Himmel über Berlin, 1987). Despite it being partially inspired by Rilke's poetry, it shows us angels which are *not* terrifying at all, but rather benign ghost-like bystanders, excluded from the human congregation and yet ever present to "testify" reality. Understandably, they desire to become mortal and experience "the way of the flesh"; however, when eventually ex-angel Damiel (Bruno Ganz) and trapeze artist Marion (Solveig Dommartin) fulfil their long repressed wish for *the* sexual relationship, what we have is precisely 'the mystique of being spiritually connected with another being', which compeletely ignores the traumatic fact of the other's desire.

As for Kieślowski's film, the point about sexual relations needs to be refined: strictly speaking Véronique is not attracted to the puppeteer, but to the knowledge he might harbour *about herself*. If eventually she decides to turn away from this knowledge, it is because it breeds anxiety. Here we should not forget that anxiety, in Lacan, is equivalent to a warning sign through which the subject gets a glimpse of its own "non-autonomy", in the sense that it becomes aware of the possibility of its own disappearance in the other's desire. After making love with the mysterious puppeteer Véronique is suddenly faced by the 'unbearable freedom' which was always the object of her search, for she discovers, in some pictures scattered on the bed, the presence of her Polish double, who had died on stage. In psychoanalytic terms, this "other life" – the romantic, more adventurous life of Weronika, which the puppeteer had already staged for her through the story of the ballerina-marionette – is nothing but the fundamental fantasy, whose foreclosure allows the subject (Véronique) to achieve self-consciousness. Kieślowski therefore suggests that the double is not an external figure but is instead lodged in the unconscious, "in us more than ourselves"; as Žižek puts it, 'the double is the object that the subject refuses to be' (Žižek 2001c: 84). It is at this point, when she encounters the scene of her own fundamental fantasy in the figure of her double, that the heroine opts to return to her father, who of course stands for symbolic authority. Let us recall Rilke's line: 'Perhaps there remains for us some tree on a hillside, which every-day we can take into our vision' – surprisingly, is not this "living" tree precisely the tree Véronique enigmatically touches whilst on the way to her father, who at that precise moment is cutting some "dead" wood? The finale confirms that Véronique has chosen security and a calm life regulated by fantasy and desire over the (potentially) deadly mission of drive.

Now, retrospectively, Weronika's *jouissance* in the first part of the film can be seen in a new light. The enjoyment in question is expressed through the medium of music, more precisely it concerns, again, the enjoyment of the voice *qua* partial object: while Weronika chooses to embark on a successful career as a soprano despite her heart condi-tion, Véronique becomes a music teacher, the implication being that somewhere in her life she has compromised her talent and opted for a more modest but safer career. In Lacanian terms, it is Weronika's choice that appears ethical. But perhaps the most original feature of *The Double Life of Véronique* has to do with its subtly self-reflexive inten-tion, expressed through the linkage illusion-representation-truth. For if Véronique's truth – her unconscious desire – emerges only in the illusion staged by the director-puppeteer, she deliberately misses it by wanting to reach beyond the stage: while her pupils are hypnotised by the spectacle, fully identifying with the representation (despite the explicit presence of the puppeteer's hands), Véronique's gaze is directed at a mirror reflecting the puppeteer's face behind the scenes. The point is that by unmask-ing the illusion, *she misses herself*, i.e. she fails to recognise the "other scene" upon whose repression she has structured her life. The Real – the traumatic Real of freedom/*jouissance* – is on the side of the illusion, while reality is for those who cannot face film.

After this incident the puppeteer slowly lures Véronique to confront the repressed content of her desire. The second part of the film is effectively a protracted seduction scene culminating in Véronique's anxious presage about her freedom. The allusions to the sexual deadlock are clear enough: while Weronika fully endorses her relationship with Antek, and dies, Véronique rejects both the lover we first see her in bed with, and the puppeteer, retreating instead into the safe haven of Father's arms. The same basic mechanism is at work in what is in many ways the most famous precursor of *The Double Life of Véronique* in European cinema, Jean-Luc Godard's *Breathless* (À bout de souffle, 1960). The obvious (and to an extent naïve) question apropos Godard's first film is: why does Patricia (Jean Seberg) turn in Michel (Jean-Paul Belmondo) to the police if she loves him? For the answer we should of course turn to Truffaut, whose influence on the story-line is instantly recognisable: as in Véronique's case, the non-existence of the sexual relationship materialises in woman's retreat when confronted by the prospect of *jouissance*. As Patricia puts it, quoting Faulkner, in the famous sequence of her hotel room, 'between grief and nothing, I will take grief'. For this choice – which speaks for her anxiety, the risk of disintegrating in the self-destructive core of Michel's desire – this independent American woman will deserve to be called *dégueulasse* (disgusting/a bitch), whether by her reckless dying lover or by the detective.[10]

We find an interesting variation to this classic theme of woman caught between the Real of enjoyment and marital security in much of Andrzej Zulawski's cinema, especially in films like *That Most Important Thing: Love* (L'important c'est d'aimer, 1975) and *Fidelity* (La fidélité, 2000). The latter is a melodrama where Clélia's (Sophie Marceau) identity is dramatically suspended between a self-destructive passion for Némo (Guillaume Canet) and her fidelity to Clève (Pascal Greggory). The variation introduced by Zulawski is that the choice of fidelity is the most extreme and excessive one the heroine could make in a world where exploitation and betrayal have become the norm. This induces me to return my previous understanding of Rohmer's "categorical imperative" as laid out in the "Moral Tales". Is it possible to conceive also Rohmer's avowal of the moral choice as intrinsically *extreme* and *excessive*, in line with Lacan's well-known thesis that 'the moral law [...] is simply desire in its pure state, the very desire that culminates in the sacrifice, strictly speaking, of everything that is the object of love in one's human tenderness' (Lacan 1998a: 275)? Although the sacrifice of *jouissance* in Rohmer is not meant to conjure up the explosive conflation of law and desire, but rather to re-introduce the pleasure principle, we should still emphasise the ambiguity of Rohmer's representation of the moral law, insofar as this law also implies, at least potentially, the return of enjoyment.

2.2 The flames of *jouissance*

Amongst the many fascinating types in Bernardo Bertolucci's epic *Novecento* (1900, 1976), one that would not disappoint the analyst is Attila (Donald Sutherland), the Berlinghieri's estate foreman who becomes the head of the local Black Shirts to embody the prototypical fascist. His obsession with law and order turns quickly into its opposite, psychotic violence and sexual perversion. As with the earlier *The Conformist* (Il conformista, 1970), Bertolucci captures poignantly the inter-dependence of the "fascistic" fixation on the law and its symptom, the explosion of psychotic and perverse *jouissance*. The lesson of this classic "return of the repressed" scenario, however, should not be sought in the mere condemnation or ridiculing of the fascist's attitude towards the law, but instead in the more problematic realisation that *the law enjoys* (see Lacan 1998b: 2). Let us explore some filmic exemplifications of this logic.

The specific film I have in mind is Carl Theodor Dreyer's breathtaking *Day of Wrath* (Vredens Dag, 1943), often regarded as a metaphorical rendition of the Nazi invasion of Denmark. Both explicitly and metaphorically, however, there is only one protagonist in this film: Anne (Lisbeth Movin), the young and somewhat disturbingly attractive wife of an austere Protestant parson named Absalon (Thorkild Roose). Set in a small rural village in seventeenth-century Denmark, the film comments on the intolerance against women suspected of being witches and consequently burned on the stakes. Apart from Anne, who eventually does burn, witch-hunting affects two other characters. The first one to go down is old Marte (Anna Svierkier), whom Anne in vain tries to save; then we learn that Anne's own mother had suffered the same death. Finally, following her passionate love affair with her stepson Martin (Preben Lerdorff Rye), as well as Absalon's death, it is Anne herself who has to face the accusations of witchcraft and meet her destiny on the stakes.

The key question to raise apropos *Day of Wrath* concerns Anne's desire as seen from her own perspective: why does she accept to go to the stakes without defending herself? The only way to explain the heroine's will to martyrdom – which accompanies her throughout the film – is by crediting her with the same *passion for the Real* which animates some of the fictional characters discussed in Part II. What burns along with Anne are those frightening jolts of enjoyment or gaps in her being which, having set masculine desire in motion, now threaten to suspend this desire's endless metonymical shift through their over-proximity. It is here that we should inscribe the parallel with Nazi-Fascism, for if we substitute Anne with the figure of the Jew we achieve an insightful metaphorical description of anti-Semitic fantasy:

> the basic trick of anti-semitism is to displace social antagonism into antagonism between the sound social texture, social body, and the Jew as the force corroding it, the force of corruption. [...] This displacement is, of course, supported by condensation: the figure of the Jew condenses opposing features, features associated with lower and upper classes: Jews are supposed to be dirty *and* intellectual, voluptuous *and* impotent, and so on. [...] But this logic of metaphoric-metonymic displacement is not sufficient to explain how the figure of the Jew captures our desire; to penetrate its fascinating force, we must take into account the way 'Jew' enters the framework of fantasy structuring our enjoyment. (Žižek 1989: 125–6)

Žižek's basic point with regard to Nazi-Fascism is that 'the corporatist vision of Society as an organic Whole' is 'the fundamental ideological fantasy' insofar as it is sustained by the reference to an exceptional feature (the Jew) which becomes the catalyst for obscene enjoyment:

> In short, 'Jew' is a fetish which simultaneously denies and embodies the structural impossibility of 'Society': it is as if in the figure of the Jew this impossibility had acquired a positive, palpable existence – and that is why it marks the eruption of enjoyment in the social field. (Žižek 1989: 126)

The paranoid construction of the Jew in Nazi propaganda is mirrored in the paranoid construction of the witch in seventeenth-century Denmark as portrayed by Dreyer. The underlying implication is that Jews as well as witches have access to a life substance (*jouissance*) prior to symbolic castration.[11] Like the Jew, Anne is enjoyment incarnated. She must burn because the excess with which she is associated *must not be recognised as one's own excess*; as in racism, hatred of the other's enjoyment is self-reflexive, it always entails *hatred of the other inside me*, of my own *jouissance*:

> The fascinating image of the Other gives a body to our own innermost split, to what is 'in us more than ourselves' and thus prevents us from

achieving full identity with ourselves. *The hatred of the Other is the hatred of our own excess of enjoyment.* (Žižek 1993: 206)

The mechanism of displacement that typifies anti-Semitism and witchcraft betrays the attempt to keep a certain fantasy scenario in place through the liquidation of the object that may well turn desire into drive. Ultimately, Anne is burnt as a *defence against the drive*: had she lived, she would have forced more people to "make themselves seen" in their excessive fascination with her (in Lacan, the *se fair/*"make oneself" seen, heard, etc., is a prerogative of drive, a signal that we are affected by it, see Lacan 1998a: 200). The key point about the connection between ideological fantasy and enjoyment is that, in the final analysis, the displaced core of *jouissance* (the Jew, Anne) defines those who perceive it: ultimately, excessive (and potentially destructive) enjoyment belongs to Power itself, to the Law that orders and executes the elimination of its disturbing surplus.

Dreyer emphasises the ambiguity of the relationship between the law and its exception. His point is that the witch is not merely eliminated as a defensive strategy, but also *enjoyed*. How? First, we have sadistic torture as it is inflicted upon Marte, in a scene that recalls the horrors of the Inquisition. Then there is direct sexual enjoyment, since Anne is possessed by both Absalon and his son Martin. More specifically, if her passionate relationship with Martin seems spontaneous and wholly plausible, her marriage to the old Absalon can only appear as an "obscene" act of prevarication on his part. Dreyer therefore unveils the disavowed enjoyment of the law, an enjoyment so great that it fulfils itself on the stakes, where it coincides with its repression, the taming of the drive.

The obscene enjoyment associated to the act of torture in Dreyer's film recalls the famous torture sequence in Roberto Rossellini's masterpiece of the same period, *Rome, Open City* (Roma, città aperta, 1945), where the law (Nazi-Fascism) is also connoted as sadistic. Recall the film's most famous passage, that of Pina's (Anna Magnani) tragic death. Before running pathetically towards her fiancé Francesco (Francesco Grandjacquet) whilst he is taken away, she is approached by a lecherous Nazi soldier who tries to grope her. What we have in this seemingly insignificant detail is the same perversion at stake in the torture sequence, which also explains Rossellini's choice of presenting the Gestapo officer responsible for Manfredi's (Marcello Pagliero) torture and death, Major Bergman (Harry Feist), as an effeminate homosexual. It is not simply that Rossellini associates Nazism with homosexuality (a naïve reading), but that by depicting the Nazi officer as a homosexual he is able to render the mixture of attraction and repulsion that qualifies his ambiguous connection with the male victim. Replicating the basic psychological mechanism staged in *Day of Wrath*, torture in *Rome, Open City* suggests that the elimination of the enemy (Manfredi is a Communist Resistance fighter) involves both the disavowal *and* the endorsement of *jouissance*, for *jouissance* returns in the act that is supposed to eliminate it.

This is why *Rome, Open City* should be read alongside a work that at first sight cannot fail to appear radically dissimilar to it, Pasolini's *Salò, or the 120 Days of Sodom* (Salò, o le 120 giornate di Sodoma, 1975). Thirty years after *Rome, Open City*, Pasolini, who was a fervent admirer of Rossellini (and of Dreyer),[12] directs a terrifying film that, in a strange way, renders explicit the Real content of Rossellini's classic Resistance narrative by fully endorsing the obscene enjoyment embodied by the Nazi-Fascist executioners of the law. Major Bergman and his colleagues have transmuted into four debauched libertines, the latter uncovering the *jouissance* of the former. Pasolini's film is primarily about the horrible fate of desire as it turns into drive, into a compulsion to repeat endlessly the same gesture which not only misses the object *but is also aware of this failure*.

2.3   Against the service of goods

My central contention apropos *Salò* is that to grasp the paradoxical significance of ethics in this film it is necessary to turn to the specific treatment reserved for its most outrageous theme, raw sexual perversion. What needs to be taken into account is the relation between power and the perverted mode of enjoyment of the libertines, insofar as the libertines' desire to enjoy the other is characterised as *a form of pleasure beyond the pleasure principle*.

It is true that Pasolini's libertine society de-individualises and fetishises the body as an instrument devoted to the generation of pleasure. Interpreting Sade, Pasolini stages the complicity between modern ratio and perversion denounced by Adorno and Horkheimer: the more our civilisation enforces its mastery over nature, the more it administers pleasure as regimented enjoyment; in its rationalised and ritualistic modes of distribution, the truly mythical and alienating quality of pleasure is extinguished, together with its profoundly antagonistic core. That said, we need to bear in mind that what is most important in *Salò* is not (perverted) pleasure in itself, but its *endless pursuit*: despite their vaunted expertise in any field of sexuality, these libertines dismiss their own orgasm (and the homeostatic comfort that derives from it). The truth about their perversion is thus to be found in the limitless repetition of the act they stage, which is based on the rejection of pleasure in favour of *jouissance*. This also allows us to account for their ban on heterosexuality. The film's universalisation of the homosexual act is to be approached through what Deleuze (1991, 120) calls 'the coldness of desexualization', for homosexuality can be conceived as disengaged from the immediate satisfaction of a utilitarian logic, a concept punctually underlined by the Duke (Paolo Bonacelli): 'The sodomitic act has the advantage of endless repetition'. However, Pasolini eventually departs from Deleuze, holding on instead to the Freudian domain "beyond the pleasure principle": the repetition of the perverted act does not simply reassert the modicum of balance of the pleasure principle from the opposite end; rather, repetition in *Salò* brings about the divisive force of *jouissance*. How? Precisely by accomplishing the passage from desire to drive: from perceiving the object as belonging in the other's *jouissance* (desire), to the awareness that *jouissance* will stick to us whatever we do, like a curse (drive). While in the logic of desire *jouissance* defines the impossibility of the Thing we crave, in the logic of drive it becomes the stain of surplus-enjoyment attached to our every act by which we miss the object. *Salò* tells us that when the wall of prohibition sustaining the economy of desire falls, we enter the shadowy domain of drive dominated by excessive enjoyment, 'since *jouissance* is, at its most elementary, "pleasure in pain", that is, a perverted pleasure provided by the very painful experience of repeatedly missing one's goal' (Žižek 2000a: 297).

In *Salò*, therefore, drive does not send us back to the pleasure principle, but instead it presents us with an exorbitant bill, that is, the traumatic awareness that the impossible Thing sustaining desire is recast as the very core of the subject caught in the loop of drive. What the libertines discover at the end of their journey into the dark realm of drive is that the "surplus of sense" that they cannot shake off *is what they are*, the hard kernel of their being. The external Thing (the Real of enjoyment) comes to coincide with "our Thing", the most intimate place inside us. Such a realisation cannot but have devastating consequences: as the final part of the film suggests, it determines the sudden collapse of the libertines' psychic balance.

This is obvious also by the way Pasolini manipulates the audience's gaze. Throughout the film he endeavours to align the spectator's point of view with that of his four debauched dignitaries, thus suggesting, or inviting, a certain alliance in evil. Let us take one of the most impressive sequences, when the Monsignor tortures his young victims in the courtyard. Significantly, we see him through the binoculars of the Duke, who is comfortably seated inside the villa, masturbating a boy. Imitating

Rossellini's crafty manipulation of the spectator's point of view in *Rome, Open City's* torture sequence, Pasolini turns us into voyeurs, forcing our visual perspective to overlap with the libertines'. By looking through the binoculars, however, we not only realise that we are staring voyeuristically, but also that the encounter with the object of our visual desire coincides with its loss: we see only partial scenes of torture, something is excluded, which means that we are compelled to resort to our imagination. This implies that the scopic drive we are progressively caught in eventually calls *us* into question, telling us that the object we strive to see is inside us, in the form of the unbearable inconsistency of our desire.

Apart from the glimpsed scenes of torture, what troubles us as we watch through the binoculars are the images of the delirious Monsignor as he cracks his whip in the courtyard, screaming furious words that we cannot hear since they are covered up by a sombrely sacred musical comment (from Orff's *Carmina Burana*). These images provide clear evidence that the Sadean executioner is left with nothing but a purposeless rage, which of course betrays the groundlessness of his desire. The terrifyingly frustrated facial expression of the Monsignor suggests that torture has turned into a strange kind of self-torture, for the more he inflicts pain to his victims, the more he effectively "becomes" the very Thing (the whip) that secretly feeds his perversion. The epilogue indicates that the libertines have endorsed transgression to the extent of reaching *jouissance*, and consequently subjective destitution, the loss of the self. One of the "binocular shots" frames three of the four libertines as they engage in an inane, utterly psychotic dance amongst their dead victims. The point is that only then, after this psychotic passage through self-instrumentalisation, we are allowed a glimpse of hope, as eventually the camera cuts to two innocent young soldiers dancing to a foxtrot melody (the film's last shot). We go from a mad dance that ratifies subjective annihilation to an innocent image of dance symbolic of rebirth.

But let us return to the parallel between these libertines and Sade's executioner. In a twist that I believe to be the trademark of Pasolini's political commitment, *Salò* shows how, potentially at least, the over-identification with the excess of the law brings about the law's own undoing, for it reveals how the obscene executioner (the unacknowledged and yet fundamental support of the law) is compelled to assume the impossible *jouissance* of the Thing as the libidinal core of what he is. The point that Pasolini seems to be making is that the more pervasive the grip of power on individuals becomes, the more the question of enjoyment will come back to haunt power itself.

The exposure of power's inner inconsistency acquires an even more stringent significance if observed from the perspective of Pasolini's notorious anti-capitalistic stance. When resisting or escaping the rule of capital becomes an impossible proposition, he seems to suggest, the most effective strategy lies in assuming capitalism's own imbalance. If *Salò* is, as Pasolini intended it to be, a political act, this is because it endorses the destructive libidinal potential inherent in capital. This is echoed in Pasolini's shocking declaration that, despite the horrors therein portrayed, he enjoyed making *Salò*. When, during the shooting, he was asked why he chose Sade, his reply was: 'Well, I am surely not planning to create an ascetically political, puritanical film. Obviously I am fascinated by these sadistic orgies in themselves too' (in Bachmann 1975: 40).[13] The Italian public and media had been long obsessed with the true nature of Pasolini's desire, more or less secretly toying with the following question: 'what if he really is a (Sadean kind of) pervert?' Again, we should insist that it is precisely the ominous ambiguity of Pasolini's position vis-à-vis the seedy underbelly of power that poses a threat to the ideological machine, for this ambiguity brings to light *the scandal of the law*, the fact that the neutral configuration of the law is moored in its nightly supplement (*jouissance*). This is why the director claimed that 'the pages of Sade are extremely revolutionary. I have created this lucid, extraordinary scandal of reason, a limitless and boundless scandal that I admire' (in Greene 1994: 208).

The 'scandal of reason' is also the subject matter of a film that Pasolini had praised, and that invites a few parallels with *Salò*: Marco Ferreri's *Blow-out* (La grande bouffe, 1973). The story of four male characters (a magistrate, a choreographer, a pilot, and a chef) who decide to "eat themselves to death", *Blow-out* shares with *Salò* precisely the focus on the enigmatic excesses of reason, on its fundamental *cupio dissolvi*. Pasolini commented that the shock-value of Ferreri's film rests on the ontological arbitrariness of the characters' "will to die": not once in the film are we given an insight into the reasons behind these characters' 'obscure fanaticism' (Pasolini 1996: 130). Even more explicitly than in *Salò*, death-drive aims here at the impossible enjoyment of one's own body, in as much as the four libertine-like protagonists are driven by the immoderate consumption of food and sex.[14] A metaphor for our consumer society, Ferreri's film anticipated and perhaps influenced *Salò* in exposing the dark side of capitalism's normative regulation of pleasures. If fully endorsed, the truth about the regulated, imposed-from-above freedom to consume is a lethal coercion to confront the Real of *jouissance*. The strength of *Blow-out* and *Salò* is that of not shirking the traumatic-liberating power of this abyssal injunction, which exemplifies the challenge that Lacanian ethics poses to the notion of "service of goods", the utilitarian, market-driven ethics of liberal tolerance. Lacanian ethics are by definition *beyond the service of goods*, for they are beyond the good *tout court*, that is to say, beyond any purpose that may be articulated in positive terms.

2.4   Minimal shocks of enjoyment

As we have seen, the role of fantasy in the sexual relationship is fundamental in providing a shielding screen that makes the relationship viable. As Žižek (2006a: 48) puts it: '[e]very subject has to invent a fantasy of his or her own, a "private" formula for the sexual relationship – the relationship with a woman is possible only inasmuch as the partner adheres to this formula'. And again:

> Any contact with a real, flesh-and-blood other, any sexual pleasure that we find in touching another human being, is not something evident, but something inherently traumatic, and can be sustained only in so far as this other enters the subject's fantasy frame. (Žižek 2006a: 51)

The absolutely vital element in this strategy, through which we convince ourselves of the possibility of the relationship, is of course *objet a*, the blurred spot, the stain, around which the fantasy is woven.

The most sophisticated *objet a* in Rohmer's entire filmography is probably Claire's knee in the previously mentioned film (*Claire's Knee*, 1970). As Jérôme, the film's bearded hero, explains to his friend and writer Aurora, Claire's knee is 'the magnet of my desire, the point where, if I could follow my desire, I would place my hand'. The director hinted at this dependence when he stated that 'she [Claire] stands for an attraction that is purely erotic, in the most refined sense of the word' (in Nogueira 1971: 121). Jérôme makes this eroticism fully explicit when, in a sentence, he sums up the logic of courtly love: 'if Claire threw herself at my feet I would turn her down'. If the aim is to miss her, her knee, which Jérôme touches in the critical moment of the film, represents *objet a* in its unredeemable ambiguity, its being both a void and the filler that momentarily lends this void a material albeit elusive presence. What instigates Jérôme's moral crisis is the movement Claire makes when, having climbed on a ladder under a cherry tree, she suddenly bares her knee in front of him. This movement represents the threatening coming forth of *jouissance* that runs through all six moral tales. To be precise, *objet a* is not only the actual object (the knee) to which Jérôme's desire gets attached, but also the sinuous curvature of space delineated by the knee's movement when it suddenly appears. It is the same kind of curvature, indicating the paradoxical coincidence of absence and presence, that Pasolini, as a child, had named "teta veleta" (an invented and meaningless expression) to describe his inexpressible sensual perturbation at the sight of the back of a knee:

> It was in Belluno, I was around 3 years old. Some boys were playing in the public gardens opposite my home, and more than anything else I was struck by their legs, especially the convex curvature of the knee from behind, where whilst running tendons flex in an elegant and violent gesture. [...] Now I know it was an acutely sensual feeling. If I think about it, I feel exactly the same tenderness, suffering, and violence of desire in my guts. It was a feeling of the unattainable, of the carnal – a feeling for which no name existed. So I made one up and it was 'teta veleta' [...] something like a tickle, a seduction, a humiliation.

Later, when discussing the same incident with writer Dacia Maraini, he added: 'I felt this same sentiment of "teta veleta" for my mother's breast' (in Naldini 1989: 8–9). It is important to notice how the function of language here is to provide a minimal neutralisation of the threat of *jouissance*, which is effectively the threat of void. This also explains why, in Rohmer's film, the hero constantly relates his experiences to Aurora: it is through their enlightened discussions that enjoyment is kept at bay – and this is, ultimately, the function of culture itself.

In one of these perfectly civilised discussions Jérôme admits that 'she [Claire] provokes in me a real and yet undefined desire. All the stronger because undefined. A pure desire, a desire of nothing. I won't do anything, but this desire bothers me.' As with most of Rohmer's heroes, Jérôme's problem from this moment on is how to get rid of the impending menace of excessive enjoyment. The originality of Rohmer's solution, indeed one of the key moments in his cinema, is that he has his hero over-identify with the object, a move that suddenly "cures him", for after this move he altogether stops desiring the girl. First, he comes in contact with Claire's knee accidentally; then, after maliciously provoking her tears over an issue concerning her boyfriend, he deliberately caresses it. As he later explains to Aurora, placing his hand on the girl's knee represented the easiest and yet most difficult gesture to perform, an 'heroic act, an act of pure will, for I never felt so strongly that something *had* to be done'. The point made here is of capital importance, as it concerns the psychoanalytic act that dispels the subject's dependence on the symptom. Jérôme speaks of his gesture as an act of 'pure will', the implication being that, although he was actively following his innermost desire, at the same time he experienced the whole thing from a passive position, the position of someone who is left with no choice and therefore performs his gestures blindly, automatically, in an unreflected fashion. This is one of those rare occasions in Rohmer's cinema where the director manages to conjure up the liberating function of the Lacanian act instigated by drive.[15] For Jérôme, touching the knee corresponds to the dissolution of the anxiety caused by the over-proximity of *objet a*.

To expand on this, let us consider a couple of passages from Fellini's *Amarcord*. An unlikely seduction sequence which is truly paradigmatic of Fellini's cinema begins with Titta (Bruno Zanin), *Amarcord*'s young protagonist, reluctantly submitting to the Catholic ritual of confession; whilst speaking to the priest he cannot avoid fantasising about the very "impure acts" for which now he ideally should repent. He recalls the hot summer day when, in a crescendo of excitement, he cycled to the local cinema hoping to approach the village beauty, Gradisca (Magali Noel). Alone in the empty theatre, smoking, rapturously glued to the screen where Gary Cooper stars in William Wellman's *Beau Geste* (1939), Gradisca indeed appears, albeit in an ironic light, as the object of desire personified. Hampered by his shyness and yet magnetically attracted to the woman, Titta moves closer and closer by constantly changing seats. Finally next to her, he conjures up the courage to place a hand on her thigh, in a move that strikes us as homologous to the one performed by Jérôme in *Claire's Knee*. At this point, however, we have the anticlimax: as if awakening from daydreaming, Gradisca turns towards Titta asking him, calmly: 'so, what is it that you're after?' Titta's reaction is summed up by his despairing commentary: 'I sat there like an idiot, unable to do or say anything!' What this comical sequence highlights is the typical deadlock of the masculine perception of feminine elusiveness, confirming Lacan's claim from *Seminar XX* that '(m)an's *jouissance* is by definition the jouissance of the idiot' (Lacan 1998b: 81). For Lacan, masculine sexuality is akin to the fundamentally masturbatory phallic enjoyment that never reaches the feminine other: 'Phallic jouissance is the obstacle owing to which man does not come, I would say, to enjoy woman's body, precisely because what he enjoys is the jouissance of the organ' (Lacan 1998b: 7).

To fully grasp the originality of Fellini's sequence, however, we should focus precisely on the partly concealed traumatic impact of the kid's desiring experience, where we not only discern idiotic masculine enjoyment vis-à-vis the elusive "stuff" of femininity, but precisely the shock of the impact with the desublimated object. Strictly speaking, therefore, the young boy *does* get what he wants, since the void *qua* sexual deadlock into which he plunges is the kernel of the desired object. This emphasis on trauma is fully endorsed in a later sequence of *Amarcord*, the hilarious passage where Titta tries his luck with the oversized tobacconist. Once she allows him access to the object of his fascination, i.e. her disturbingly immense breasts (what better image for the lost maternal object?), the kid is once again faced with the unbearable proximity of *a*, as a consequence of which he falls ill (in the next sequence we see him in bed, feverish, complaining to his mother about his misfortunes with women). Here we should recall Žižek's reading of Kieślowski's *A Short Film About Love* (Krótki film o milosci, 1988), 'a masterpiece on the (im)possibility of courtly love today': as soon as the young protagonist "gets what he wants", i.e. moves from the fantasmatic threshold of the window from which he was spying the older woman, to her flat, where she offers him to touch her vagina (*qua* Thing), his voyeuristic fantasy suddenly disintegrates into the nightmarish Real, and he is driven to suicide (see Žižek 1997: 65–6). Without the protective screen of fantasy (the window, the telescope from which he was looking), the object of desire risks turning into what in the tradition of courtly love was known as *die Frau-Welt* (the woman who stands for terrestrial life):

> she looks beautiful from the proper distance, but the moment the poet or knight serving her approaches her too closely (or when she beckons him to come nearer so that she can repay him for his faithful services), she turns her other, reverse side towards him, and what was previously the semblance of fascinating beauty is suddenly revealed as putrefied flesh, crawling with snakes and worms, the disgusting substance of life. (Žižek 1997: 66)

To conclude with Rohmer, it is striking to notice how rigidly his cinema is constructed on the opposition of *objet a* and the aseptic universe of language, to which moral choices are consigned. What goes almost unnoticed is the fact that a number of unpalatable themes in Rohmer's pseudo-naturalistic cinema are a priori excluded from treatment: death, politics, violence, disease, homosexuality, the State, authority, bureaucracy, work, etc. As for the characters, they are aged invariably between adolescence and maturity, from bourgeois or petit-bourgeois back-grounds, all in good health, articulated, fairly good-looking (without particular imperfections), and apolitical. This is the price Rohmer's cinema has to pay to come into being in its crystalline form. Passions remain, true, but self-regulated or mediated by reason, diluted as in a Platonic dialogue. Amorous passion itself, just like the feminine object of desire, is conceived as an artwork, to be studied or admired from a distance. Rohmer's universe is thus a universe of controlled transgressions, where moral responsibilities are opposed to the a-historical laws of drive. Potential perversions, where they surface, are immediately gentrified and sublimated, as in *Claire's Knee*. Desire never reaches the Real of despair or *jouissance*, it can only allude to it. Insofar as it draws its allure on a self-evident mechanism of repression, Rohmer's pseudo-naturalistic cinema allows us to locate with relative ease the fundamental deception of cinema as an act of creative representation. Rohmer's astute deception, in other words, is *paradigmatic of the basic cinematic gesture as such*, for film narratives can only come into being by excluding/repressing part of their contents:

> We only attain the level of true Theory when, in a unique short-circuit, we conceive of a certain formal procedure not as expressing a certain aspect of the (narrative) content, but as marking/signalling the part of the content that is excluded from the explicit narrative line, so that – therein resides the proper theoretical point – *if we want to reconstruct 'all' of the narrative content, we must reach beyond the explicit narrative as such, and include some formal features which act as the stand-in for the 'repressed' aspect of the content.* (Žižek 2001c: 58)

As anticipated, at the heart of Rohmer's moral universe there is the problem of enjoyment, perceived as a threat to the laws of "beauty and order" that, in his view, define the universe as such (see Rohmer 1990: 70–80). For Rohmer, enjoyment, in its Lacanian connotation, is a secondary fact whose intervention threatens to spoil and corrupt our balanced immersion in the symbolic order of language, communication, and aesthetic contemplation, as reflected in the exasperated naturalistic smoothness of his style. It is first and foremost a question of precedence. If, as we shall see in Part II, Bergman conceives *jouissance* as a primordial substance without which the universe would not exist, in Rohmer the universe begins emphatically with the Word – which, incidentally, explains why he always proclaimed himself indifferent to Bergman's cinema.[16]

The truly fascinating aspect of Rohmer's cinema, however, is that, at a second glance, the relationship it entertains with the Real cannot fail to appear ambivalent. In the very first shot of *Chloe in the Afternoon*, Frederic opens the bathroom door revealing his wife's naked body from behind. Although this minimal "shock of nudity" is immediately absorbed in a narrative where of course characters spend most of their time talking and not having sex, it nevertheless functions as a symptom – a condensation of repressed enjoyment – which momentarily "burns" the screen. And since the symptom is characterised by its repetition, we should not be surprised to encounter other similar shots depicting feminine nudity from behind: first, roughly half way through the film, when the English au pair girl rushes out of the bathroom naked to take care of Frederic's and Hélène's new-born baby; and at the end when Frederic takes off Chloe's bathrobe unveiling for the camera (in close up) her beautifully shaped posterior. The question of *whose* point of view is involved here is not an idle one. In Hélène's case, it is clearly a subjective shot from Frederic's perspective. With the au pair, however, it is the camera who first registers the occurrence and only a few seconds later Frederic appropriates the point of view when he briefly enters the room – at this stage, though, we are not aligned with his point of view. Finally, in Chloe's case, we have a more radical split between Frederic and the camera, for Chloe is placed in between the two, with the camera alone having the privilege of observing her behind. What we witness, therefore, is a progressive shifting of points of view, from the subjective shot to the objectively driven gaze of the camera. The effect of this slight estrangement is typically Brechtian in its intention, since we, the audience, are called directly into question: how do we feel about this *objet a*? Would we act in the same way as Frederic? The director, in other words, puts the moral question straight to us. What if, however, we can answer this question only by bringing Rohmer himself into the equation? What if the above shot is symptomatic also of his *jouissance*? Ultimately, the symptomatic recurrence of the same shot testifies to Rohmer's readiness to accept the challenge posed by the return of the excluded remainder which, precisely as excluded, allows his creativity to flourish. It is in these apparently insignificant instances, when it briefly over-identifies with its exception, that Rohmer's cinema reveals its true colours and best intentions. For despite its aseptic temperament, it is a cinema that enjoys.

As a somewhat inopportune parallel, what comes to mind apropos this understated insistence on females' bottoms in *Chloe in the Afternoon* is not only Gradisca's posterior but also, again, *Salò*. In a memorable sequence of Pasolini's film, the libertines inspect their victims' posteriors with a view to electing 'il culo più bello' (the most beautiful arse). From this angle, the difference between Pasolini and Rohmer is therefore the difference between full-blown, exhibited over-identification with *objet a* – which not only turns into *cupio dissolvi* but also, with it, into a strategy of liberation – and a modest, inconspicuous, rarefied and yet equally insightful enjoyment of the symptom. As a middle ground we could, of course, include Truffaut's ecstatic fascination with women's legs, as for instance in *The Man Who Loved Women*: 'Women's legs are like compass points, circling the globe and giving it its balance and harmony'; or, even more acutely, the deadly obsession with legs in some Buñuel films such as *Viridiana* (1961) and *Tristana* (1970). In all these cases we are alerted to the inherent limitation of desire recognised by Lacan (1998b: 23):

> As is emphasised admirably by the kind of Kantian that Sade was, one can only enjoy a part of the Other's body, for the simple reason that one has never seen a body completely wrap itself around the Other's body, to the point of surrounding it and phagocytizing it. […] Enjoying has the fundamental property that it is, ultimately, one person's body that enjoys a part of the Other's body.

2.5   Rape as fantasy

One of the clearest examples of Rohmer's ambiguous attitude towards enjoyment can be found in his costume drama *The Marquise of O…*(Die Marquise von O…, 1976), where the narrative is centred on the act that more explicitly connotes the disturbance associated with *jouissance*: rape. The first observation to make is that the central event (rape) is relegated to the space of pure fantasy. There is hardly a hint of sexual violence in the film, and yet as the Marquise's pregnancy develops we are encouraged to imagine the disturbing scenario that has led to such a situation. A number of incidents contribute to increasing the ineffability of the key event: (1) the fact that the Marquise (Edith Clever) was unconscious when raped, which if on the one hand increases the monstrosity of the act, on the other hand it triggers a whodunit type of scenario, imbued with a sense of suspense, where the principal concern becomes the identification of the villain; (2) the main suspect is the Russian Count (Bruno Ganz), who had previously saved the heroine from the attack of a group of Russian soldiers and had then become infatuated with her; (3) the problem of rape is obscured by the way the narrative develops, focusing on the way in which the Marquise is humiliated and eventually ostracised by her family who refuse to believe her ignorance about the pregnancy;

(4) the disturbing potential of the only shot that, retroactively, might have induced us to hypothesise rape is neutralised via a pictorial reference, since the image of the Marquise's unconscious body lying sensually on the bed, as she is gazed at by the Count, is an explicit quotation from Füssli's most famous painting, *The Nightmare* (1781); (5) the story ends with the reconciliation between the Marquise and the Count.

All these elements contribute to isolating the hard kernel of *jouissance* that sustains the narrative by turning it into a rarefied, purely hypothetical event impervious to empirical knowledge. The truth of this operation of displacement is that rape here materialises the impossibility of the sexual relationship, the horrifying radicalisation of fantasy – i.e., the moment when fantasy *qua* protective screen turns into *fundamental fantasy*, the subject's innermost desire that *cannot be subjectivised*.

The indistinctness of love and violence, fantasy and trauma, is also the most intriguing theme at work in Pedro Almodovar's *Talk to Her* (Hable con ella, 2002). Here Benigno's (Havier Cámara) sexual violence on Alicia (Leonor Watling), the dancer he has grown obsessed with, is portrayed as an ambiguous sign that not only we cannot immediately decipher, but also, more importantly, that does not necessarily ratify the monstrosity of the male rapist. On closer analysis, what makes Benigno's and the Count's ignominious acts so surprisingly similar (given the abyssal distance between Almodovar's and Rohmer's cinemas), and to an extent forgivable (in narrative terms), is the all-important detail of the unconscious status of their respective female victims. If the Marquise was unconscious after the shock of the Russian invasion, Alicia was in a coma after being run over by a car. In both cases rape is therefore supplemented by what we should not be afraid to call by its name, i.e. necrophilia, for at the time of the violence the two victims were "as good as dead", simply unaware of what they were suffering. From the point of view of courtly love, the implications are obviously very significant. Since the place occupied by the Lady is by definition empty (she functions as a screen onto which the knight anchors his desire), the sexual act with a female partner who is not aware of it comes very close, at least in theoretical terms, to the traumatic encounter with the true core of the Lady, which in turn confirms that *Woman does not exist*. What Almodovar and to an extent Rohmer fail to develop is the question of the traumatic impact that such a discovery would cause on their male characters. Unless we are talking about either perversion or psychosis (and, in Benigno's case, we are clearly dealing with psychosis), the encounter with the Lady can only result in subjective destitution.

In Cédric Kahn's *Red Lights* (Feux Rouges, 2004) we are presented with an interesting variation on the strategy of obfuscating and thus transcending the obscene core of *jouissance* evoked by rape. The double trauma at the heart of the film (the wife suffering rape and the husband's subsequent killing of the fugitive convict guilty of that violence) manages to evoke the Real of the sexual relationship in metaphorical terms. The key insight is Kahn's awareness that the couple *must* confront this unbearable Real in order to attempt to overcome their conjugal crisis. As a journey to the Real, which I am tempted to describe as a postmodern version of Rossellini's *Voyage to Italy* (Viaggio in Italia, 1954), the film is successful in highlighting the necessity of trauma for regeneration. The most captivating aspect is the portrayal of the double trauma, for its obvious lack of realism (how likely is it that the same man meets accidentally both wife and husband in the space of a few hours and in totally different circumstances?) speaks for its metaphorical significance: what we are dealing with is the enjoyment of both characters, their respective attachment to an inherently traumatic fantasy. This attachment acquires the unstoppable strength of the drive; most importantly, we realise it represents the only way forward for the characters, the only way they can salvage their marriage. Was she really raped, did he really kill? Significantly, both events, similarly to the rape scene in *The Marquise of O…*, are suspended, turned into derealised, insubstantial fantasy objects – we do not see them, we can only put the pieces together afterwards and guess. More explicitly than Rohmer's film, however, *Red Lights* encroaches upon the frightening landscape of the unconscious, the desert of the Real where the unbearable truth of fantasy has to be confronted in order for the fantasy to be woven again. The point of view from which we follow the narrative is Antoine's (Jean-Pierre Darroussin), the fantasy at stake is his. And his problem is Hélène (Carole Bouquet), his wife, insofar as she is more successful than him in every aspect of their lives: work, personal appearance, etc. The apparent imbalance in their marriage projects us into Antoine's fantasy underworld, and the narrative unfolds as his attempts to deal with sexual difference. His is indeed a clever strategy, similar to the one at work in dreams: first he loses his wife; then he has her raped by a fugitive convict, the epitome of the villain; and finally, of course, he kills the convict himself, restoring the credibility of his position as a husband. Fundamentally, what is displaced through this fantasy is none other than *Antoine's own impotence*, the very feature that here sanctions the non-existence of the relationship; or, put differently, his traumatic desire to rape his wife.

The shocking question of the connection between desire and sexual violence is confronted head-on in Marco Bellocchio's *The Conviction* (La condanna, 1991), whose merit is to explicitly state that the sexual act *in itself* is traumatic (since, deprived of its traumatic dimension, sex would be utterly desexualised and dehumanised). In the baffling opening scene of the film, Sandra (Claire Nebout) finds herself locked inside a castle after visiting its museum. Since it is impossible to establish whether or not she has deliberately provoked her fate, this incipit would seem to highlight the elusiveness of feminine desire. To contrast the specificity of the feminine position, we are soon after introduced to woman's asymmetrical partner. While Sandra, locked inside the castle, is admiring Leonardo da Vinci's *Madonna Litta*, Giovanni (Vittorio Mezzogiorno) suddenly appears behind her, proceeding to explain the meaning of the painting (an explanation which, inevitably, Sandra does not agree with). Interestingly, Sandra is not surprised by the presence of this complete stranger, which increases our perplexity apropos her desire.

This ambiguity is explored further in the following sequence, which focuses on the sexual act. Firstly, it is impossible for us to make out whether the two characters are actually having sex or it is all just an act; if their movements and grunts suggest real copulation, the scene is nevertheless theatrical, resembling the kind of ceremonial mating foreplay performed by animals. Secondly, we are unable to establish the amount of violence involved. True, at one point Sandra runs away, Giovanni chases her and takes her forcefully; yet, it is evident that we are not watching a standard rape scene, as Sandra is portrayed in such a way as to suggest that she is willing to be taken by force. The obvious feminist counter-argument here would be that we are watching a rape scene from a male (chauvinist) point of view. However, what about Liliana Cavani's "post-Holocaust" drama *The Night Porter* (Il portiere di notte, 1974), where Lucia (Charlotte Rampling), a concentration camp survivor, openly endorses her scandalous "desire to be raped" by her former SS captor/torturer Max (Dirk Bogarde)? Twelve years after the end of the Second World War Lucia chances upon Max while in Vienna with her husband, an accomplished orchestra director. Despite her initial horror, she is unable to resist the fascination that the memory of Max exerts on her. One brief rendezvous is enough to instigate in Lucia the irresistible recollection of the abuse Max used to inflict on her, to the extent that she immediately leaves her husband and ties herself absolutely to her vicious lover. Liliana Cavani, a woman, does not shirk what she clearly regards as the feminine fundamental fantasy, a masochistic primal scene in which the Freudian "a child is being beaten" turns into "a woman is being raped".[17]

> It is precisely the status of fantasy that brings us to the ultimate point of the irreconcilable difference between psychoanalysis and feminism, that of rape (or the masochistic fantasy sustaining it). For standard feminism, at least, it is an a priori axiom that rape is a violence imposed from without: even if a woman fantasizes about being raped, this only bears witness to the deplorable fact that she internalized male attitudes. The reaction here is one of pure panic. The moment one mentions that a woman may fantasize about being raped or at least brutally mishandled, one hears cries: This is like saying that Jews fantasized about being gassed in the camps [...] the problem with rape, in Freud's view, is that it has such a traumatic impact not simply because it is a case of such brutal external violence, but because it also touches on something disavowed in the victim herself [...] the core of our fantasy is unbearable to us. (Žižek 2004: 97–8)

Žižek (2006a: 55) elaborates further on this understanding of rape in *How to Read Lacan*:

> [...] while (some) women really may daydream about being raped, this fact not only in no way legitimizes the actual rape, but renders it all the more violent. Let us take two women: the first is liberated and assertive, active; the other daydreams in secret about being brutalized, even raped, by her partner. The crucial point is that, if both of them are raped, the rape will be much more traumatic for the second woman, *on account of the very fact that it will realize in 'external' social reality the 'stuff of her dreams'*. There is a gap that for ever separates the fantasmatic kernel of the subject's being from the more superficial modes of his or her symbolic or imaginary identifications. It is never possible for me to assume (in the sense of symbolic integration) the fantasmatic kernel of my being: when I venture too close, what occurs is what Lacan calls the *aphanisis* (the self-obliteration) of the subject: the subject loses his/her symbolic consistency, it disintegrates. And perhaps the forced actualization in social reality itself of the fantasmatic kernel of my being is the worst, most humiliating kind of violence, a violence that undermines the very basis of my identity (of my self-image).

In Italian cinema, we find another filmic reference to the feminine fundamental fantasy in Lina Wertmüller's *Swept Away* (Travolti da un insolito destino nell'azzurro mare d'agosto, 1974). In this film the rapport between arrogant Northern capitalist Raffaella (Mariangela Melato) and Southern working-class Gennarino (Giancarlo Giannini) has often been labelled as misogynistic. When they first make love on the beach, for instance, Raffaella begs Gennarino to 'sodomise' her. Although poor Gennarino does not know the meaning of such a word, the reversal of roles has already taken place: after exploiting and humiliating him, the rich woman has fallen desperately in love with the uncouth working-class man who now, out of revenge, brutalises her both mentally and physically. What should not be missed is that this reversal of roles is described by Wertmüller (another female director) as an intrinsically obscene feminine fantasy. After they are rescued from the deserted island and brought back to civilisation, Raffaella lacks the courage to sustain this fantasy and, instead, abandons Gennarino, by now infatuated with her, to the none too merciful cares of his coarse wife. Now perhaps we are in a better position to understand why, during the trial scene in Bellocchio's *The Conviction*, Sandra, who has pressed charges against Giovanni for sexual violence, states that 'he [Giovanni] stirs deep-seated realities that everyone has the right to keep hidden': what she refers to is the very abyss of feminine *jouissance*, the unnameable enjoyment that constitutes Sandra's fundamental fantasy. Her following tears are evidence for this, since they suggest that she has ventured too close to the Real of her desire.

2.6   Religion, masturbation and Jung

As a fake form of transgression aimed at reappropriating enjoyment from whoever might be seen as "stealing" it from us (society, work, sexual partner, etc.), masturbation is eminently indicative of the subject's jealous defence of his or her own private fantasies. In Fellini's *Amarcord* a group of schoolboys perform collective masturbation inside a car. In a similar manner to a group of friends sharing a meal around a table, each boy has his own private access to enjoyment through a unique fantasy of woman. The crucial point is made when one of the boys, while masturbating, "oversteps the mark" by mentioning, in a groan of pleasure, the name of a girl (Aldina) who already functions as another boy's private fantasy. As expected, this "fantasy infringement" is experienced by the latter as a theft of enjoyment. If we were to look for an overarching definition of Fellini's cinema, perhaps the metaphor of masturbation would not be misplaced, since the basic gesture of his filmmaking concerns the defence and stubborn justification of his own private fantasy universe. Furthermore, like every masturbator Fellini thrives on prohibition, which in his case is often kindly provided by the Catholic Church. In most of Fellini's works, desire is strictly correlative to the overwhelming presence of the religious agency that decrees the sinfulness of one's actions.

It is easy to discern a similar strategy in Buñuel, who was fully aware of the extent to which his cinema depends on an instance of prohibition (apparently he used to claim that 'sex without religion is like cooking an egg without salt'). Educated by Jesuits, Buñuel always acknowledged the connection between Catholicism and desire, also in relation to his own biography: 'Ironically, this implacable prohibition [related to his religious upbringing] inspired a feeling of sin which for me was positively voluptuous' (Buñuel 1985: 14–15). In Buñuel's films the repressive character of religion is both mocked and fiercely attacked, although it is clear that the director's imagination is sturdily dependent on the very transgression engendered by the religious ban.

The more blatant case of disavowal with regard to religion, in Buñuel, is probably *Viridiana* (1961), the scandalous film about a beautiful novice nun who suffers two rape attempts and eventually drops her inhibitions to accept an only slightly veiled invitation to a *ménage à trois*. Regarded as an anti-Catholic film, *Viridiana* was immediately banned in Franco's Spain and harshly criticised by the Vatican. However, are we not confronted here by a classic example of the basic Buñuelian ruse? Religion is once again instrumental to the key question posed by his cinema, the enigma of the impossibility to satisfy a simple desire. The central character Viridiana, a blonde nun played by the gorgeous Silvia Pinal, was inspired by an obscure Italian saint of the sixteenth century whose life Buñuel had read about avidly when studying with the Jesuits. The point is that the erotic charge of the film is vastly dependent on the fact that the feminine object of desire is clad in nun's clothes, and behaves accordingly. The attack against Catholic idealism (the paupers Viridiana seeks to help eventually turn against her) does not manage to conceal the film's *jouissance*, which emerges fully in those rare instances when Viridiana bares a part of her body: a perfectly chiselled leg first; then, in a revealing shot from above, her bosom, when the lecherous don Jaime (Fernando Rey), having drugged her, attempts to take advantage of her. Not to mention the later sequence where one of the paupers endeavours to rape her after immobilising Jorge (Francisco Rabal), who is forced into an impotent voyeuristic position; or the various references to the heroine's repressed libido, as when she is invited to milk a cow whose long nipples are obvious phallic symbols. The film is indeed voyeuristic to the bone, if not overtly fetishistic (especially in the figure of Don Jaime and his obsession with legs).

One of Fellini's many dream sketches, dated December 1974, shows the director flying in a hot-air balloon with Pope Paul VI, whom Fellini always disapproved of as the quintessence of the paternalistic authority of the Catholic Church (as a cardinal, in the early 1960s, he had also strongly attacked *La dolce vita*). In this dream the Pope warns Fellini about a huge woman who suddenly appears in front of them, defining her as 'the great fabricator and dissolver of clouds'. Significantly, when discussing his dream Fellini identified the woman as a lawyer he had met a few years earlier and had desired with great intensity, to the point of fainting (in Fellini 1987: 38). Are we not back to the axis law–church–woman? Like the reference to fascism, religious authority in Fellini's cinema is often (unconsciously) linked to femininity, insofar as it corresponds to a 'fabricator and dissolver' of desire.

It is no coincidence that Titta, in *Amarcord*, reminisces about his heated encounter with Gradisca when in church, whilst submitting to confession; and, as we have seen, Uncle Teo's desire is "tamed" by a nun. Analogously, Guido's (Marcello Mastroianni) heated memories of Saraghina (Eddra Gale) in *8½* are sustained by the notion of sin and the harsh reprimands of the local clerical community. Again, Fellini requires the services of the Catholic Church insofar as the latter provides those references to prohibition, sin, and redemption (grace) which, in a perverse loop, prove to be absolutely central to the production of fantasy and desire. If anything, the problem with Fellini's cinema (and Buñuel's) is how to break with the pathological compulsion to engender desire through transgression. Because of its reliance on the dialectic of law and its transgression, it is a cinema that obeys the masculine logic of the exception, inasmuch as sin *qua* exception sustains the law instead of opposing it. From this angle, Fellini's pervasive Catholicism is in desperate need of a Christ who, as Paul put it in Galatians (3: 13), may "redeem us from the curse of the law". Why is it, for example, that despite all his extramarital affairs as well as his continuous indulging in masturbatory fantasies of other women, Guido, in *8½*, is unable to break with his wife Luisa (Anouk Aimée), and even feels closer and closer to her as the film draws to its end? Amongst other things, *8½* demonstrates how transgression (betrayal) and the law (marriage) are not opposed but are rather two sides of the same coin. Marriage thrives on (various forms of) transgression, and vice versa.

With *8½* Fellini wants to justify what in previous films, up to *La dolce vita*, had troubled him: the fact that he had nothing to say (politically, socially, etc.). Now he comes to the conclusion that, as Guido (Fellini's alter-ego) states at one point, 'even if I have nothing to say, I want to say it anyway!' The final sequence, when Guido at last begins working on a film about which he has no idea, confirms that Fellini had been looking for a way to rid himself of the pressure to make films with at least a hint of historical or socio-political conscience. It works as a liberating moment, insofar as it implies that the director can now indulge freely, without guilt, in his fantasies, without having to anchor them in historical reality. In his last monologue Guido states, soberly: 'this confusion *is* me... and doesn't scare me anymore'; and to his wife: 'life is a celebration... let's live it together'. While on the one hand these lines seek to affirm the coincidence of dream and reality, order and confusion, on the other hand they also attempt, in vain, to abolish the traumatic, non-symbolisable excess that accompanies dreams and fantasies.

It is no surprise, then, that Fellini chose Jung as his spiritual mentor. It was during the filming of *La dolce vita* that he was introduced to Jung's ideas by Ernest Bernhard, a Jungian analyst who lived near him in Rome (incidentally, in 1965 Fellini also made a pilgrimage to Jung's home in Zurich). Why Jung? In Fellini's own words:

> What I admire most ardently in Jung is the fact that he found a meet-ing place between science and magic, between reason and fantasy. He has allowed us to go through life abandoning ourselves to the lure of mystery, with the comfort of knowing that it could be assimilated by reason. (Fellini 1976: 147)

Jung provided Fellini with a theoretical framework that encouraged him to find comfort in fantasy, while at the same time allowing him to dispel his sense of guilt towards society:

> I have always thought I had one major shortcoming: that of not hav-ing general ideas about anything. The ability to organize my likes, tastes, desires in terms of genre or category has always been beyond me. But reading Jung I feel freed and liberated from the sense of guilt and the inferiority complex that the shortcoming I touched upon always gave me. (Fellini 1988: 164)

Armed wth Jung's theory of the "collective unconscious", the director could now revel in his dreams, play confidently with his creativity, just like Guido at the end of *8½*. The Jungian unconscious, conceived as a series of archetypal images shared as a hidden reservoir by the whole of humanity, opened the way to a comfortable, non-threatening understanding of fantasy (see also Bondanella 1992: 153).

If Jung worked as the cultural reference that helped Fellini legitimate his frictionless immersion in fantasy, with Buñuel the same purpose was achieved through his adherence to Surrealism in its therapeutic function. Buñuel's surrealist ambition was to conceive the whole of reality as innocent fantasising, an endless dream that would not comprise any repressed content. Testament to this ambition is, more than anything else he has done, his penultimate film, *The Phantom of Liberty* (Le Fantôme de la liberté, 1974). Not accidentally he claimed: 'Chance governs all things; necessity, which is far from having the same purity, comes only later. If I have a soft spot for any one of my movies, it would be for *The Phantom of Liberty*, for it tries to work out just this theme' (Buñuel 1985: 171). The heartfelt homage Buñuel pays to chance in this film is the exact equivalent of the absolute faith Surrealism had in the liberating power of free associations, automatic writing, and, in short, unrestrained imagination:

> Fortunately, somewhere between chance and mystery lies imagination, the only thing that protects our freedom, despite the fact that people keep trying to reduce it or kill it off altogether. I suppose that's why Christianity invented the notion of intentional sin. When I was younger, my so-called conscience forbade me to entertain certain images – like fratricide, for instance, or incest. I'd tell myself that these were hideous ideas and push them out of my mind. But when I reached the age of sixty, I finally understood the perfect innocence of the imagination. It took that long for me to admit that whatever entered my head was my business and mine alone. The concepts of sin and evil simply didn't apply; I was free to let my imagination go wherever it chose, even if it produced bloody images and hopelessly decadent ideas. When I realized that, I suddenly accepted everything. 'Fine', I used to say to myself. 'So I sleep with my mother. So what?' Even now, whenever I say that, the notions of sin and incest vanish beneath the great wave of my indifference. (Buñuel 1985: 174–5)

Here we should recall, however, that Buñuel's last film, three years after *The Phantom of Liberty*, shot when the director was 77, was *That Obscure Object of Desire* which, as we have seen, works as a powerful statement on the strict correlation between prohibition and desire. In other words, in Buñuel's final film imagination is far from innocent. Like Fellini, Buñuel does not seem to account for the intimately and necessarily self-reflexive character of fantasy. What ultimately emerges in these two directors, despite their frequent efforts to prove the opposite thesis, is that "there is no such thing as *innocent* fantasising".

The truth about Fellini's disposition to abandon himself freely to imagination explodes, for example, in films such as *Fellini Satyricon* (Satyricon, 1969), a work where the "comfort of fantasy" turns into a nightmarish, hallucinated vision of pre-Christian Rome. Given its fragmented nature and lack of overarching narrative frame, Petronius' work, from which the film is adapted, offered Fellini the perfect opportunity to create something that could reflect Jung's concept of the collective unconscious, at the same time oddly unfamiliar and comfortably close to home: 'a great dream galaxy sunken in the darkness and now rising up to us amid glowing bursts of light' (Fellini 1988: 172–3). *Fellini Satyricon* can thus be regarded as one of the most significant exceptions in Fellini's filmography. Practically every aspect of it is out of key with the director's customary style, giving form to a strangely distorted panoply. Apart from the atypical use of photography, camerawork, lighting, set and costumes, perhaps the most striking piece of evidence for the excessive status of this film comes from its use of music. As Nino Rota confirmed (in Hughes 1971: 180), Fellini demanded from him not the usual type of score aimed at generating sentimental and emotional identification in the audience, but an atonal composition reliant mainly upon distorted electronic sounds. What makes Fellini a great artist is that he did not content himself with keeping within the limits of his creative universe; instead, he constantly probed the disavowed foundations of that universe.

2.7   Taming the gaze: politics meets the peep show

Marco Bellocchio's *Good Morning, Night* (Buongiorno, notte, 2005) is the third and latest Italian film to date to deal with the kidnapping and assassination of Christian Democrat president Aldo Moro – after Giuseppe Ferrara's *The Moro Affair* (Il caso Moro, 1986) and Renzo Martinelli's *Five Moons Plaza* (Piazza delle Cinque Lune, 2003). Moro was kidnapped by the Red Brigades on 16 March 1978 and executed on 9 May, 55 days later, after his captors had unsuccessfully attempted to negotiate his release with the Italian state. Although Bellocchio does not hide his views on the event, his film has more to do with fantasy than with political history. First, it is not meant as an investigation into the obscure background to the tragic conclusion of Moro's captivity (a background against which many commentators have advanced numerous conspiracy theories). Bellocchio refuses to explore the historical role of the Red Brigades; his depiction of Mario Moretti (the Red Brigades' leader), for example, simply throws into relief his fanatical intransigence and dogmatism. Similarly, the polemical dimension of the film is at best of secondary importance, although the director does not waste the opportunity to discredit both the Christian Democrats' leadership and the Vatican, denouncing their opportunistic strategy of non-collaboration with the Red Brigades as implicitly criminal. In a nutshell, Moro is represented as a victim of the delirious vision of the terrorists, who in turn share responsibility with the dominant right-wing current of Moro's party, politicians who opposed Moro's strategy of the "Historical Compromise" which implied an alliance with the Italian Communist Party.

In view of this, the inevitable first question would have to be: what is the aim of *Good Morning, Night*, if it is not a directly political one? As stated by the director, when he was commissioned the film he accepted on condition that he would be allowed a degree of "unfaithfulness" with regard to history. This unfaithfulness is easily locatable in the final visionary twist of the narrative, when Chiara (Maya Sansa), the only female in the commando of four kidnappers, dreams that Moro leaves the flat where he was kept prisoner unscathed. What some critics have found indigestible is both Bellocchio's alleged restoration of the figure of Aldo Moro, and his portrayal of Chiara's secret humanity, which comes to full fruition in the final sequence of the film. Chiara's character is modelled on that of Anna Laura Braghetti, the *brigatista* author of *Il prigioniero* (The Prisoner, 1998), a memoir in which she describes the 55 days of Moro's captivity against the biographical backdrop of her own militancy in the Red Brigades. Despite often fitting the standard image of the confused young woman caught in the whirlpool of 1970s armed struggle, in her book Braghetti acknowledges her full support to her comrades' decision to kill Moro – in fact, in 1980 she herself carried out the execution of Vittorio Bachelet, a high-ranking representative of Italy's judicial system. What immediately appears problematic, therefore, is the connection between the Braghetti character and the "unfaithful" visionary dimension that intimately erodes and eventually subverts the realism of the film, both on a historical and stylistic register. Bellocchio plays the card of the *brigatista*'s repressed unconscious sensitivity, which discreetly punctuates the narrative mainly through her dreams, brief successions of images that are apparently disconnected with the main narrative line or develop with it a loosely metaphorical relationship. In one such instance, for example, Braghetti dreams of the execution of partisans during the Resistance, thus implicitly equating fascists and *brigatisti*.

My main point here concerns the status of the relationship between the two contrastive textual dimensions of the film. By introducing a visionary ending to the Moro affair, Bellocchio seems to focus on what Walter Benjamin called 'splinters of messianic time' (Benjamin 2003: 397), potential utopian breaks in the flow of history out of which the glimmer of a different historical outcome transpires. The status of this break is crucial, and constitutes by far the most intriguing aspect of the film. As the title itself suggests, and as is confirmed by the heavy use of chiaroscuro, the film is constructed around the juxtaposition of light and darkness, whose function is to denote a conflict between the warped consciousness of the terrorists (darkness) and the unconscious liberating potential embodied by the female character (light). From this angle, the film lends itself to be read as a glorification of the intrinsically subversive capacity of the moving image, allied with femininity, against the aseptic instrumental involution of modern (masculine) rationality. This emphasis on the liberating potential of what I am tempted to call the feminine cinematic unconscious is indeed a theme that has dominated Bellocchio's work for at least the last two decades.

The problem is that the film endows the image of the "cinematic unconscious" with a positive and fairly unproblematic status, as Moro's final morning stroll through Rome's periphery confirms. The fundamental weakness concerns the director's misuse of psychoanalytic theory, which can be documented in his filmography. In the mid-1980s many commentators believed that Bellocchio had fallen under the sway of his psychoanalyst, Massimo Fagioli. Since the start of the 1970s, Fagioli had been organising seminars of collective analysis, through which he openly attacked the dominant psychoanalytic discourse in Italy and Europe, attacks which eventually led to his expulsion from the "Italian Society of Psychoanalysis". Bellocchio started attending Fagioli's seminars in the late 1970s, and soon developed with him a number of collaborative projects in film. Critics were often sceptical of this partnership, dismissing Bellocchio's films as mere applications of Fagioli's anti-Freudian theories, which are based on what he calls *immagini interiori* – images corresponding to figurations of a "healthy and friendly" unconscious. If we recall that Freud's own rejection of cinema was instigated by his scepticism towards the idea that unconscious drives could be expressed figuratively, it is clear that Fagioli's belief in the beneficial representability of the unconscious could not be more remote from the Freudian tradition.

With reference to Fagioli's thought and influence on Bellocchio's work, my argument develops as follows. First of all, as repeatedly admitted by both parties, the collaboration cannot be taken to imply that Bellocchio's cinema became a mere reflection of Fagioli's theories. The relationship remained open and antagonistic. Furthermore, even if we were to admit Fagioli's overwhelming influence, this does not prevent Bellocchio's films from developing an unconscious side *beyond* their conscious narrative strategy. In fact, as already suggested, in Lacanian terms the cinematic unconscious would have to be defined as a paradoxical *knowledge that does not know itself*, a form of knowledge which is detached from the symbolic significations a film might wish to attain, and yet remains inevitably glued to it in the form of symptomal knots. To explore this point, let us focus on the classic cinematic feature that unobtrusively runs through the entire narrative of *Good Morning, Night*: voyeurism. Chiara is somewhat compulsively attracted to the peephole on the door of Moro's cell, repeatedly spying on him, for reasons that she does not seem to be aware of but that no doubt disturb her enormously. Before we assess the significance of this voyeuristic compulsion we should consider the symbolic weight carried by the Aldo Moro character. Although Bellocchio refused this reading, Moro here functions very much as a charismatic paternal presence, easily eclipsing the *brigatisti*'s pathetic and infantile attachment to the cause. This, incidentally, also provides some clues as to why Bellocchio dedicated his film to the memory of his father, a conservative figure with whom he always had a very conflictual relationship. As for Chiara's voyeurism, it seems legitimate to understand it as an attempt to negotiate some kind of bond with the paternal metaphor in front of her. But what is actually at stake in voyeurism? In Lacanian terms, the object of our scopic drive, the thing in the visual field that originally sets our visual desire in motion, is none other than the gaze itself, insofar as the gaze is the blind spot in the visual field that the eye cannot see and that, at the same time, always-already looks back at the subject.

In Chiara's case, however, we do not get as far as the gaze. In contrast to Antonioni's *Blow-up*, Bellocchio's film does not unravel the gaze *qua* object of the scopic drive. On the contrary, it suggests that the object of Chiara's visual desire is a very precise image, the image of a free Aldo Moro. What a Lacanian reading tells us, however, is that this image of freedom is ultimately equivalent to Chiara's unconscious desire, as she looks compulsively into the peephole, *to be seen* by an invisible and free-floating gaze – by Moro's gaze insofar as it is free to float outside his prison and thus able to return Chiara's. It is here that we encounter the crucial inconsistency of Bellocchio's position, which concerns the overlapping of the gaze as a primordially lost object and Moro's liberated gaze. The problem is that Chiara, insofar as she looks voyeuristically, deep down

longs for the over-identification with the gaze *qua* lost object – a shattering over-identification which, as such, would cause the breakdown of
her symbolic identity. As always with voyeurism, the excessive libidinal
investment in the act of looking ultimately speaks for a masochistic drive,
without which the subject (in our case Chiara) would be unable to free
herself from her symbolic context (her attachment to the ideology of the
Brigate rosse). My contention is that by failing to capitalise on its decisive
intuition, Bellocchio's film remains somewhat idealistic, since it tells us
that the unconscious wish expressed by Chiara's vision is not the gaze
in its empty, virtual, and thus truly traumatic guise, but rather its gentrified version, in as much as it belongs to Moro, the eroticised object. The
upshot is that the gaze is here granted very precise historical and political connotations: effectively, as anticipated, Moro is re-inscribed into
the picture as a father figure, that is to say as Lacan's Master-Signifier,
the signifier that brings order and meaning into a chaotic, potentially
psychotic universe.

The surprising thing to note, then, is the circular, non-progressive
dimension of the film, which reminds one of the logic articulated by
Freud's *Totem & Taboo*: the symbolic order is first radically disturbed by
the kidnapping of the Father; Chiara, however, is stricken with guilt,
and her dream works as a way to *put the Father back into his place*, thus
re-establishing the previous balance and banning forever the very notion
of parricide. Paradoxically, this entails that Bellocchio employs the
unconscious as a means to generate a degree of symbolic pacification.
Perhaps such an outcome tells the truth about Bellocchio's well-known
rebellious, anti-authoritarian stance, whose ultimate aim is to re-
politicise imagination, and with it the utopian spirit of 1968. The point
unintentionally made by the film is that such a rebellious spirit relies
heavily on the figure of the Father/Master, a figure inevitably invested by
discordant libidinal stimuli such as love, hatred, admiration, and envy.
In turn, this would seem to confirm Lacan's (in)famous address to the students during May 1968: 'What you aspire to as revolutionaries is a Master.
You will have one!' (Lacan 2006: 207). Bellocchio's position would thus
seem to coincide, strictly speaking, with the position of the hysteric, for
the staging of Moro's liberation appears as an unconscious strategy to
regain a Master who can then be bombarded by endless demands.

But let us return to the filmic representation of Moro's escape. As
anticipated, there is nothing particularly excessive or shocking about
this release of unconscious libidinal energy. Rather, as underlined by the
musical comment from Schubert, it echoes Fagioli's idea of the *incon-
scio mare calmo* (the unconscious as a calm sea), the idea that drives

are fundamentally healthy. In line with the previous argument apropos Lacan's theory of the gaze, my main objection is that such an image *cannot* be regarded as correlative to the unconscious. This can be further clarified via a reference to Freud's theory of dreams. How does an unconscious wish inscribe itself in a dream? Freud claims that the unconscious wish cannot materialise in the dream-text directly, but has to attach itself to "day-residues", fragments from the dreamer's recent waking experience. These fragments constitute part of the explicit dream-text, and their overall function is to disguise the illicit unconscious wish, thus allowing it to elude the censorship of the ego. The real kernel of the unconscious is not the dream-text, whether explicit or latent, but the desire that inscribes itself through the very distortion embodied by the narrative content of the dream. That is to say: the unconscious is the *form* of the desire that attaches itself to a certain narrative, whilst the content of a dream is, as Freud famously put it, "the guardian of sleep", a narrative whose main role is to absorb the shock potential of the forbidden unconscious desire. This means that the desire at stake in Freud's theory of dreams can only be defined as a deflagration of illicit libido, or even, in a Benjaminian sense, as a leap into a radically different temporality, the desire for an Event to intervene from a different time-frame. In relation to film, the unconscious of the Freudian tradition makes itself available as a kind of unrepresentable gravitational pull that "shapes" what we see, conferring upon it its own specific distortion.

With films, as well as dreams (and any other symbolic structure), the crucial psychoanalytic question is not "What does this narrative mean?", but rather "What fundamental act of repression, or foreclosure, allowed this narrative to emerge as it is?" The unconscious is precisely what needs to be foreclosed so that a certain narrative can emerge. What is at stake in the unconscious is therefore the opposite of a synthetic function: the negative force of the imagination, the capacity of our mind to dismember what immediate perception puts together. From this viewpoint, Moro's discreet escape works as a visual prop for the unconscious wish aimed at the shattering encounter with the gaze. That is to say: the kernel of Chiara's desire is of a psychotic nature; her fantasy of Moro's freedom is the ultimate defensive mechanism against the devastating power of imagination, which, as such, would truly set *her* free. The main objection I put to Bellocchio, therefore, is not that he has too much faith in imagination, but that *he has not enough*. If truly endorsed, imagination coincides with Lacan's *fundamental fantasy*, the traumatic dimension where "the unconscious happens".

3
Unbearable Freedoms: the Real of Sexual Difference from Rossellini to Fassbinder

Having established the centrality of drive for a theory of cinema that may wish to concern itself with Lacanian ethics, what is left to do is verify the impact of any cinematic attempt to throw a bridge towards "the hazy shores of freedom". It may come as a surprise that the majority of the directors mentioned below are seen as exemplary bearers of a strong Christian sensitivity towards the question of liberation, especially in its connection with masochism. The Christian legacy they represent, however, is based on what can only appear as the shocking assumption that the place of God is empty. More precisely, at the heart of the cinema I discuss in relation to the problem of freedom there is the revelation that God, to say it with Lacan, is unconscious.

3.1 Enjoying gravity

In *Gravity and Grace* Simone Weil writes of the spiritual physics of art as 'a double movement of descent: to do again, out of love, what gravity does' (Weil 1987: 137). This understanding of gravity needs to be radicalised if we are to link film and psychoanalysis: *gravity has to do with the ground only insofar as the ground has to do with the unconscious.* As a symbolic structure of interrelated signs film is sustained, quite literally, by symptomatic knots of unconscious enjoyment. To the extent that cinema is, in its ultimate configuration, precisely this mindless enjoyment, which is not the spectator's "visual pleasure" but the way cinema enjoys itself regardless of its teleology, of the conscious message it carries.

At the end of Antonioni's *The Cry* (Il grido, 1957), Aldo (Steve Cochran) climbs atop the tower of the furnace where he used to work, whilst Irma (Alida Valli), his ex-lover, follows him from a distance. As he moves up Irma calls his name aloud – a call that, to quote the screenplay, 'is the only thing in the world that could pull him out of his depression'.

The screenplay continues: 'He leans over the railing and reels for a moment as if to resist a sudden vertigo. Irma looks up from below. [...] She emits a bloodcurdling scream. In the silence, her loud, long outcry accompanies Aldo's fall, covering the sound that his body makes as it strikes the ground' (in Chatman 1985: 40). As with Rossellini's *Germany Year Zero* (Germania anno zero, 1947), film here does exactly what pre-scribed by Weil: it repeats, *out of love*, the lesson of gravity. It is crucial to stress that Aldo's fall, like Edmund's in Rossellini's film, cannot be explained away as a suicide, the tragic gesture of a man who has been trampled all over by life. Despite what is suggested through narrative continuity, this is not a conscious leap into the void, but the result of the vertigo suddenly experienced by the hero – a vertigo meant to capture the impossibility of his relationship to Irma.

Jacques Rancière (2006: 9) writes that '[c]inema, in the double power of the conscious eye of the director and the unconscious eye of the camera, is the perfect embodiment of Schelling's and Hegel's argument that the identity of conscious and unconscious is the very principle of art'. This notion of film as an encounter between active and passive, the conscious power of the director and the infinite power of the automaton-like passiv-ity of the camera – which is also the way Rancière reads Deleuze's dialectic of movement-image and time-image – seems particularly insightful if we read "passivity" alongside the Lacanian Real. For Lacan, this phan-tomatic Real of enjoyment, *jouissance*, constitutes the foundation of "everything that stands". The potential of cinema is to unravel the dialec-tic of symbolic meaning and its Real supplement through which meaning itself can be, as it were, reset to zero, and consequently reconfigured. Although cinema is, as Žižek claims, the pervert's art by definition, inso-far as it tells us how to desire (how to fantasise), it simultaneously invites us to locate this Real in which every meaning is necessarily anchored. Ultimately, by locating the Real in cinema we are able to make sense of the key Žižekian theme that links liberation to trauma – the "liberation hurts" theme.

In European cinema we have a number of examples of this conver-gence of trauma and liberation in relation to sexual difference. One of these is provided by the Michel Piccoli character's shooting of his wife in Marco Ferreri's *Dillinger is Dead* (Dillinger è morto, 1969). In this claustrophobic tale of human alienation, an engineer breaks with his empty bourgeois life without ever becoming fully aware of his inten-tions. One day he comes home from work to find his wife in bed with a headache and a cold meal on the table. We follow him in a number of apparently routine activities such as cooking, setting up a projector, and flirting with the maid, after which he comes across a gun, assembles it, and paints it. Eventually, he shoots his wife while she is asleep, and immediately after leaves home to take a boat heading for Tahiti, with the prospect of a new relationship with a young woman he meets on board. What should not be missed about his progressive slipping into psychosis that leads to uxoricide is the gesture of pointing the gun *against himself* whilst looking in the mirror, which recalls Travis' (Robert De Niro) famous "you talking to me?" monologue in Martin Scorsese's *Taxi Driver* (1976). This gesture tells us that the real aim of his murderous act, in itself nothing but a misplaced "passage à l'acte", was to kill off what was "in him more than himself", his own attachment to his bourgeois milieu. This is another instance in which a symptomatic reading of film would seem to confirm that the act of liberation is primarily self-directed and it involves a degree of psychosis. Even stylistically there is nothing to explain here, only the pure, "psychotic" self-referentiality of the image.

Despite what we might infer when considering its traumatic content, *Dillinger is dead* speaks for the paradoxical vitality of the death-drive. Far from relating to death as such, the Lacanian death-drive designates *the opposite of dying*; death-drive is

> a name for the 'undead' eternal life itself, [...] the way immortality appears within psychoanalysis, an uncanny *excess* of life, an 'undead' urge which persists beyond the (biological) cycle of life and death. [...] The ultimate lesson of psychoanalysis is that human life is never 'just life': humans are not simply alive, they are possessed by the strange drive to enjoy life in excess, passionately attached to a surplus which sticks out and derails the ordinary run of things. (Žižek 2003: 62)

Commenting on agency in Rossellini's cinema, Rancière (2006: 13) saw very perspicaciously how 'the character's extreme liberty coincides with his or her absolute subjection to a command. [...] it is a dialectic of impotence and excessive power'. The paradox is that when we act we are in fact *acted*, we enter a kind of "uncharted territory" where we perform our gestures as if guided by an invisible hand: 'in an authentic act – Žižek writes – the highest freedom coincides with the utmost passivity, with a reduction to a lifeless automaton who blindly performs its gestures'. This means that the act occurs without any fantasmatic support, whereas activity is secretly sustained by an underlying fantasy. Consequently, the act radically divides the subject, who is unable to 'assume it as "his own", posit himself as its author-agent – the authentic act that I accomplish is always by definition a foreign body, an intruder which simultaneously fascinates and repels me, so that if and when I come too close to it, this leads to my *aphanisis*, self-erasure' (Žižek 2000a: 374–5).

It is plain to see how this apprehension of the act and the previously mentioned notion of drive are correlated. We accomplish an act only if we empty our subjective framework from its wealth of subject positions, only if we are *driven* towards a "derailing" experience that compels us to detach from our symbolic context. Far from relying upon an idealistic position, this emphasis on substanceless subjectivity takes us straight into the heart of militant materialism:

> Materialism is not the assertion of inert material density in its humid heaviness – such a 'materialism' can always serve as a support for Gnostic spiritualist obscurantism. In contrast to it, a true materialism joyously assumes the 'disappearance of matter', the fact that there is only void. (Žižek 2004: 25)

Or, more comprehensively put, materialism means that

> we should assert that 'objective' knowledge of reality is impossible precisely because we (consciousness) are always-already part of it, in the midst of it – the thing that separates us from objective knowledge of reality is our very inclusion in it [. . .] the correct materialist position [. . .] is that *there is no universe as a Whole*: as a Whole, the universe (the world) is Nothing – everything that exists is *within* this Nothing. (Žižek 2002a: 180–1)

The properly political point concerns the reappropriation of this void, this nothing, through a universal cause such as, first and foremost, the subject. Therein lies the reason of Žižek's fascination with biogenetics. What we get with biogenetic planning is the anti-humanistic emphasis on the potential disappearance of 'the illusion of the autonomy of personhood' (Žižek 2004: 18). Thinking the human body as a technologically modifiable unit and the self as an insubstantial genetic formula also means connecting the subject with its empty/virtual core. The new existential scenario opened up by biogenetics takes us back to the "old" scenario described by Lacanian psychoanalysis, with its emphasis on the non-existence (or virtuality) of the subject. This is why we should treasure Michelangelo Antonioni's (and Rossellini's) lesson: his cinematic subjects embrace virtuality precisely in this psychoanalytic guise.

In his enlightening discussion of Rossellini's aesthetics, Rancière claims that 'for Rossellini, there is no beautiful shot that is not a moment of grace in the strongest, Pauline sense of the term; no beautiful shot that does not give its absolute consent to the encounter with the thing or person it was not searching for'. Without mentioning it, Rancière hints at the encounter with the unconscious substance that qualifies the Lacanian act. This is why the parricide and eventual suicide committed by young Edmund (Edmund Meschke) in *Germany Year Zero* (Germania anno zero, 1948) cannot be explained through the ideological content of the film:

> The film would be infinitely reassuring if all it did was to urge us to condemn dangerous words and protect a child who is being crushed under the weight of a world in ruins. But all that really weighs on Edmund is the crushing weight of the liberty of year zero. The Nazi catechism cannot produce the act, and remorse cannot drive him to suicide. There is no cause in either case, but only vertigo, the attraction exerted by the void of unlimited possibility: the gaping window of the bombed out building, the window that is also the source of the light that forms the white squares Edmund pretends to shoot at with his imaginary pistol. (Rancière 2006: 131)

Similarly, according to Žižek Edmund stands for 'the subject of the signifier, i.e., for the subject insofar as it is reduced to an empty place without support in imaginary or symbolic identification'. Thus, Edmund's jump demarcates the collapse of meaning, the ground zero of ideology:

> What propels him into act is an awareness of the ultimate insufficiency and nullity of every ideological foundation: he succeeds in occupying that impossible/real empty place where words no longer oblige, where their performative power is suspended. This is 'Germany, Year Zero': Germany in the year of absolute freedom when the intersubjective bond, the engagement of the Word is broken. True, we can call this also 'psychosis', but what is 'psychosis' here if not another name for freedom? (Žižek 2001b: 36)

The attraction to the "void called subject", the unbearable lightness of the fall, is a key component of Rossellini's cinema. I am thinking of Pina's (Anna Magnani) death in *Rome, Open City*, or Michele's (Sandro Franchina) suicide in *No Greater Love* (Europa '51, 1952); or, as Rancière remarked apropos *Francis, God's Juggler* (Francesco, Giullare di Dio, 1950), 'the call presented by St Francis of Assisi, God's Juggler, who teaches his brothers that the way to decide where they must go and preach is to spin round and round, as kids do, until vertigo throws them on the ground and points them in the right direction of the call' (Rancière 2006: 132). These observations are meant to bolster my claim that the emergence of subjectivity in Rossellini's neorealist films is to be linked dialectically to an utterly heterogeneous feature that critics have variously named epiphanic, miraculous, elliptical, sacred,[18] a feature which ultimately stands for the Rossellinian subject's unconscious assumption of his or her repressed desire.

The best way to track this passage from realism to the Real is by looking at what many consider the most accomplished of Rossellini's "Bergman films", *Voyage to Italy*, which chronicles the breakdown of an English couple's marriage during their trip to the south of Italy. The unconventional narration reminds one of Antonioni, for the plot is reduced to the bone and filled with *temps morts*, while the camera focuses on insignificant details concerning the journey south of the increasingly detached Alex (George Sanders) and Katherine Joyce (Ingrid Bergman). As with most of Antonioni's films, we are denied access to primary narrative information (the reasons behind the couple's crisis). The emphasis shifts instead on the Italian landscape, which gradually fills up and widens the gap between man and woman. Of the two, Katherine is the one whose actions indicate a potential way out of the couple's stifling sentimental impasse, as she gains a distance from this impasse by directing her attention to the external world. Alone, she drives through Naples, visits museums and catacombs, and eventually – this time with her husband – the ruins of Pompeii, growing more and more engrossed in the natural spectacles she beholds, 'the physicality and rawness of the ancient world, the ubiquity of death in life' (Brunette 1996: 166).

The visit to Pompeii leads to the controversial final sequence, which I shall discuss in sub-chapter 3.7. For the moment, suffice it to observe how Rossellini's film makes the implicit statement that sexual relationships are ontologically unworkable, insofar as they are fraught with an objectal excess that cannot be integrated into the whole, a Real remainder whose indelible persistence in the inter-subjective field throws any preconceived idea of harmony off balance. Commenting on *Voyage to Italy*, Rancière (2006: 132–3) identifies this excess/remainder in 'a sound we cannot hear, the sound of the pebbles Katherine Joyce tells her husband about in the sun-drenched terrace of Uncle Homer's villa. These pebbles had been thrown at her misty, rain-splashed window by a young man, barely more than a child, who was later found chilled to the bones in the garden'. The subtext is James Joyce's short story *The Dead*, where the cause of the intangible ennui in the relationship between Gabriel and Gretta Conroy suddenly acquires a name: Michael Furey, the young passionate poet Gretta refers to nostalgically. The status of this allusion is indeed symptomatic of the role played by fantasy *qua* third constitutive element of the relationship, for the moment this disavowed fantasy is openly exchanged or "made public", the relationship is suddenly at risk of crumbling.

As for Rossellini's realism, the disavowed surplus sustaining the whole can be identified in the representation of "authentic" Italy. Authenticity here is a misnomer, and as such it ought to be clarified via a reference to the indestructible, "undead" quality of the external world as it opens up in front of Katherine's eyes. As in Joyce's short story, the dead here (particularly in the Pompeii sequence where an archaeologist digs out a man and a woman caught by the volcanic eruption whilst in bed together) *are more alive than the living*, but precisely because they embody the Lacanian lamella, the libido-object that cannot die, persisting after biological death and undermining any attempt at symbolic signification. This lamella is the lifeblood of Rossellini's Italy, constantly intruding, slipping through the fractures of the narrative – as epitomised in the wonderful passage where Katherine, whilst visiting mount Vesuvius, takes cognisance of the boiling lava and the process by which it produces the uncanny phenomenon of ionisation: when lighting a torch or a cigarette in proximity of the lava, thick smoke immediately arises from every nearby crater, as if by magic. What better figuration of the Lacanian Real! A formless, slimy, dangerous substance endowed with the power to change instantly the configuration of external reality.[19] *Voyage to Italy* is a voyage to *this* Real.

As with the best "road movies", then, the theme of the journey here is eminently metaphorical, suggesting not only the literal crossing of borders, but most of all a journey to an unknown, threatening place – ultimately, the unconscious itself: 'an entrance one can only reach just as it closes (the place will never be popular with tourists)' (Lacan 2007: 711). A similar journey is at stake in some Ingmar Bergman's best films such as *Wild Strawberries* (Smultronstället, 1957) and *The Silence* (Tystnaden, 1963). In the latter, for instance, the place of arrival is definitely *not* a tourist location (there are tanks in the streets), but the foreign city of Timoka. This is not the name of a real city, as Bergman initially thought, but an Estonian word meaning "belonging to the executioner". As is well known, Bergman often suffered from panic attacks when in foreign surroundings (see Steene 1975: 8); the significance of the film is therefore to be sought in the director's willingness to confront his deepest fear, which of course coincides with his most authentic desire, his fundamental fantasy, and can be appreciated in a recurrent dream he had at that time:

> I am in an enormous, foreign city. I am on my way towards the forbidden part of town. It is not even some dubious areas of ill repute with its steaming flesh pots, but something much worse. There the laws of reality and the rules of society cease to exist. Anything can happen and everything does. I dreamed this dream over and over again. The irritating thing was, I was always on my way to the forbidden part of the city, but I never actually reached it. Either I happened to wake up, or it changed into another dream. (Bergman 1995: 108–9)

Going back to gravity, there are many "leaps into the void" in European cinema, whether metaphorical or not, and it would be pointless now to start enumerating them. I shall only mention the ending of Robert Bresson's *Mouchette* (1967). My overarching point here is that Bresson's cinema of disembodied gestures owes its originality to the inscription of vertiginous acts which may redeem or liberate through passive acceptance or sacrifice. Mouchette (Nadine Nortier) kills herself in a very unusual way: she rolls down a slope and into a river of the French countryside, a move she tries three times before accomplishing it. As in the following *A Gentle Woman* (Une femme douce, 1969), which opens with the heroine jumping off the window of her flat, the obvious implication is that suicide is liberating. The story-line in *Mouchette* (as in *Germany Year Zero*) presents us with enough sociological reasons to make us sympathise with the poor peasant girl's predicament. The central motif, however, has to do with her discovery of sexuality, and her suicide effectively symbolises the Real of sexual difference. During the film she is exposed to a number of situations which introduce her to the problem of enjoyment: she sees her classmates flip upside down on a rail, thus flashing their underwear in her face; when passing a doorway, a boy calls out her name and drops his trousers; she witnesses a sexual competition between the gamekeeper Mathieu (Jean Vimenet) and poacher Arsène (Jean-Claude Gilbert) over Louisa (Marine Trichet), the barmaid; she is briefly courted by a young man at the fair in the famous sequence of the bumper-cars; in the key passage of the film, finally, she is deflowered by Arsène, whom later she refers to as 'my lover'. The whole point is that Mouchette is learning to desire the Lacanian way, i.e. *through other people's desire.* For her, becoming a woman involves learning to place a fantasy screen between herself and the other(s); she attempts to do that, for example, by progressively taking the place of her dying mother in her squalid domestic environment. Her problem, however, is that she is not allowed to fantasise. A modicum of "fantasy space", for instance, is what she is desperately seeking in Arsène's place before he violates her.[20] Her final suicide is thus symbolic of *her failure to become a woman*: before rolling into the river, she wraps herself in the white dress she was supposed to cloth her dead mother in. On the way to femininity, Mouchette would like to emerge as a mother; she fails, and in this failure we catch a glimpse of femininity itself. The film is sharply divided between "perverse" phallic sexuality and feminine enjoyment (Mouchette, Louisa, and Mouchette's mother are all representative of a type of enjoyment that defies the purely sexual/phallic dimension), and this irredeemable gap is what the heroine's suicide ultimately crystallises. Bresson's typically claustrophobic universe is the feminine universe of symbolic identification without exceptions.

3.2   I suffer, therefore I am

Rainer Werner Fassbinder's cinema is also a voyage to the Real, and amongst the most recklessly unashamed ones in European film. The trait of Fassbinder's cinema that makes it absolutely relevant today is its ability to explore the tortured connections between desire, power and liberation, on both a personal and collective level. Particularly intriguing is the director's ambiguous stance on the question of masochism as a strategy of liberation. When one looks at Fassbinder's composite oeuvre, it is difficult not to notice the centrality reserved to the treatment of masochism, which is what is truly at stake in his interest in abject characters portrayed as victims. The relationship between victim and executioner is at the pulsating heart of Fassbinder's imagination. One thing must be clear from the start. When I refer to masochism as a strategy of liberation I do not mean "the theatre of sadomasochism", which is merely a way to dupe the guard of the superego (to pretend that we are contravening its injunction to enjoy whilst we are actually enjoying pain). In *Seminar VII*, Lacan (1999: 239) stated that '[t]he economy of masochistic pain ends up looking like the economy of goods', which means that 'pathological sado-masochism ultimately involves a "utilitarian" pain *for* the sake of pleasure and, as such, does not go beyond the pleasure principle' (Chiesa 2007: 180). And even less am I referring to the postmodern logic of victimisation which, as Žižek has convincingly argued, is part and parcel of today's ideological predicament. What I am aiming at involves, rather, the painful confrontation with Lacan's fundamental fantasy, upon whose foreclosure the process of subjectivation is based: 'what the fundamental fantasy stages is precisely the scene of constitutive submission/subjection that sustains the subject's "inner freedom"' (Žižek 2000a: 280).

The ruse of "masochistic theatre" is nicely captured in the famous scene from Buñuel's *The Phantom of Liberty* where a sadomasochistic couple meticulously arranges for an oddly-assorted audience (including three monks) to congregate in a hotel room with the excuse of sharing some Port and engaging in civilised conversation. After changing secretly into their S&M attire, the two suddenly perform their "whipping act" in front of the stunned audience, even complaining when, a few moments later, these unwitting onlookers start flocking out of the room in shock and disbelief. The point to emphasise is that such performances do not disturb the smooth functioning of the symbolic order, precisely because they openly rely on its efficiency: firstly, 'the faked spectacle of punishment' (Žižek 2000a: 281) can function only previous to the stipulation of a symbolic contract between the masochist and his dominatrix; secondly, it is sustained by a third gaze, i.e. it is performed for the big Other.

In Fassbinder's cinema we experience an altogether different, more complex approach to masochism. In this respect, the first thing to do is recognise a basic elusiveness in the director's own position, a slight disparity between what he *consciously* argues for and what his films *unconsciously* reveal. As for his cinematic use of and political interest in masochism, his stance seems fairly clear: 'There is no such thing as masochism without sadism. And relationships between people are always sado-masochistic as a direct result of their upbringing' (in Rayns 1979: 93). According to Fassbinder, the distorted character of contemporary sexual or more generally social relationships is to be understood as a historically specific dysfunction emanating directly from the contradictions of our socio-political milieu. This is why the key character in his cinema is "the victim" and the key theme 'the manipulability, the exploitability of feelings within the system that we live in, and that at least one generation or more after us will certainly have to live in' (Fassbinder 1992: 28). On the other hand, he also adumbrates a more profound and to an extent indefinable role played by masochism, one that not only reflects and denounces social injustice but also hints at liberation: 'only those individuals who can accept their own masochism are on the way to being healthy. [...] Yes, to enjoy pain is always cleverer than simply to suffer it' (in Rayns 1979: 94). Fassbinder's position on masochism, as it emerges in his writings, can therefore be summed up as follows: 1. Perverted human (sexual) relationships are the result of social injustice. 2. The way out of this predicament involves directly assuming the very dysfunction.

The immediate remark to make concerns the first point. Considering the sexual deadlock as an epiphenomenon, i.e. the result of a more fundamental disturbance (class difference), only makes sense if conceived against the background hypothesis of a "healthy" universe where sexual difference, as well as class difference, would be eliminated. There is a moving sequence in *Gods of the Plague* (Götter der pest, 1970) where Franz Walsch (Harry Baer), the Gorilla (Günther Kaufmann), and Margarethe (Margarethe von Trotta), imagine their escape to a Greek island, where they would live on fishing, hunting and drinking wine. Similarly, the whole of *Rio Das Mortes* (1970) is built around the longing for an alternative life in Peru. These examples capture the key tension and dominant mood in Fassbinder's cinema (especially of the earlier phase), which is one where the sleepwalking hopelessness of his stylised crooks and drifters is somewhat magically related to a utopian/anarchic space outside modern alienation, without however giving in to its lure. Utopia for Fassbinder also seems to mean the end of sexual difference, a social community where the loved one is gleefully shared with one's best friend.[21] Such a society 'would function without hierarchies, without fear, without aggression' (Fassbinder 1992: 19), something akin to a democratic order *not* based on repression. If on the one hand this view reminds us of Fassbinder's sympathy for anarchic movements, on the other it ties in with the Marxian thesis of the classless society to come. It is here that we should emphasise how strongly Fassbinder's cinema resists ceding to its utopian temptation and, instead, keeps proposing, obsessively, the dialectic of degradation and liberation.

In a similar manner to Pasolini, Fassbinder knew that every true process of liberation from a given power edifice implies a painful passage through a dark, at least minimally masochistic scenario, since the subject is first and foremost required to gain a distance from his/her obscene libidinal attachment to, or investment in, what keeps him/her in check. The problem is therefore that freedom cannot be embraced effortlessly. When, for instance, he was asked why the servant Marlene (Irm Hermann) walks out at the end of *The Bitter Tears of Petra von Kant* (Die Bitteren Tränen der Petra von Kant, 1972), when Petra (Margit Carstensen) offers her freedom and equality, Fassbinder gave a very precise answer:

Because the servant accepts her own repression and exploitation, and is therefore afraid of the freedom she is offered. What goes with freedom is the responsibility of having to think about your own existence, and that is something that she has never had to do; she has always simply followed orders, and never had to make her own decisions. When she finally leaves Petra, she is not, I think, heading for freedom but going in search of another slave-existence. [...] It would be wildly optimistic, even utopian, to imagine that someone who has done and thought nothing for thirty years except what others have thought for her would all of a sudden choose freedom. (in Rayns 1979: 84–5)

One thinks here of Lars Von Trier's *Manderlay* (2005), which shows how problematic a question emancipation from slavery (let alone the introduction of democracy) is – or, for that matter, *Viridiana*, where Buñuel cruelly mocks his heroine's idealism. Interestingly, at one point the naïvety of *Manderlay*'s heroine Grace (Bryce Dallas Howard) transfers from the social arena to the bedroom, encountering there the same substantial impasse: the handsome black slave she had idealised in the name of what we might call her "multicultural ethos" turns out to be disturbingly over-aggressive.

The persistence with which Fassbinder stages the eroticisation of pain accounts for his awareness that what is at stake in masochism is not only submission, but also, crucially, our most profound attachment to life. What Fassbinder relentlessly attempts to represent is the masochistic experience as something akin to the fundamental fantasy, which 'provides the subject with the minimum of being, it serves as a support for his existence – in short, its deceptive gesture is 'Look, I suffer, therefore I am, I exist, I participate in the positive order of being' (Žižek 2000a: 281). And the point is that our unconscious masochistic attachment to life needs to be consciously (and painfully) assumed if we are to free ourselves from its spell.

But let us go back to sexual difference. In Fassbinder's cinema there is clearly no such thing as freedom in sexual, as well as class, relationships. From his first films to *Querelle de Brest* (1982), the universality of class difference finds a veritable echo in the universal resonance of sexual difference. *The Bitter Tears of Petra von Kant*, with its constantly oscillating emphasis on sexual (Petra and Karin) and class (Petra and Marlene) difference, is a perfect case in point. It chronicles the torrid lesbian relationship between Petra, a successful and arrogant fashion designer in her mid-30s, and Karin (Hanna Schygulla), a cunning young woman cynically after a career in modelling; as such it amounts to a prototypical story of power struggle in the sexual relationship. Although the film features only women (women caught in a bourgeois/patriarchal narrative),[22] the impasse it explores is presented as ontological, irrespective of historical or gender-related considerations. The revealing aspect is (as always with film) form, that is to say the specific aesthetics the film embraces. The narrative's thematic claustrophobia and bleakness are reflected successfully in its style, for the entire story takes place in Petra's apartment, conceived as a theatre stage. Typically, Fassbinder exploits filmic resources with great inventiveness (deep focus compositions, tracking shots, etc.) and, more importantly, in such a way that they materialise the narrative's deepest concern. In this case, it is a matter of building an invisible cage around the main character. Thus humiliation, including self-humiliation (Petra is an auto-biographical character), becomes a stylistic cipher. In infusing narratives of degradation with aesthetic pleasure, Fassbinder's cinema as a whole reinforces the concept that liberation can only be the result of "self-beating". Formally, the aim is to draw us as close as possible to the hopeless condition of his fictional characters, to the point that we might find ourselves empathising with their condition of radical exclusion. Fassbinder achieves this by constantly juxtaposing Brechtian estrangement and classic (Hollywood) identification techniques.

In this respect, the question of femininity is central. Fassbinder's cruelty is not directed at women, as many critics noted, with indignation, when *The Bitter Tears of Petra von Kant* was released. It is mainly self-directed, insofar as the self matters *objectively*, as the most trustworthy representative of the external world, a world engaged in an endless struggle with its own contradictions. One of the basic lessons of psychoanalysis is that to be able to look at the world we first have to pass through the self, and take its division into consideration. This is why it would be a mistake to explore Fassbinder's work through the "identity politics" paradigm. Not only have questions of race, gender and ethnicity always been secondary, for him, to the question of class: 'I'm often irritated by all the talk about women's liberation. The world isn't a case of women against men, but of poor against rich, of repressed against repressors. And there are just as many repressed men as there are repressed women' (in Rayns 1979: 85); but also, at a deeper level, the question of sexual difference is treated by him as homologous to that of class difference, in the sense that *it disturbs the same universal split*. If Fassbinder has often preferred to work with female characters, then, it is because of the rich complexity he saw in feminine sexuality (see Rayns 1979: 89), and because of his personal affinity with it in terms of sensitivity. This complexity concerns mainly woman's basic ambiguity towards oppression: 'I know some fairly emancipated women who enjoy being repressed and at the same time fight against their repression. It's a state full of contradictions' (in Rayns 1979: 91). Once again, we should insist that Fassbinder – like Pasolini, Bergman, Godard, and to an extent Von Trier – is profoundly fascinated by this contradiction, which is more likely to emerge in femininity and effectively amounts to the enigma of masochism. One thinks of Godard's 1960s films, where woman is often represented as a commodity, an image exploited by consumerism; again, the key point is that, in films such as *Vivre sa vie* (1962), to this position of exploitation corresponds woman's readiness to fully assume it (see Sontag 1964).

As for Fassbinder, a work like *Fox and His Friends* (Faustrecht der Freiheit, 1975) shows the extent to which gender, for him, is a psychological condition inextricably related to class. As a gay film, it goes as far as it can to demonstrate that the identity issue is *less* relevant than the question of class difference. The striking point about this film, and a sign of Fassbinder's genius, is that it dares *not* to represent gays as a victimised minority; on the contrary, the "gay universe" is explicitly linked to the oppressing class, to the extent that it is even associated with Nazi ideology. Franz Bieberkopf, nicknamed Fox and played by Fassbinder himself, is a young working-class (unemployed) gay man who wins the lottery, falls in love with Eugen (Peter Chatel), is drawn into upper-class gay circles, and is eventually ripped off, humiliated, driven to despair and, finally, to suicide by his rich friends. The film's charm, irrespective of its bleak narrative, is that despite being totally immersed in a gay universe it is actually more concerned with the issue of class exploitation. Being gay is never presented as a problem; rather, it is seen as the norm. This is explicitly stated, for example, in the scenes where Eugen's parents are shown as being more worried about their social status and financial condition than their son's "deviant" sexual inclinations. The gay middle-/upper-class world is denounced by Fassbinder as being corrupted, hedonistic and evil, which works well as an indictment not only of the dominant gay world itself but more importantly of the dominant class.

The crucial theme of the film, however, has to do with Fox's more or less unconscious death-drive. As with most of Fassbinder's heroes, he is depicted as complicit in his own downfall, which means that we are not merely dealing with a case of social Darwinism. More significantly, we find here the same overall strategy often used by Pasolini, inasmuch as the film as a whole is constructed around the figure of a poor devil whose inevitable demise proves instrumental to the uncovering of the oppressors' sadistic perseverance in evil. It is not only that without figures like Fox – or, say, Accattone (Franco Citti) in Pasolini's eponymous 1961 debut-feature – any denunciation of the brutal heart of power would prove unpersuasive, but rather that it is only in the character's Fall that one is encouraged to read the signs of a new beginning. True hope can only emerge from hopelessness.

The key Christian *topos* of Fall and Redemption – in itself a central theme in European cinema – is a dominant trait of Fassbinder's sensitivity. Apropos this double movement, Žižek highlights how Redemption is already *implicitly* contained in the Fall:

> the Fall is *in itself* already its own self-sublation, the wound is *in itself* already its own healing, so that the perception that we are dealing with the Fall is ultimately a misperception, an effect of our distorted perspective [. . .]. We rise again from the Fall not by undoing its effects, but in recognizing the longed-for liberation in the Fall itself. (Žižek 2003: 86)

In its ruthless cruelty, the final sequence of *Fox and His Friends* – depicting two kids as they mercilessly search Fox's dead body after his suicide – speaks for the director's fascination with the Fall, the very humiliation suffered by Christ-like figures like Fox. The existential parable of these figures suggests that their real aim is *to alienate themselves completely from their symbolic universe*. In the film's brilliant final sequence, staged in a finely stylised underground station bathed in shades of blue (a colour suggesting "freedom in detachment"), cruelty is indeed redoubled. First the two kids rob Fox of the last of his money (the 8,000 marks he got from selling his sports car) as he lays dead; then, one of his old working-class friends walks past him with Max (Karlheinz Böhm), the rich man he had seduced him at the start of the film, but eventually both walk away to avoid getting into trouble. Fassbinder denies his hero even the consolation of posthumous working-class solidarity, for – in a passage that reminds us of the ending of Robert Bresson's *The Devil Probably. . .* (Le diable probablement. . . 1977), where the dead hero is robbed by his best friend – he *wants* him to appear uncompromisingly alone, humiliated, reduced to an anonymous lifeless body. The character's masochistic streak is thus reflected and subsumed in the director's broader vision, where human pathos is counterbalanced, if not eclipsed, by the sheer determination to stage the masochistic scene. Ultimately, Fassbinder's filmmaking and biography meet. In both, the unbearable awareness of oppression feeds the assurance that freedom belongs to a condition of painful self-contraction brought about by the endorsement of the fundamental fantasy. For this reason, the direct translation of the film's German title ("the first law of freedom") is more accurate. For Fassbinder, indeed, freedom begins with utter degradation.

We should not forget, however, that at the heart of Fox's demise there lies the same old obstacle of Fassbinder's cinema, the sexual deadlock. For Fox and Eugen the sexual relationship is indeed impracticable, since one gives everything (Fox), while the other simply takes (Eugen). It is not directly a matter of femininity vs masculinity, but rather gullibility (the nickname Fox is indeed ironic) vs greed and exploitation. When it comes to the melodramatic representation of sexual difference, Fassbinder tends to operate along the same lines: he consciously displaces the sexual deadlock onto the deadlock of class exploitation. If the emotional focus of almost all his films is a more or less melodramatic situation highlighting the tragic impossibility of relationships, the underlying argument he presents, as a rule, ends with the acerbic condemnation of social inequality. In ideological terms, therefore, Fassbinder would seem to distance himself from the Lacanian axiom of sexual difference. For him, the gap between the sexes is a historical consequence of a more profound malaise concerning the perverse (capitalist) organisation of the social sphere (capital does not spare the bed). As a 'romantic anarchist' (Fassbinder 1992: 67), he constructed most of his works around the melancholic utopia of unadulterated relationships in a society spared from capitalistic exploitation.

We are now in a position to refine the understanding of the two poles of Fassbinder's sensitivity: on the one hand a nihilistic obligation to emphasise the self-relating negativity of the subject, which emerges through death-drive and the staging of masochism *qua* fundamental fantasy; on the other, the persistence of melancholy, i.e. the fantasmatic attachment to a utopian condition of plenitude to come.

Masochism features strongly in all of Fassbinder's melodramas, which, as is well known, were greatly influenced by Douglas Sirk. Here the Lacanian theme of the impossibility of the sexual relationship comes into full view, especially in the underlying equation of marriage and sadomasochism. In an early classic like *The Merchant of Four Seasons* (Händler der vier Jahreszeiten, 1971), set in 1950s Germany, the displacement of sexual difference onto social alienation seems at first sight too prominent, too programmatic to channel sufficient emphasis into the main character's masochistic drive. The explanation for the failure of the relationship between Hans (Hans Hirschmüller), a street fruit vendor, and Irmgard (Irm Hermann), his petit-bourgeois wife, is presented to us through a series of vaguely stylised flashbacks. Hans had served in the Foreign Legion and later joined the police, where he had been fired for lack of discipline. Before marrying Irmgard, he had naïvely fallen for the idea that a gift of flowers would win him a marriage proposal with another woman, 'the great love of his life' (played by Ingrid Caven, at the time married to Fassbinder), but she had rejected him on the grounds of his humble job. Fassbinder thus provides us with a coherent elucidation of his character's inability to achieve personal happiness and integrate in his social milieu, in what is meant to be another highly critical film of the West German society of the Adenauer economic miracle.

To locate the film's unconscious core, however, we need to look elsewhere, first and foremost in the insistence with which the camera cuts off Hans from his environment, suggesting either that, as in a Greek tragedy, his fate was always-already sealed, or, more insightfully, that he somehow *seeks* his own undoing. The obstinacy of the camera's gaze is correlative to the empty stare in his character's eyes, which from the beginning alludes not only to his being doomed, but more precisely to his *secret enjoyment* of that tragic condition. This comes to the fore in the penultimate scene of the film, where Hans, having found the strength to momentarily step out of the daily grind that slowly consumes him, drinks himself to death in front of his petit-bourgeois relatives. Despair and, eventually, suicide, play a double role in Fassbinder, serving both as a direct critical indictment of warped social relations and as a strategy to conjure up an image of redemption. What matters supremely to Fassbinder is the shattering encounter with the "void called subject", for deep down he knows that only there an image of liberation from social oppression may arise. Being complicit in their downfalls, Hans and Fox voice both a powerful indictment of capitalist exploitation, and a metaphorical leap into freedom. In a passage that closely echoes Pasolini's theory on the metaphorical resemblance of death and editing (see Pasolini 1995: 237–41), Fassbinder commented thus on the significance of death:

> Life doesn't become manageable and accessible until the moment when death is accepted as the true aspect of existence. As long as death is treated as a taboo, life remains uninteresting. A society based on the exploitation of human beings has to treat death as a taboo. (Fassbinder 1992: 29)

Fassbinder's films indicate that the taboo of death can be challenged if "death" is coupled with "drive". Metaphorically speaking, masochism for him implies the suspension of the character's immersion in the symbolic order, achieved through the insistence of drive.

Let us recall the main argument. In Lacanian psychoanalysis the emergence of pure subjectivity coincides with what Žižek describes as an 'experience of radical self-degradation' whereby I, the subject, am emptied 'of all substantial content, of all symbolic support which could confer a modicum of dignity on me'. The reason why such a humiliating and potentially perverse position of self-degradation is to be assumed, he argues, is that within a disciplinary relationship (between "master and servant"), self-beating is, in its deepest configuration, nothing but the staging of the other's secret fantasy; as such, this staging allows for the suspension of the disciplinary efficacy of the relationship by bringing to light the obscene supplement which secretly cements it. Žižek's central point is that this supplement ultimately cements the position of the servant: what self-beating uncovers is 'the servant's masochistic libidinal attachment to his master', so as 'the true goal of this beating is to beat out that in me which attaches me to the master' (Žižek 2002a: 252). Ultimately, we are back to the fundamental fantasy, for what we witness there, in this non-subjectivisable scene, is the unbearable fascination with one's submission that clandestinely sustains subjectivity itself.

From this angle, the fundamental fantasy should be regarded as a key political category. Žižek's analysis highlights the key question referred to at the start of this section: it is not enough for us to be aware of our state of subjection to change things, as that very subjection is sustained by the disavowed pleasure (*jouissance*) we find in being caught in it:

> When we are subjected to a power mechanism, this subjection is always and by definition sustained by some libidinal investment: the subjection itself generates a surplus-enjoyment of its own. This subjection is embodied in a network of 'material' bodily practices, and for this reason we cannot get rid of our subjection through a merely intellectual reflection – our liberation has to be *staged* in some kind of bodily performance; furthermore, this performance *has* to be of an apparently 'masochistic' nature, it *has* to stage the painful process of hitting back at oneself. (Žižek 2002a: 253)

Ultimately, the passage from "oppressed victim" to "active agent of the revolution" requires a move whereby the subject endorses that disavowed excess anchoring his identity in the socio-symbolic order *qua* power mechanism: 'the only true awareness of our subjection is the awareness of the obscene excessive pleasure (surplus-enjoyment) we derive from it; this is why the first gesture of liberation is not to get rid of this excessive pleasure, but actively to assume it' (Žižek 2002a: 254).

3.3 Melodramas of mutilation

> The bourgeois principle of contract between equal subjects can be applied to sexuality only in the form of the *perverse* – masochistic – contract in which, paradoxically, the very form of balanced contract serves to establish a relationship of domination. (Žižek 1994: 109)

In this section I am going to sketch a number of well-known European films where the success of the sexual relationship paradoxically overlaps with the profound imbalance brought about by mutilation, and the consequent establishment of an explicit rapport of domination. Let us start with *Martha* (1974), arguably Fassbinder's most accurate statement on the question of sadomasochism. It is the story of the bourgeois marriage between the 31-year-old librarian Martha Heyer (Margit Carstensten) and Helmut Salomon (Karlheinz Böhm), a businessman. Form offers again the key to access the universal concern of Fassbinder's art. Although we are supposed to reflect on the female character's upbringing, with her pathological attachment to her father, the way the director describes Martha's first meeting with Helmut speaks for something different. I am referring to the wonderfully intricate single take with the 360 degree shot around both characters, which not only captures their mutual attraction but also – more explicitly than, say, the famous shot in Hitchcock's *Vertigo* – connects formalism with the inherent imbalance of the relationship.

If there are few doubts concerning the husband's sadistic leanings, Fassbinder is more interested in Martha's masochism – well beyond his conscious critical intention, which is that of showing 'a marriage as clearly as possible as a sadomasochistic relationship' (Fassbinder 1992: 141).[23] The question to ask is: to what extent is Martha complicit in the process that progressively leads to her complete subjugation, oppression, and mutilation? Apropos the controversial role played by women in his films, Fassbinder (1992: 149) claimed:

> I find women more interesting. They don't interest me just because they're oppressed – it's not that simple. The societal conflicts in women are more interesting because on the one hand women are oppressed, but in my opinion they also provoke this oppression as a result of their position in society, and in turn use it as a terror tactic.

And, specifically about the Margit Carstensten character:

> If Martha at the end of the film is no longer among the living, then she reached what she most deeply wanted [...]. In fact, the film tells a story that goes like this: what makes the woman happy? Most men can't oppress as perfectly as women would like. (in Rayns 1979: 110)

Here Fassbinder touches on the film's real concern. Humiliation after humiliation, Martha winds up utterly subjugated, and at the same time isolated from the outside world, prey to her husband as much as to her paranoid fantasies. Her occasional acts of hysterical resistance are all in vain, for, ultimately, they are powerless in the face of her unconscious desire to "exit the world of the living". In the last sequence we see her in a wheelchair manoeuvred by her husband, permanently paralysed after a car crash caused by her paranoia. The conclusion to draw is two-sided, confirming the "unconscious intentionality" of Fassbinder's cinema: (1) The non-existence of the sexual relationship is marked by its shockingly perverted nature whereby both parties enjoy their roles. In this respect, the ending functions as a sarcastic statement, or provocation, on the idealistic pursuit of happiness in marriage, since Fassbinder acerbically suggests that the attempt to realise the sexual relationship necessarily turns into a *real*-isation, i.e. it can only fulfil itself in the Real of disfigurement and domination. (2) The real paradox voiced by the film, however, concerns femininity. Martha does not merely stand for pathological masochism, unconsciously enjoying her status of submission to Helmut; she also represents the passage through "symbolic death" which alludes to an act of "resetting". This, it would seem, is the properly unconscious dimension of the film.

It is striking to notice how many European films rely on an image of mutilation to comment on the constitutive lack of sexual relations. The wheelchair, for instance, functions as a perfect metonymic object in Buñuel's *Belle de jour* (1967), although instead of *real*-ising itself, the masochistic debt of the female character is here simply cancelled. The key observation to make is that Séverine (Catherine Deneuve) stops imagining obscene masochistic scenarios only when the husband, having been shot, is confined to a wheelchair. Why? Let us first deal with the heroine's fantasy underworld. In typical Buñuelian fashion, Séverine's fantasy unsettles the narrative from the very start, when, in a dream, she sees herself being maltreated by her husband during a journey on a horse carriage. Eventually she is tied to a tree, whipped and sexually abused by one of the servants – crucially, not by the husband, who instead watches the whole scene whilst imparting orders. The message is instantly clear: woman's unconscious connection with *jouissance* is what allows her to endure her "normal" bourgeois life/marriage. This is indeed an exemplary rendition of the rapport between illicit *jouissance* and the smooth functioning of the symbolic order: the latter (Symbolic) cannot exist without establishing a secret liaison with the former (Real). Buñuel's stroke of genius, however, has to do with the film's finale. When we see Pierre (Jean Sorel), the husband, reduced to a living dead after being shot by the rogue Marcel (Pierre Clementi), who had fallen in love with Séverine, we realise that the relationship has finally, if tragically, managed to accomplish itself. As if by magic, Séverine's disturbing fantasies disappear – she herself tells her paralysed husband that she does not dream anymore. Again, why? Because her husband's dead-like passivity works as a guarantee that his desire has been tamed, that it is fully under control. In such a situation, the Lacanian *Che vuoi?* ("What do you want from me?", the distressing question at the heart of desire *qua* other's desire) is annulled; Séverine does not need to ask herself what he wants (from her), *because the problem of his desire has been eliminated*. The irony is that we have *the* relationship – one that is not supplemented and spoiled by the obscene third of fantasy – only within a situation of extreme imbalance, where the other is thoroughly objectified, reduced to an inanimate being (a point which is also proved by the previously discussed finale of *Fellini's Casanova*).

An analogous argument applies to the third vignette of Max Ophuls' *Le plaisir* (1952), while Roman Polanski's *Bitter Moon* (1992) and Lars Von Trier's *Breaking the Waves* (1996) present us with alternative scenarios. In Ophuls' wonderfully rarefied adaptation of Maupassant's short story, a painter falls in love with his model, then grows bored with her and leaves her. Overcome by grief, she throws herself off a window, breaking her legs. Only at that point, with the girl in the wheelchair, does the painter rediscover his love for his muse, even deciding to marry her. The final voiceover spells out the film's lesson: 'Happiness has nothing to do with joy'. The happiness in question is exactly of the same kind as that of the films discussed above, insofar as it involves the paradoxical neutralisation of the Real of sexual difference through the other's mutilation.

Bitter Moon initially unravels a similar scenario, although it is Oscar (Peter Coyote), the man, who (accidentally) breaks his leg after dumping his girlfriend Mimi (Emmanuelle Seigner). To re-establish a viable rapport Mimi pays a visit to Oscar in hospital, sadistically hauls him from his bed to the floor thus turning him into a paraplegic. From then on she will be in charge, proudly manoeuvring his wheelchair – the point being that only then the "normal couple" is formed, for *objet a* is finally "extracted" from the other. As Lacan (1998a: 268) famously put it: '*I love you, but, because inexplicably I love in you something more than you –* the objet petit a *– I mutilate you'*. Polanski, however, goes a step further than *Belle de jour*, suggesting that mutilation does not eradicate fantasy: even as a cripple, Oscar keeps spoiling the game, reducing everyone to a prop for his phallic enjoyment. Most of the film, in fact, focuses on his voyeuristic perversions as the couple meet their repressed doubles Nigel (Hugh Grant) and Fiona (Kristin Scott Thomas) on a cruise. Oscar's perversion reaches its climax in the final scene where, after watching Mimi have sex with Fiona, he proceeds to kill his wife and then blows his head off. Beyond the bombastic spectacularisation of sexuality – a far cry from Polanski's minimalist debut feature *Knife in the Water* (Nóz w wodzie, 1962) – the film's tragic ending captures poignantly the Real of the sexual deadlock.

Insofar as it calls into question perverted phallic enjoyment, Lars Von Trier's *Breaking the Waves* mirrors the image of masculinity presented in Polanski's film. Paralysed from the waist down after an accident at work, Jan (Stellan Skarsgård) tells his wife Bess (Emily Watson) that the only way she can keep him attached to life is by sleeping with other men and then describing the experiences back to him in detail. Bess, a profoundly religious girl from a small Presbyterian community in Scotland, duly obliges. Instead of focusing on the perverse circuit of masculine sexuality, Žižek highlights a key question related to Bess's sexuality:

> Jan's *jouissance* is clearly phallic-masturbatory: he uses Bess to provide him with the fantasmatic screen that he needs in order to be able to indulge in solipsistic, masturbatory *jouissance*, while Bess finds *jouissance* at the level of the Other (symbolic order), that is, in her words. The ultimate source of satisfaction for her is not the sexual act itself (she engages in such acts in a purely mechanical way, as a necessary sacrifice) but the way she *reports* on it to the crippled Jan. (Žižek 2005: 333)

In Part II, this insight on feminine sacrifice – in itself central to Von Trier's cinema – will be unpacked in connection with Lacan's notion of feminine *jouissance* of the Other. For the time being, suffice it to observe that Jan's perversion, like Oscar's, need not be regarded as an exceptional derailment of masculine desire, but instead as fully consistent with its logic.

In Buñuel's *Tristana* (1970) we are still firmly anchored in the masculine logic of desire. When Tristana's (Catherine Deneuve) leg is amputated for medical reasons, and replaced with a prosthetic one, Don Lope (Fernando Rey) is secretly overjoyed, for he knows that his young lover will never be able to leave him again. The leg, as Hitchcock clearly detected,[24] can legitimately be regarded as the film's main character, in as much as we can read in it, *qua* partial object, an ineffable and disturbing excess. Not surprisingly, it is after the eviction of this excess that the implicitly perverse character of the relationship emerges in full: deprived of her leg, Tristana becomes vulgar, jaded and bitter, as when on the balcony she bares her breasts in front of deaf-mute boy Saturno (Jesús Fernandez). The very fact that she finishes off Don Lope after his falling ill with pneumonia not only signals her revenge against the old man, but also suggests that without her sublime object she has lost the ability to manipulate him.

Liliana Cavani's *The Night Porter* (1974) pushes the sadomasochistic autonomy of the couple to its outermost limit, its self-obliteration, as Max (Dirk Bogarde) and Lucia (Charlotte Rampling) finally opt for a "beautiful death" rather than renounce their amorous tie. It is interesting here to compare Cavani's film with a classic *amour fou* narrative such as Truffaut's *The Woman Next Door* (La femme d'à côté, 1981), for in both stories the final deflagration of the Real is preceded by the endorsement of a *perverse* solution to the enigma of the non-existence of the relationship. But if in Cavani's case perversion is explicitly stated (sadomasochism), with Truffaut it is unsuccessfully disavowed, for the central problem of the tragic love affair between Bernard (Gérard Depardieu) and Mathilde (Fanny Ardant) is that it is fuelled by its illicit character: the obstacle (the lovers' respective spouses) is simultaneously the condition of possibility of the affair itself.

Pedro Almodovar's *Talk to Her* (Hable con ella, 2002) provides an interesting variation on the sadomasochistic theme. Almodovar's worthy intuition in this film is that of depicting the perfect relationship as one between a psychotic man (Benigno, played by Javier Cámara) and a woman in a coma (Alicia, played by Leonor Watling). Although *Talk to Her*, in line with most of Almodovar's films, is based on the opportunistic exploitation of such postmodern clichés as sexual transgression and shifting identities, what makes it appealing is the fact that, as already highlighted, it dares to focus on the taboo of rape, simultaneously connecting it with the question of sexual difference. The sexual act is here represented as highly ambiguous: is it rape or is it an act of love, even "pure love" since Benigno is a virgin? Apart from the obvious ethical problem that Benigno's act raises, this is a legitimate question insofar as it helps us radicalise the impact of sexual difference on Almodovar's cinema. Benigno insists that his relationship with Alicia is perfect, claiming that ordinary couples rarely have such a good understanding of each other. Despite the apparent nonsense of this assertion, it nevertheless manages to tap into a deeper truth: does not the rapport between a psychopath and a sleeping beauty provide us with the perfect formula for the successful relationship? As in its poignant "film within the film" – where the "shrinking man" turns into a sort of penis, thus truly satisfying his partner – *Talk to Her* confirms that a relationship is guaranteed to succeed only after the taming of the other's fantasy. In *Talk to Her*, then, we truly reach an ideal couple: Alicia materialises the lifeless/empty core of *objet a* which, as such, can only satisfy a psychotic partner.

To conclude with Fassbinder, in his *Chinese Roulette* (Chinesisches Roulette, 1976) mutilation does not affect one of the partners, but their young daughter, who is a cripple – the same idea, incidentally, is used by Bergman in *Autumn Sonata* (Höstsonaten, 1978) – and metaphorically incarnates the impossibility of the sexual relationship. Fassbinder's film succeeds in materialising – both formally, through extremely evocative visual imagery, and narratively – the deadlock inherent to the relationship in such a way that it appears as a Real surplus of the symbolic pact between man and woman (marriage). We begin with the description of a deceptively harmonious marriage between Gerhard (Alexander Allerson) and Ariane (Margit Carstensen) a bourgeois couple in 1970s West Germany. When husband and wife depart for their respective business trips, daughter Angela (Andrea Schober), knowing that they are in fact meeting respective lovers, concocts so that they will both arrive at their holiday house on the same day. At that point, the first reaction of shock is quickly pacified by languid bourgeois hypocrisy – they laugh it off and begin a "weekend à quatre". Again, it is left to Angela to spoil the false state of harmony. As she arrives at the house she proposes to play a psychologically brutal guessing game between two teams (the "Chinese Roulette") whose aim is to identify a member of the opposite team by asking a series of questions. It is through this game that the unsettling disavowed content of what each thought about Ariane emerges, as she is likened to a concentration camp commander. What strikes one here is the daughter's chilling laughter after revealing the mother's identity: a truly obscene laughter that betrays Real enjoyment whilst embodying the impossibility of the relationship.

3.4 Masochistic expenditure and superego jouissance

If the staging of a masochistic gesture is the only way for the subject to cut the Gordian knot of his or her libidinally-invested subjection to the law, the economy of masochism simultaneously brings into contention the insidious figure of the Sadean executioner, the embodiment of the law's dark underside. Here we should go back to the previously mentioned thesis on the consubstantiality of law and superego pressure, in connection with Lacan's postulation that the law, fundamentally, enjoys: 'I will remind the jurist that law basically talks about what I am going to talk to you about – jouissance. Law does not ignore the bed' (Lacan 1998b: 2). Already in 1962, with his essay 'Kant avec Sade' (see Lacan 2007: 645–68), Lacan objects to the fact that Kant, in his positing the autonomous and self-determining character of the law, conveniently forgets to include in the picture the law's obscene addendum, that is, the underworld of enjoyment (*qua* practices of domination) introduced by Sade. The problem we are faced with is how to expose this obscene superegoic addendum – since, if the law enjoys, this means that the law is fundamentally imbalanced, sustained by a scandalous, irrational and strictly-speaking unlawful (criminal) will to enjoy. Paraphrasing Žižek's comment on a passage from P.D. James's *A Taste for Death* (see Žižek 1994: 93), we could say that what compels the executioner of the law to show his enjoyment is "the experience of having his desire to kill the victim coincide with the victim's death-drive". The point not to be missed is that, as Gilles Deleuze noted in *Coldness and Cruelty*, what supremely frustrates the sadistic executioner is the masochistic fervour of his victim: a genuine sadist could never tolerate a masochist victim. The immediate reason for this frustration is that masochism forces the sadist to acknowledge that the object of his desire – the body of the other – is already the object of the other's desire, and as such it can only provide a kind of ersatz enjoyment. Consequently, the sadist realises that he has been thoroughly objectified, cynically used by the masochist as an instrument to generate his own (the masochist's) "pleasure in pain". Put differently, the masochist makes visible the extent to which the (executioner of the) law is enslaved to the lack that pertains to desire; the *jouissance* of the masochist affirms its speculative identity with the *jouissance* of the law, hence revealing the strict correlation between the self-affirming character of the law itself and its groundlessness.

In a reference to Michael Haneke's controversial *The Piano Teacher* (La Pianiste, 2001), Žižek (2002b: 20–1) makes the same point by calling into question Lacan's notion of anxiety:

> In his (unpublished) seminar on anxiety (1962–63), Lacan specifies that the true aim of the masochist is not to generate jouissance in the Other, but to provide its anxiety. That is to say: although the masochist submits himself to the Other's torture, although he wants to serve the Other, he himself defines the rules of his servitude; consequently, while he seems to offer himself as the instrument of the Other's jouissance, he effectively discloses his own desire to the Other and thus gives rise to anxiety in the Other – for Lacan, the true object of anxiety is precisely the (over)proximity of the Other's desire. That is the libidinal economy of the moment in *The Piano Teacher* when the heroine presents to her seducer a detailed masochistic scenario of how he should mistreat her: what repulses him is this total disclosure of her desire.

The relationship between executioner and masochist offers itself as an interesting variation on the classic Hegelian couple lord–bondsman (master–slave). In the *Phenomenology of Spirit*, Hegel claims that it is through his complete submission to the lord that the bondsman actually gains self-consciousness, insofar as he externalises himself in the objects of his labour: 'the bondsman realizes that it is precisely in his work wherein he seemed to have only an alienated existence that he acquires a mind of his own' (Hegel 1977: 119). As the standard Marxist interpretation has it, it is therefore the bondsman, and not the lord, who can claim to occupy an autonomous subject position. However, does not the figure of the masochist challenge the lord/executioner precisely by undermining the belief in such autonomy? What the masochist makes manifest is the fact that his "being-for-itself", his autonomy, is grounded in the unfathomable abyss of his own enjoyment, which is homologous to the Hegelian notion of absolute negativity. Hegel indeed emphasises this point when he insists on the link between the bondsman's self-consciousness-through-labour and 'absolute fear': 'If consciousness fashions the thing without the initial absolute fear, it is only an empty self-centred attitude; for its form or negativity is not negativity per se, and therefore its formative activity cannot give it a consciousness of itself as essential being' (Hegel 1977: 119).

To sum up: masochism can be understood as a way to bring out the dark underside of the law, demonstrating how the law (power) is always supplemented by an obscene injunction to enjoy, which ultimately reveals the self-destructive character of the law as well as its fundamental inconsistency and changeability. The following passage from Deleuze (1991: 88) focuses with unequalled accuracy on the absurdity of the law:

> We all know ways of twisting the law by excess of zeal. By scrupulously applying the law we are able to demonstrate its absurdity and provoke the very disorder that it is intended to prevent or to conjure. [...] A close examination of masochistic fantasies or rites reveals that while they bring into play the very strictest application of the law, the result in every case is the opposite of what might be expected (thus whipping, far from punishing or preventing an erection, provokes and ensures it). It is a demonstration of the law's absurdity.

We can also see, now, how Lacan turns around Kant's claim that the moral law is the measure of the subject's freedom: it is not that the unbearable pressure of the moral law coincides with disinterestedness and freedom (Kant), but that freedom can only be posited as an unbearable (implicitly traumatic) pressure to face the empty kernel of the law. The daring equation between freedom and masochism thus targets the tautological foundations of the law: the real scandal is that, as Deleuze (1991: 82–5) put it apropos Kant's *Critique of Practical Reason*, 'the law [...] is self-grounded and valid solely by virtue of its own form. [...] the object of the law is by definition unknowable and elusive'. Such a perspective implies the psychoanalytic awareness that 'the object of the law and the object of desire are one and the same, and remain equally concealed'; or, as Lacan (1998a: 275–6) claims at the end of *Seminar XI*, that

> the moral law [...] is simply desire in its pure state, the very desire that culminates in the sacrifice, strictly speaking, of everything that is the object of love in one's human tenderness – I would say, not only in the rejection of the pathological object, but also in its sacrifice and murder. That is why I wrote Kant avec Sade.

Kant and Sade provide two opposite examples of how to "disturb" the Real. Kant's moral law designates the intervention of subjective freedom within the order of Being: the ethical act is self-grounded, authorised only in itself, regardless of utilitarian considerations or natural propensities ("the starry heavens above me and the moral law within me", from the *Critique of Practical Reason*). With Sade, freedom is also conceptualised as a rupture with causality, with natural order, as an unconditional injunction to enjoy. The paradox noted by Lacan is that in both cases, regardless of the radically different points of enunciation, we have a break with the Freudian pleasure principle, i.e. an intervention of drive.

By coupling Sade with Kant, Lacan underlines the non-pathological thrust of the categorical imperative: Sade's "unconditional injunction to enjoy" is correlative to Kant's "unconditional injunction to do one's duty", as both are ultimately delivered from any utilitarian concern with the actual attainment of the object (in other words, they are "desire turned drive"). What 'Kant avec Sade' reveals, therefore, is that, if developed through to its bitter end, Kant's revolutionary insight into morality conflates with Sade's notion of absolute excess. Lacan claims that the moral law cannot serve as a stabilising device which prevents us from encroaching upon the abyss of the noumena; quite on the contrary, it represents the Real "in disguise", an irresistibly transgressive injunction. And, again, the distinctive feature of Žižek's position seems to be that the scandal of the law can only be fully articulated from the point of view of the masochist vis-à-vis the Sadean executioner. If a subject does not need the law to punish him, for he can do it himself outside the remit of the law, the latter inevitably loses its coercive character and exhibits its fundamental lack of purpose, its being anchored in *jouissance*. The masochist teases out and identifies with the libidinal (irrational and self-destructive) kernel of the law.

A fine example of this logic is Elio Petri's masterpiece, *Investigation of a Citizen Above Suspicion* (Indagine su un cittadino al di sopra di ogni sospetto, 1970), a film that explores the enigma of the law (it begins with the following quotation from Kafka: 'Whatever impression he may leave on us, he serves the law, and therefore he belongs to the law and eludes human judgement'). It tells the story of a nameless police inspector (Gian Maria Volontè) who kills his debauched lover Augusta Terzi (Florinda Bolkan) and then proceeds to leave clues around as if to purposefully place himself in the line of investigation. On the day of the killing, he is also promoted from head of the homicide department to head of the political police, where he is admired for his repressive methods. The first part of the film lends itself to being viewed as a demonstration of the limitless, utterly discriminatory power of the law, at least in the historical context here represented (post-1968 youth rebellion): the inspector kills Augusta Terzi, it seems, precisely to prove to himself that he is untouchable. In the second part, however, his theorem slowly falls apart, as the very factor that makes power absolute and irresistible is exposed as the cipher of its boundless fragility. The libidinal foundations of the law, in other words, are shown to be the very cause of the law's undoing. Petri exposes the link between criminal authority and the erotic fascination it exerts, suggesting that the "letter of the law" owes its power to an unconscious libidinal investment based simply on its senseless enunciation. Let us recall Žižek's reading of Pascal's argument in favour of symbolic authority:

> According to Pascal, the interiority of our reasoning is determined by the external, nonsensical 'machine' – automatism of the signifier, of the symbolic network in which the subjects are caught [...]. It follows, from this constitutively senseless character of the Law, that we must obey not because it is just, good, or even beneficial, but simply *because it is the law* – this tautology articulates the vicious circle of its authority, the fact that the last foundation of the Law's authority lies in its process of enunciation. (Žižek 1989: 36–7)

What brings about a change in our perception of the law in Petri's film is the progressive breakdown of the inspector's disciplined *forma mentis*. The person responsible for his breakdown is none other than his deceased lover. Though not explicitly emerging as the key character of the film, Augusta Terzi stands for that vital reference to masochism which forces power to confront its inconsistency. The film's "hidden" kernel, therefore, should be uncovered by pursuing its central symptomal feature, i.e. the masochistic fervour of the victim. Formally, this symptom fragments the narrative through a number of flashbacks telling us precisely how much Augusta enjoyed masochistic rituals, with a particular preference for necrophilic fantasies. It is through these flashbacks that the partly disavowed truth of Petri's film emerges, for what really breaks down the subjective defences of the inspector is the fact that *he is unable to forget the enigma of his victim's masochistic enjoyment*. Again, what proves unbearably frustrating for the executioner is the possibility that his victim might actually enjoy being punished. This awareness of the other's *jouissance* is what drives the Volontè character insane, uncovering the thoroughly specious if not overtly perverted nature of his inflexible reliance on the law.

In this respect, the film's final sequence shows the extent to which institutions are engaged in dissimulating their own transgressive core. In this nightmarish, quintessentially Kafkaesque passage the inspector fantasises about his crime being paternalistically forgiven by higher-level authorities; in his fantasies, in other words, the Volontè character captures the essence of the law, the fact that it constantly supplements transgression with its dissimulation. On the whole, Petri's film suggests that the law is ultimately a formal fact invested by *jouissance*, and not merely a question of content; from this angle, it goes well beyond its explicit (conscious) intention, which is the denunciation of the repressive, proto-fascist type of power operative in Italy immediately after 1968. This also suggests that the equation between repressive Law and fascism advocated by many post-1968 Italian political films in their anxiety to denounce the corruption of the Italian system, is fundamentally misplaced. The common flaw of films like Petri's *Investigation*, Pasolini's *Salò*, Bertolucci's *The Conformist*, as well as Marco Bellocchio's *Slap the Monster on Page One* (Sbatti il mostro in prima pagina 1972) and Francesco Rosi's *Illustrious Corpses* (Cadaveri eccellenti, 1976) – to mention but a few – is that they tend to disregard the fact that *law is law* regardless of its fascistic excesses. This is why *Salò* functions better as a metaphor for our tolerant consumer society than as a direct indictment of fascism.[25] The point is that the core of the law is Real irrespective of its different historical frameworks: whether liberal-democratic or explicitly totalitarian, the law remains rooted in its tautology, in the enigma of its form so eloquently narrativised by Kafka. In denouncing the intrinsically fascistic trait of the law what we risk overlooking is precisely its universal formal dimension, which is also its "absurdity", the excessive force with which it destabilises the domain of the pleasure principle.

After all this, we should nevertheless keep in mind that Lacan does not celebrate superego *jouissance* as the ultimate ethical goal of psychoanalysis. Lorenzo Chiesa (2007: 175) has emphasised this point:

> If, on the one hand, Sado-Kantian ethics represents for Lacan an important milestone in the history of ethics insofar as it has done with the servicing of goods [...], on the other hand, his appreciation of Kant and Sade should not be overestimated. The ethics of psychoanalysis is certainly anti-Kantian and anti-Sadean. One of the underlying leitmotifs of Seminar VII is precisely the necessity to distance the ethics of psychoanalysis from these two authors, and how difficult it is to delineate such a demarcation in a clear way.

One of today's key arguments concerning Lacanian ethics has to do with the possibility of distinguishing between superegoic transgression as inherent to the law, and an ethics which would allow us to bypass the ferocious figure of the superego. If there is a vital and necessary question to ask about Lacanian ethics it is probably the following: can we connect with the structuring void of the symbolic order without passing through the Real of superego *jouissance*? As I have suggested apropos Fassbinder's cinema, one way to start answering this question is by positing death-drive as the agency enacting, or actualising, symbolic death. Insofar as it triggers the (traumatic) passage from alienation to separation, symbolic death leads to the New. In this respect, in most of Fassbinder's work we witness a remarkable coincidence of aesthetics and ethics which often reminds us of Antigone's choice as described in *Seminar VII*. It is an absolute choice motivated solely by the (implicitly masochistic) desire to embrace desire's lack, thus entering the domain of symbolic death. One can see, however, how the basic problem remains: how is this "pure desire" of desire's lack, beyond the superego, actually brought about?

3.5 Anxiety and the act

> The psychotic *passage à l'acte* is to be conceived of as a desperate attempt of the subject to evict *objet a* from reality by force, and then gain access to reality. (Žižek 1994: 77)

The shocking opening of Ingmar Bergman's "German film" *From the Life of the Marionettes* (Aus dem Leben der Marionetten, 1980) works as a gruesome but precise exemplification of a psychotic *passage à l'acte*, while the rest of the narrative unravels in a series of flash-backs and flash-forwards as an attempt to explain the reasons behind it. A man later identified as Peter Egermann (Robert Atzorn), a respectable businessman, kills a prostitute, later identified as Ka (Rita Russek), short for Katarina, and then proceeds to rape her anally. At the end of the first sequence colour fades into black and white, and will only return in the film's final moments. Bergman's thesis becomes clearer as other characters are introduced, starting with Peter's wife, a successful stylist also named Katarina (Christine Buchegger) and his psychoanalyst Martin (Morgen Jensen). When, in the first flash-back (14 days before the killing), Peter pays a visit to the psychoanalyst, he tells him about his disturbing dream where he kills his wife, with whom he cannot have a satisfactory relationship.

So, what is Peter's problem, exactly? In a word, anxiety. As is well known, Lacan claims that anxiety is *the only feeling that does not lie*, since it surfaces when the object of desire (or the desiring other) gets too close to us, suffocating us with *jouissance*. Suddenly we are unable to symbolise reality, for the necessary distance between us and the external world collapses. Ultimately, however, the object of anxiety is the subject who suffers from it: 'I myself (the subject), as the object-cause of the Other's desire, am the object whose overproximity triggers anxiety: that is, anxiety emerges when I am reduced to the position of the object exchanged/used by the Other' (Žižek 2000a: 364). We are now in a better position to understand why Peter gets it all wrong. As a psychotic, he deals with anxiety by attempting to violently evict *objet a* in the other, so as to regain the ability to "make sense" of reality. What he misses is the necessity to renounce the object, in as much as this very object does not belong to the other. This is what Lacan (1998a: 276) refers to at the end of *Seminar XI*, where, after claiming that pure desire culminates in the sacrifice of the object, he specifies:

> This is an extreme position, but one that enables us to grasp that man can adumbrate his situation in a field made up of rediscovered knowledge only if he has previously experienced the limit within which, like desire, he is bound. Love, which, it seems to some, I have down-graded, can be posited only in that beyond, where, at first, it renounces the object.

Peter, instead, seeks to obliterate the object in its disturbing over-proximity. As a desperate attempt to "cork" the symbolic field, his gesture, which he fantasises about for the whole film, is to be inscribed in the logic of phallic *jouissance*.

In the scene following Peter's monologue, Bergman stresses how the psychotic's relationship with *objet a* is necessarily one of incredible fascination. Instead of leaving after the session, Peter hides in a dark corner of Martin's study, unseen by his analyst. The latter picks up the phone and calls none other than Peter's wife, with whom, it transpires, he is having an affair. When she arrives, Peter is still there, hidden, spying on their fondling. As they are about to have sex Katarina suddenly holds back, explaining that her husband is part of her, that she carries him with her everywhere she goes. If they quarrel, fight and hit each other, she adds, it is because they do not want to grow up, they prefer to remain immature: 'Our nerves have grown together in some strange, uncanny way'. It is significant that during the most intense parts of the conversation between Katarina and Martin, the camera slowly zooms in on Peter's face, encouraging us to believe that the scene is being played out *for him*, or even that it is *his own* voyeuristic fantasy. The role of fantasy here is, of course, extremely ambiguous. On the one hand it feeds on Peter's anxiety, confirming the dangerous over-proximity of *jouissance*; on the other hand it also allows him to momentarily re-inscribe a distance between himself and his wife.

The film's central theme is not, as it would appear, Peter's inability to connect with his wife, to get to the core of who she really is – as in his first dream, where he wants to have sex with her but he is unable to. The real problem for him is not impotence, nor is it his latent homosexuality derived from his excessive attachment to his mother (the analyst's final explanation). Rather, it concerns the fact that his attachment to his wife (and hers to him) is disturbingly real, thus thwarting symbolisation. As in the above scene in the analyst's study, he needs more fantasy. In this sense, the psychoanalytic baggage of the film does not manage to conceal its truth. Eventually, Peter's anxiety leads to psychosis. And if the psychotic act remains, strictly speaking, a fake, i.e. a case of displacement (he murders a prostitute who reminds him of his wife), the act *qua* uxoricide appears eventually in the Real of his dream, where, as he claims, he felt more alive than when he was awake: 'Am I really alive? Or was my dream in effect the only brief moment of life I had?' The interesting point to highlight is that in this dream the actual murder remains properly unconscious, i.e. it does not fit the narrative coordinates of the dream itself. All of a sudden Peter sees his wife's dead body next to him, and all he can do is assume that he has killed her. This is indeed psychosis, an act we can only appropriate after committing it, for it demands our over-identification with the Real of enjoyment, and the consequent momentary collapse of our sense of selfhood. At the end of the film we find Peter's wife looking at him in his prison cell, in what is clearly a quotation from *Psycho* (1960). The nurse comments to Katarina that he still suffers from anxiety attacks, and that at night he takes an old tattered teddy bear to bed with him. This is not surprising, since his *passage à l'acte* – both in reality and in his dream – was, as such, an a priori abortive attempt to remove *objet a*.

In Godard's "militant films", sexual difference is regularly associated to class exploitation, in a way that reminds us closely of Fassbinder. The rape scene in *Numéro deux* (1975), for instance, is presented as the logical culmination of the alienating effect that work has on a married couple's sexual life: Pierre (Pierre Oudrey), reduced to impotence by his factory job and unable to satisfy his wife Sandrine (Sandrine Battistella), manages to be aroused only when he discovers that she has slept with another man, and rapes her (anally) to avenge himself. Here we need to abstract from the nevertheless significant socio-political dimension of the film. The point is that this rape *qua* violent *passage à l'acte*, as in Bergman's film, materialises sexual difference in its universal mode, and not only as a consequence of capitalist alienation. The fact that Sandrine is turned into a "desirable object" for the husband by another man's penis brings to light the good old trick of phallic *jouissance*: everything depends on fantasy. In this respect, we could argue that despite its militant turn, deep down Godard's cinema keeps depicting woman as the deadly, sublime object of desire that Patricia once was for Michel in *Breathless* or, even more explicitly, Marianne (Anna Karina) for Ferdinand (Jean-Paul Belmondo) in *Pierrot le fou* (1965).

Claude Chabrol's *The Unfaithful Wife* (La femme infidèle, 1968) is also constructed around a fake psychotic act borne out of anxiety and the intolerable pressure to which it gives rise. Indeed, one of the central preoccupations of Chabrol's cinema, well beyond questions of direct socio-political relevance, is the rapport between the limitations of the masculine strategy of sublimation and the psychotic solution. More explicitly than many of his contemporaries, Chabrol is fascinated by the possibility of an act that may release his male characters from the unbearable over-proximity of *objet a*. This is particularly evident for the so-called "Hélène cycle", those films of the late 1960s and 1970s where Chabrol casts his then wife Stephane Audran in the leading role. However, there are plenty of signs in his previous films too. We find apt examples of this logic in the episode of Marie's (Bernadette Lafont) rape in *Le beau Serge* (1958); in *The Cousins* (Les cousins, 1959), where Florence (Juliette Maynel) is first contended by Charles (Gérard Blain) and Paul (Jean-Claude Brialy), but ends up with the sadistic Clovis (Claude Cerval), one of the first "beast figures" in Chabrol's cinema; in *Web of Passion* (À Double Tour, 1959), where Léda's (Antonella Lualdi) murder reflects an entire family's inability to come to terms with her beauty and freedom; in *Les Bonnes Femmes* (1960), where the four female protagonists are portrayed as objects of desire constantly threatened by rapacious men, until Jacqueline's (Clotilde Joano) death at the hands of psychopath motorcyclist André (Mario David).

It is in the later *The Unfaithful Wife*, however, that psychosis acquires for the first time centre stage. Indeed, psychosis comes naturally for a character like Charles (Michel Bouquet), an archetypal Chabrolesque hero whose conjugal life is based solely on bourgeois etiquette and an obdurate attachment to social status. When he discovers that Hélène (Stéphane Audran), his wife, has a lover (Victor, played by Maurice Ronet), he decides to pay a civilised visit to him so as to settle matters in a gentlemanly way (i.e., to safeguard his bourgeois reputation). Once in the lover's flat, he begins a very urbane conversation with him; however, the mere sight of his wife's lighter, which he had given to her as a present, is enough to trigger in him a violent reaction that leads to Victor's brutal murder. Once again, as in the opening scene of Bergman's *From the Life of the Marionettes*, we are confronted with a case of displacement, which also explains why the film does not simply work as an ironic indictment of bourgeois mores. Strictly speaking, the hero's problem is that he refuses to face the true nature of his anxiety, which is rooted, despite Chabrol's mocking of bourgeois subjectivity, in the *universal* quandary of sexual difference.

This explains why, as he is taken away by the police at the end of the film, Charles can finally whisper to his wife 'I love you madly': it is not Lacan's notion of love as the "beyond of the object" which is established here, but rather the very framework of fantasy (distance) that enables the circulation of desire. Not dissimilarly from the finale of Kieślowski's *Three Colours: White* (Trois couleurs: Blanc, 1994) – where the hero contemplates his ex-wife from a distance, as she tells him in sign language that they shall remarry – the physical distance between husband and wife in the last shot of *The Unfaithful Wife* suggests that the destructive potential of anxiety has been, at least momentarily, domesticated. Paradoxically, imprisonment in both films is what makes the relationship sustainable. In Kieślowski's, the hero's tears at the sight of his wife behind bars are "fake tears", suggesting that in fact there is nothing he fears more than a reunion sanctioned by the contract (the *égalité* referred to in the title) of marriage. From this premise it follows that Karol's (Zbigniew Zamachowski) impotence, which structures the entire narrative, is nothing but a stratagem through which he aims to heighten the status of Dominique (Julie Delpy) to that of the unreachable Lady.[26]

We find this very same idea in Chabrol's underrated *Weddings of Blood* (Les noces rouges, 1973): after the two lovers Pierre (Michel Piccoli) and Lucienne (Stéphane Audran) have confessed their crimes (the killings of Pierre's wife and Lucienne's husband), they are handcuffed and taken away in a police car. Although these crimes are indirectly unmasked by Hélène (Eliana De Santis), Lucienne's daughter, what becomes apparent with the final close-up of the two lovers' handcuffed hands clutched together is that deep down they wanted their clandestine love story to end up in prison, since only in captivity can their fantasy of the successful relationship continue to be woven. What we have here is, again, the motif of the necessity of the third gaze: the *amour fou* between Pierre and Lucienne was always sustained by the reference to their respective "official" partners (the obstacle-*qua*-condition-of-possibility theme). Once the spouses are eliminated, their rapport suddenly reveals its pointlessness. When, in the final shot, they are asked by the police inspector why they did not run away together, Pierre, grasping Lucienne's hand, replies: 'we have never dreamed of leaving'. Ultimately, what truly scared them was the prospect of remaining alone together.

One thinks here of the famous ending of Louis Malle's *Les Amants* (1958): after their idyllic encounter in the woods, where lovemaking seems to sanction an indestructible bond, the two lovers drive away on their own, leaving behind family and annexed bourgeois values, convinced that the whole universe is contained in the their respective gazes. However, this romantic cliché is slightly and yet crucially disrupted when, in the car, Jeanne (Jeanne Moreau), the heroine who has finally found the courage to leave her rich husband, experiences a momentary lapse in the seemingly unbreakable fabric of her new romance. It is this doubt – which also, imperceptibly, traverses Bernard's (her young lover, played by Jean-Marc Bory) mind – that saves the film from its hopeless romanticism, suggesting that the Real of sexual difference has all but been eliminated. And there is more. When they stop for food, Malle tells us how Jeanne is going to deal with the already surfaced deadlock of sexual difference: she is going to have a child. This is indicated by the way her eyes follow the child who waits on them, returning the change after their meal, and then by the way she turns towards the mirror behind her, as if to catch the reflection of the woman she will become. Only after this understated but all the more crucial revelation can they proceed on their journey – and, this time, as Bernard remarks, the sun is finally shining.

Chabrol's *The Butcher* (Le boucher, 1969) provides us with a captivating variation on the theme of psychosis as fake *passage à l'acte*. The naïve but necessary question apropos this narrative is the following: why does butcher Popaul (Jean Yanne), the "gentle beast" in love with chic middle-class school mistress Hélène (Stephane Audran), keeps on butchering young women? Chabrol's contingent explanation (Popaul's obsession with blood has to do with his having served as an army butcher in Algeria and Indo-China), in fitting the cliché of the unstable war survivor, is not enough. Rather, Popaul's psychotic explosions – which are never shown – should, again, be regarded as symptomatic of his missed (displaced) encounter with *objet a*, incarnated of course by Hélène herself. It is not, however, that Hélène could have saved him had she let herself be loved (as the standard critical reading has it)[27] but rather that by denying herself to him she simply aimed at safeguarding her elusive status. From this perspective, the motif of Hélène's repressed sexuality (she has enforced celibacy upon herself after a failed love affair) also sounds unconvincing. Instead of just incarnating frigidity, Hélène materialises the feminine awareness that, as it were, her own flesh is nothing but a fill-in for a constitutive lack. The problem – and at the same time the merit – of the film is that, if on the one hand Popaul indeed sees Hélène as the sublimated Lady of courtly love (as, explicitly, in the Louis XIV costume dance sequence), on the other hand, unlike the medieval Knight, he also draws closer and closer to her. This self-destructive movement comes to a head in the brilliant final confrontation in Hélène's house, when, instead of stabbing *her*, Popaul plants the knife into *his own* body. Metaphorically, this gesture signals the avoidance of an intrinsically fake *passage à l'acte*, confirming the Lacanian argument that the *jouissance* of *objet a* is always-already a *jouis-sans*, the enjoyment of the very lack of enjoyment:

> One of the major tasks of psychoanalysis is to make the subject accept the real *objet a* as *lack*. If *jouissance* is *jouis-sans*, enjoying 'more' or 'less' makes sense only from a perverse standpoint which takes the *presence* of *jouissance* for granted. There is only one fundamental difference at work here: one can either accept or fail to accept the lack that *jouis-sans* is. Even when the subject's fundamental fantasy (as barrier) is undone once and for all, as happens in the case of psychosis, what is at stake is not an 'increase' of *jouissance* but an incapacity of the Symbolic to manage the potentially destructive lack of *jouissance* that *jouis-sans* is. (Chiesa 2007: 184–5)

Finally, we have a significantly different case of psychosis in Fassbinder's early naturalistic drama *Why does Mr R Run Amok?* (Warum läuft Herr R. Amok? 1970). The unnamed white-collar protagonist begins by telling his friends five quick jokes and ends up bludgeoning to death his neighbour, his wife, and his sleeping son, after which he goes to work and hangs himself. Why? The director does not hide the answer, to the extent that the question of the title can only sound rhetorical: his protagonist is a repressed petit-bourgeois. If there is a cinematic example of Freud's thesis of the return of the repressed, this is it. Most of the film focuses on the monotonous life of Herr R (Kurt Raab), spent between work, family, and television. This quiet man seems to accept rather willingly such a normal, at times humiliating but also relatively comfortable life. One day he is at home trying to watch a football match on TV. Next to him his wife and a neighbour are conversing, the neighbour describing in an endless monologue a recent skiing holiday where she made her boyfriend jealous by flirting with the ski instructor. Turning up the TV volume does not help. When his wife hops to the kitchen, he brandishes a heavy candle holder and smashes it repeatedly on the neighbour's head, until she drops dead. Within seconds, the rampage extends to wife and son, although we do not see much violence, and there is no spillage of blood. The final image of Mr R is that of his own dead body in his office toilet.

As with Ferreri's *Dillinger is Dead*, psychosis here would seem to relate to a scenario dominated by superego pressure – insofar as the superego, in Žižek's reading, is the internalised agency that enjoins us to *enjoy* our socially determined symbolic role. The key question, cleverly touched on by Fassbinder's references to silly jokes at the start of the film, is that of 'the inherent reflexive eroticisation of regulatory power mechanisms and procedures themselves' (Žižek 2000a: 261). The problem for the protagonist is indeed *the* problem of the contemporary western subject at the mercy of superego pressure: he experiences his symbolic role in society as the result of a free choice *which he is supposed to enjoy*. To understand the role of psychosis in strategies of liberation we must consider the subject's necessity to detach from his or her unconscious attachment to power mechanisms. In psychosis the subject assumes this libidinal attachment to the symbolic order, thus achieving a minimal distance (dis-attachment) from it. In Žižek's reading of Lacan,

> the symbolic Order is a given that can be effectively transgressed only if the subject pays the price of psychotic exclusion; so on the one hand we have false imaginary resistance to the symbolic Norm and, on the other, psychotic breakdown, with the full acceptance of alienation in the symbolic Order (the goal of psychoanalytic treatment) as the only 'realistic' option. (Žižek 2000a: 262–3)

This would seem to confirm what I have previously argued with regard to the staging of masochism. The Lacanian answer to the question of how to free ourselves from a given symbolic network and its surplus of unconscious libidinal attachment is 'to risk a gesture by means of which death is "courted" or "pursued"', which suggests that

> Lacan reconceptualized the Freudian death drive as the elementary form of the ethical act, the act as irreducible to a 'speech act' which relies for its performative power on the pre-established set of symbolic rules and/or norms. [. . .] For Lacan, there is no ethical *act* proper without taking the risk of such a momentary 'suspension of the big Other', of the socio-symbolic network that guarantees the subject's identity: an authentic *act* occurs only when the subject risks a gesture that is no longer 'covered up' by the big Other. (Žižek 2000a: 263–4)

3.6 Redemptive violence

In *Medea* (1970), Pasolini's passionate defence of the Real is summed up by the Centaur (Laurent Terzieff), who at the start of the film claims that 'only those who are mythical are realistic, and only those who are realistic are mythical'. Despite Pasolini's dismissal of Hegel, this sentence functions as an unequivocal endorsement of the Hegelian notion of *reflexivity*, in that it can be taken as a dialectical apology of the sacred or mythical dimension of reality: 'the sacred world is in no way superseded by its own desacralisation, as the centaur points out. The sacred and the profane continue to exist side by side' (Pasolini in Willemen 1997: 68). Hegelian reflexivity here implies that the sacred and the profane (or, in Lacan's terms, the Real and the Symbolic) only exist through their reciprocal over-determination: just as it is impossible to portray the sacred without referring to the profane, by the same token any cultural context hinges upon that which resists cultural integration absolutely. The Lacanian implications are self-evident, for the Real is the very blotch whose displacement allows for the cultural (symbolic) field to surface, while simultaneously precluding its universalisation by antagonising it from within. In *Medea*, Pasolini's strategy appears driven by a determination to dialecticise the couple Real/Symbolic, starting from the empirically based assumption that the socio-symbolic order (late-capitalistic liberal democracy) is engaged in a global project aimed at eliminating any reference to pure externality. The point made by Pasolini's mythical films, *Theorem* (Teorema, 1968) included, is a prophetic one: the more reason imposes itself as a purely instrumental tool that administers democracy and civilisation, the more aggressively tragedy will strike; the more "knowledge" is a dead letter in the hands of capitalism and its relentless effort to convert social antagonisms into regulated market competition, the more hatred and destruction will spread.

Pasolini uses myth to comment on modernity, for myth allows him to address the questions of violence, trauma and evil from a dialectical perspective. Oedipus kills his father, Medea kills her sons, the schizophrenic protagonist of *Pigsty* (Porcile, 1969) kills and eats human flesh, the mythical guest in *Theorem* brings separation and the collapse of bourgeois subjectivity. What must not be overlooked is that this sacred violence is invariably linked to, and over-determined by, the explicit reference to the contemporary world: in *Oedipus Rex* (Edipo re, 1967) an autobiographical Oedipus grows up in the North of Italy during the 1920s and, after a detour through ancient Greece, returns, blind, to the Bologna and Milan of the 1960s; in *Pigsty* and *Theorem* the contemporary bourgeois setting is constantly pinned back against its meta-historical underside; in *Medea*, the ancient and barbaric universe of the heroine is juxtaposed to the modern world founded by Jason. Pasolini is not interested in mythical violence *per se*, but only insofar as these ancient traumatic narratives give him a chance to comment on his world. The standard criticism should thus be reverted. These films do not depict 'the dilemma of a subject caught between historical consciousness and the temptation to escape into metahistory' (Viano 1993: 237); on the contrary, they attempt to demonstrate that there can be no historical consciousness without the positing of an ahistorical kernel. More precisely, the gap between history and meta-history is reflected back into history itself, which therefore appears "traversed" by its own lack. In this respect, Pasolini's entire work has been the object of a critical misunderstanding of colossal proportions, for his insistence on the sacred and the irrational was never the measure of an egotistical retreat into an imaginary world; instead, it was meant to historicise (i.e. dialecticise) the Real *qua* ahistorical bar of impossibility, whose primordially-repressed status is what sustains the framework of the possible. Thus, when in the late 1960s Pasolini confessed his fascination with such notions as 'barbarism' or 'the heroism of evil' (in Duflot 1993: 83–5), he was addressing, admittedly in a partial and theoretically inadequate way, the fantasmatic core of his own desire, the kernel of *jouissance* fully confronted in his cinematic production.

Put differently, we could argue that these so-called mythical films do not try to contain the horror of pure violence, for they "know" that what is at stake in this horror is the fundamental feature of the revolutionary act. Walter Benjamin's essay 'On the Critique of Violence' provides a useful framework within which to situate Pasolini's representation of violence. The basic premise of the essay, which emanates from the bedrock of Benjamin's messianic utopianism, is the profoundly pessimistic criticism of lawmaking and law-preserving violence, i.e. of any form of violence related to the exercise of law and power. Instead of dispensing *tout court* with violence, Benjamin elaborates upon the idiosyncratic notion of 'divine violence', which he defines as a form of violence absolutely disengaged from means and ends, and yet inherently political. For example, he is prepared to subscribe to Sorel's defence of redemptive violence in the proletarian general strike (as opposed to the violence of the political general strike), but only because it can be conceived as a "purer" form of destructive intervention (its aim being the annihilation of the state) that is absolutely detached from any reference to law and power. Furthermore, it is interesting to notice that before arriving at the definition of divine violence, Benjamin criticises what he calls 'mythic violence' for its explicit link with the lawmaking function: 'Far from inaugurating a purer sphere, the mythic manifestation of immediate violence shows itself fundamentally identical with all legal violence, and turns suspicion concerning the latter into certainty of the perniciousness of its historical function, the destruction of which thus becomes obligatory' (Benjamin 2003: 249).

In this context, the question indirectly raised by Pasolini's films can be seen as concerning the reconfiguration of the classic Marxian notion of proletarian violence into the strictly-speaking theological notion of divine violence. Apropos Benjamin's differentiation between divine and mythic violence, then, Pasolini's films of the late 1960s speak for the former despite having myth as their subject matter, since violence is performed by a subject who "disappears behind the act", in the specific sense that the grounds for his or her involvement cannot be known in advance. More than the irreconcilable opposition between western teleology and myth, and more than a Jungian retreat into archetypes (see Viano 1993: 238–40), these films express Pasolini's partially unconfessed desire for a violent intervention that "wipes the slate clean", just like in Benjamin's vision: 'Mythic violence is bloody power over mere life for its own sake; divine violence is pure power over all life for the sake of the living. The first demands sacrifice; the second accepts it. [...] if the existence of violence outside the law, as pure immediate violence, is assured, this furnishes proof that revolutionary violence, the highest manifestation of unalloyed violence by man, is possible, and shows by what means' (Benjamin 1996: 249–51).

The choice of Medea is in this sense exemplary, for the barbaric high priestess of Colchis brings to fruition the subversive potential already at work in films such as *Oedipus Rex*, *Theorem* and *Pigsty*. The very fact that *Medea* is often regarded as a failed film, and simultaneously a kind of exception in Pasolini's filmography, paradoxically confirms its vital importance (in Lacan it is always in the exception that we find the repressed truth of a given signifying chain). The film's aesthetic and narrative shortcomings (lack of narrative cohesion, endless ellipses, superficial treatment of most of the characters) are functional to the absolute centrality of the character of Medea. No wonder in this film Pasolini's normally encumbering presence, his autobiographical baggage, seems to disappear. With *Medea*, he confronts head-on the inassimilable core of *his own* desire, which coincides with the destructive enjoyment unleashed by his heroine; as a consequence, Pasolini is "erased from the picture", his *aphanisis* literally deriving from an excess of enjoyment. If *Oedipus Rex* did stage a desire that Pasolini was aware of (the Oedipal complex), *Medea* goes a step further into the uncharted (unconscious) territory of the feminine act. What Medea's enigmatic final words ('Nothing is possible anymore!') allude to is the limit of the subject's expenditure, where the sacred overlaps with unthinkable evil.[28]

From a different angle, it would appear that Medea accomplishes the Kierkegaardian "religious suspension of the ethical", which, as Žižek (2001d: 148–51) often reminds us, designates the formal dimension of the ethical gesture *par excellence*: first she kills her brother Absyrtus out of love for Jason; later, out of hatred for him, she kills their two sons. What we need to emphasise here is that the formal structure of Medea's cruel acts makes visible the liberating potential of a sovereign gesture of self-relating violence. Let us consider these two acts more closely. The explicit motivation behind the killing of Absyrtus is one of survival: having stolen the Golden Fleece, Medea and Jason escape from the land of Colchis, but are followed by Medea's father (Aeetes) and his soldiers; by dismembering Absyrtus' body and scattering its pieces along the way, Medea effectively delays the chasing army. However, the real aim of this act is a much more subtle one: what Medea wants to achieve is not just a break with the pursuing army, but a break with her own emotional attachment to her family, through which she would be able to dedicate herself unconditionally to Jason. By the same token, the final killing of her sons cannot be simply liquidated as a gesture of supreme vindictive cruelty, for no hatred would justify such a monstrosity. Instead, the real target is, again, Medea's own libidinal attachment: the only way for her to overcome her love for Jason (i.e., to traverse and dispel the libidinally invested fantasy of their relationship, which is the only passionate attachment she has left) is by killing the dearest thing they have in common; after such a shock, nothing (between them) will be possible.

We must therefore value both of Medea's acts as horrifying confrontations with the abyss of the Real, to be intended literally as the formless, pulsating life-substance of the human body, that which Freud (1997: 20–33) refers to in his famous analysis of his dream about Irma's throat. Lacan (1988: 154–5) describes the object of Freud's account as 'the flesh one never sees, the foundation of things, the other side of the head, of the face, the secretory gland *par excellence*, the flesh from which everything exudes, at the very heart of the mystery, the flesh in as much as it is suffering, formless, in as much as its form itself is something which provokes anxiety', and later as the 'lamella', that is, 'libido, *qua* pure life instinct, [...] immortal life, or irrepressible life, life that has need of no organ, simplified, indestructible life' (Lacan 1998a: 198).

With this premise, it does not seem exaggerated to claim that Medea is the first fictional subject to come face to face with the abyss of negativity,

Hegel's "night of the world", that *is* the subject. Her predicament is one of progressive isolation: having first betrayed her family for Jason, she is later betrayed by her husband, ending up alone and dejected. As a result, she is forced to face the paradox of subjectivity: either "live in loss" (in eternal mourning), or outsource loss through loss itself, i.e. through an act of violence that effaces the very memory of loss. The subversive potential of this situation can be grasped by transposing the situation itself onto a political level. Medea can either accept her condition of subordination and marginalisation within Jason's newly-founded modern state (and, for example, piously devote herself to her children), or she can "out-violence" Jason's power by assuming the very negativity of her condition. Only by choosing the second option does she manage to truly antagonise her husband-rival.

In this respect, could we not argue that Medea goes a step further than Antigone, the Lacanian "heroine of the act" *par excellence*? If Antigone's self-destructive inflexibility was still aimed at safeguarding a certain symbolic constellation (the family mores as opposed to the law of the paternal state), Medea's act dissolves the last vestiges of symbolic unity, exposing the abyss at the heart of the subject interpellated in the family network. Jacques-Alain Miller was the first to recognise that the figure of Medea has all the credentials to satisfy the Lacanian definition of *une vraie femme*: 'For Lacan, the act of a true woman is not necessarily as extreme as Medea's, but it has the same structure, in that she sacrifices what is most precious to her in order to pierce man with a hole that can never be filled' (Miller 2000: 19). In a way that reminds one of Pasolini's own personal predicament, Medea does not negotiate her position of victim within the socio-symbolic order; on the contrary, she radicalises the attitude of victimisation by assuming the libidinal attachment embedded in her subordinate position. This is the only way she can free herself from what she seemed irredeemably attached to.

Again, the Hegelian subtext should not be missed, for Medea comes to embody Hegel's theme of the coincidence of the Particular and the Universal. The Particular participates in the Universal only 'in so far as his identity is truncated, marked by a lack; in so far as he is not fully "what he is" – this is what Hegel has in mind when he speaks of "negative universality"' (Žižek 1994: 146). This is how we should read the notorious passage on women and society in the *Phenomenology of Spirit*, where woman is addressed as 'the everlasting irony of the community': since woman, according to Hegel, is the particular individual unable to perceive the universal breadth of state politics, and only interested in power within the narrow confines of family life, she is effectively the 'internal enemy' of the community, insofar as 'the community only gets an existence through its interference with the happiness of the Family, and by dissolving self-consciousness into the universal' (Hegel 1977: 288). The proper conclusion to draw here is that in embodying the Particular *qua* internal enemy of the community, woman is directly connected with the very negativity that always-already characterises the Universal as such, irrespective of political universality (the state). Hegel's point is therefore that 'an individual ("self-consciousness") can relate to the Universal beyond the community only through her negative relationship towards the family – that is, her betrayal of the family, which entails the family's dissolution (this negativity is exactly what the corporatist metaphor of society *qua* large family strives to obliterate)'. Is this not *exactly* the final position occupied by Medea (and Antigone), who in sacrificing the family effectively aims to expose 'the inherent limitation of the standpoint of social totality itself' (Žižek 1994: 148)? I am also thinking of Ingmar Bergman's *Summer with Monika* (Sommaren med Monika, 1953), and especially the famous shot, which so thrilled Godard (see Godard 1986: 37), where the protagonist, played by Harriet Andersson, stares defiantly into the camera just before betraying her fiancé, father of her child, and rejecting family life altogether.

3.7 The miracle of love

So, to conclude, back to the deadlock of sexual difference. To ask a simple question: is there any hope at all? There is, at least, the condition that Žižek often describes as "the miracle of love", which in his view involves the proper *answer of the Real* (see Žižek 2003: 92–121). The meaning of this assertion carries different connotations. Before discussing them, let us remind ourselves that Lacan's understanding of love, fully in line with Freud's, is firmly anchored in the notion of narcissism: *velle bonum alicui* (to love someone, as in St Thomas Aquinas' theory of love) is for Lacan the same as *se vouloir son bien* (to wish oneself one's own well-being). In the psychoanalytic field we are concerned with, the framework of love *qua* altruism no doubt retains a 'specious character', insofar as it involves 'the insertion of the *autoerotisch* in the organized interests of the ego' (Lacan 1998a: 191–3). In brief: 'To love is, essentially, to wish to be loved' (Lacan 1998a: 253); if, as we have seen, drives are on the side of the object, love 'allows no transcendence to the object included' (Lacan 1998a: 194). This is why Lacan (1998a: 205) prefers the 'myth of the lamella' to Aristophanes' myth of love intended as the search for 'one's sexual other half': what we truly search for is always the part of *ourselves* that we have lost forever, and that can only surface, as lack, in the libido-object named lamella represented by *objet a* in all its forms.

However, it is precisely *objet a* that is able to point us to an alternative understanding of love, developed by Lacan (1998a: 271–2) at the end of *Seminar XI* in connection with his discussion of the rapport between analysand and analyst known as transference:

> Any analysis that one teaches as having to be terminated by iden-tification with the analyst reveals, by the same token, that its true motive force is elided. There is a beyond to this identification, and this beyond is defined by the relation and the distance of the *objet petit a* to the idealizing capital I of identification.

Immediately after, Lacan (1998a: 273) returns to this crucial question of the "beyond of identification":

> It is from this idealization that the analyst has to fall in order to be the support of the separating *a*, in so far as his desire allows him, in an upside-down hypnosis, to embody the hypnotized patient. This crossing of the plane of identification is possible.

The experience which involves the crossing of the plane of identification, whereby the loved one (the analyst) comes to occupy the place of the hypnotised other (the loving one/analysand), is of capital importance if we are to grasp the meaning of love as something which 'can be posited only in that beyond, where, at first, it renounces its object' (Lacan 1998a: 276). Lacan's interest in the notion of love in relation to transference relies on his fascination with the fact that, as anticipated in connection with Truffaut's cinema, love may emerge from a thoroughly artificial sit-uation – such as, for example, the analytic treatment. Analysis suggests that, precisely because love is by its very nature deceptive (we love the other for what he/she does not have), it may develop into a "miraculous exchange of lacks". Despite being an illusory fantasy of Oneness rooted in narcissism ('love, while it is true that it has a relationship with the One, never makes anyone leave himself behind', Lacan 1998b: 47), it has a chance to move beyond narcissism into a domain where it persists despite the mutual awareness of the illusion itself.

It is here that we should introduce Žižek's interpretation of love as "the answer of the Real", which expands on this last point. First of all, the Real emerges in love insofar as there we exchange, as anticipated, what we do not have (strictly speaking, *objet a*, the fantasmatic X we are for the other, which in its deepest configuration amounts to a lack). The paradox is that the loved one owes its special status to something (*objet a*) that he/she does not actually possess. Given this deadlock, love can only emerge as a kind of de-potentiation of our subjective condition as objects of desire. That is to say: we become "worthy of love" when we abdicate the privileged position of object of desire and somehow make manifest to the other that those very feature(s) that made us unique and special in his/her eyes in fact are a missing link in our subjective configuration. In this sense love is, literally, an answer of the Real: we engage in a loving relationship by acknowledging that our status as object of desire is an embodiment of void. Love, therefore, functions by subtraction; it involves a risky passage from object to subject, insofar as the loved one (in Lacan's terms, the analyst), self-assured in his/her position as object of desire (or "subject supposed to know"), suddenly appears in the eyes of the loving one as *lacking it*, as frail and vulnerable – which is precisely what always-already characterises the position of the loving one:

> Therein consists, according to Lacan, love's most sublime moment: in this inversion when the beloved object endeavours to deliver himself from the impasse of his position, from the impossibility of complying with the lover's demand, by assuming himself the position of the lover, by reaching his hand back to the lover and thus answering the lover's lack/desire with his own lack. (Žižek 2001b: 58)

Love, then, can only be experienced by a subject aware of its radical inconsistency: 'Only a lacking, vulnerable being is capable of love: the ultimate mystery of love [...] is that incompleteness is, in a way, higher than completion'. The difference between sexuality and love should by now appear obvious. While in sexuality we get caught up in the dialectic of desire and fantasy – since the sexual partner 'functions as a prop for our indulging in fantasies' – 'it is only through love that we can reach the Real (of the) Other' (Žižek 2003: 115–16). However, although the disparity between the lover and the loved one dissolves in the answer of the Real, 'the asymmetry persists' (Žižek 1994: 104), which is precisely what makes love a *miraculous* event that permits us to endure the deadlock of the sexual relationship.

To illustrate this point I would like to refer once again to the cinema of François Truffaut, more precisely to another of his underrated and most criticised films, *Mississippi Mermaid* (La Sirène du Mississippi, 1969). The Hitchcockian plot of this work is strictly centred on the vicissitudes of a couple, Louis Mahé (Jean-Paul Belmondo) and Julie Roussel/Marion

Vergano (Catherine Deneuve). Even more obviously than in most of his other films, Truffaut here focuses on the impossibility of the relationship, in this case a true "battle of the sexes". The Deneuve character's double identity provides the key twist in the plot. Louis, a wealthy tobacco magnate based on Reunion Island, marries Julie after corresponding with her through personal ads. Madly in love with his new bride, he sets up a joint access to his personal bank account. Julie, predictably, withdraws most of the funds and disappears. Having hired a private detective, Louis later finds out that his wife's real name is actually Marion Vergano, and that, with the help of a male accomplice, she had eliminated Julie Roussel and taken her place to defraud him. As he bumps into her on the French Riviera, where she is working as a prostitute in a local dance hall, he is determined to kill her. However, when she claims that she was forced into deceit by her former gangster boyfriend, adding the pathetic story of her unhappy childhood as an abused orphan,[29] he decides to give her another chance. In fact, he realises that he is still besotted with her, even resolving to kill Detective Comolli (Michel Bouquet) who was about to have her arrested. Now on the run from the police, the two continue to bicker, fight, and make up, until the final revelation of what we could call, resorting to Hitchcock's famous phrase, "the degradation of love" (a phrase used by Truffaut himself to describe his film, see Gillain 2005: 158). On their way to the Swiss border, they take refuge in a mountain shelter. It is here that we have the "miracle of love", one of the most risky passages in all of Truffaut's filmography – and indeed one of the most significant. In line with her cynical character, upon realising that Louis has next to no money left, Marion decides to kill him by pouring some rat poison in his soup. Already ill, Louis fathoms her intentions by glancing accidentally at some newspaper drawings of Snow White. As Marion feeds him more poisonous soup, however, he reacts in a way that cannot but appear surprising, telling her that *he is willing to accept his death as the final humiliation from the woman he loves*. This phrase, which signifies Louis' total degradation and utter fragility in the face of love, has a miraculous effect on Marion, who is first overwhelmed with guilt and then vows to never abandon him. The end of the film thus introduces love as the answer of the Real: the loved one (Marion) returns the gaze of the loving one (Louis) and constitutes a link with him on the basis of their own radical incompleteness.

If we endorse this reading, the ending of Truffaut's film can be compared to the endings of two masterpieces of European cinema, Michelangelo Antonioni's *The Adventure* (L'avventura, 1960) and Roberto Rossellini's *Voyage to Italy* (Viaggio in Italia, 1954). In the famous closing shot of *The Adventure*, the emotional deadlock between Claudia (Monica Vitti) and Sandro (Gabriele Ferzetti) is visualised as the sharp contrast between the cement wall filling up Sandro's side of the picture and the view of Mount Etna behind Claudia. The director himself stated apropos of this finale:

> I really don't know if the relationship between these two halves will endure or not, though it is quite evident the two protagonists will remain together and not separate. The girl will definitely not leave the man; she will stay with him and forgive him. For she realises that she too, in a certain sense, is somewhat like him. (in Di Carlo and Tinazzi 1996: 34)

Elsewhere, he added that the only way for his two characters to stay together is by

> establishing a relationship based on reciprocal compassion, or comprehension, which implies a form of resignation that is not weakness, but rather the only force allowing them to remain together, to stay alive, to be opposed to catastrophe. (in Tinazzi 1976: 83)

Sandro and Claudia, not unlike Marion and Louis, realise that they can only overcome the "catastrophe" of sexual difference through 'reciprocal compassion, or comprehension'. This implicitly validates Žižek's claim that

> I am truly in love not when I am simply fascinated by the agalma ['treasure', *objet a*] in the other, but when I experience the other, the object of love, as frail and lost, as lacking 'it', and my love none the less survives this loss. (Žižek 1994: 104)

Or even, in a more militant fashion:

> Today, more than ever, the lesson of Marguerite Duras's novels is pertinent: the way – the *only* way – to have an intense and fulfilling personal (sexual) relationship is not for the couple to look into each other's eyes, forgetting about the world around them, but, while holding hands, to look together outside, at a third point (the Cause for which both are fighting, to which both are committed). (Žižek 2003: 38)[30]

It is not a coincidence that the two final shots of Antonioni's and Truffaut's films depict the couple from behind, gazing together at (in Truffaut's case also "moving towards") a third point, the outside world which, alone, can make their rapport viable.

The finale of Rossellini's *Voyage to Italy* confirms and strengthens this view. As the marriage of the English couple falls apart, the female character Katherine Joyce (Ingrid Bergman) suggests a potential way out of the stifling sentimental impasse by slowly gaining a distance from it and directing her attentions to the external world – whereas Alex Joyce (George Sanders) grows increasingly bitter with jealousy. It is only at the end, after the visit to Pompeii, that the Joyces seem to unexpectedly find a solution to their dilemma. Whilst driving out, they drift into a religious procession in honour of San Gennaro. The car is forced to stop, engulfed by the crowd. Then somebody shouts 'Miracle! Miracle!', which propels the crowd forward, snatching Katherine away from Alex. After a few seconds of panic, Alex manages to rescue his wife and, reunited in a comforting embrace, the two finally find the courage to declare their love to each other. Critics have been fairly unanimous in spotting the intrinsically false character of this reconciliation, on the grounds that it does not appear to be a spontaneous one, but instead engendered by fear and estrangement. Rossellini himself went in this direction when he commented that

> the only way a *rapprochement* could come about was through the couple finding themselves complete strangers to everyone else. [...] The couple take refuge in each other in the same way as people cover themselves when they are seen naked, grabbing a towel, drawing closer to the person with them, and covering themselves any old how. (in Brunette 1996: 169)

However, what if it is precisely in the somewhat forced and unnatural context of the final embrace that the dimension of true love is to be found? What if the notion that love is the result of a harmonious and transparent consolidation of feelings between two individuals is ultimately false? What we have here is another "reunion in degradation", with film testifying to the paradoxical miracle of love as the encounter between two lacks.

The "excremental" dimension is exactly what the classic European film about romantic love, David Lean's *Brief Encounter* (1945), misses. Let us take the nice metaphor that kick-starts the unconsummated affair between Alec (Trevor Howard) and Laura (Celia Johnson): when they meet for the first time, he takes a bit of grit out of her eye, the implication being that she can now *see better* in relation to what she really wants, since the man she truly desires is standing there in front of her. The problem with this idealisation of the relationship is that it disavows its presupposition: the obstacle to the accomplishment of the illicit affair between Alec and Laura is *its very cause*, its condition of possibility. For this reason Laura's guilt, her reluctance to go all the way with her lover for fear of breaking the law of marital fidelity, cannot fail to appear false, to the extent that it should be turned around: her final choice of fidelity always-already relies on a degree of "betrayal in fantasy", which is precisely what allows her to sustain the relationship with her husband. By giving up on the affair when Alec is offered a job in Johannesburg, the two lovers effectively immortalise the affair itself in fantasy – ultimately, cinematic fantasy at its purest, since the whole film is told in flash-back by Laura as her memory of the affair. This massive investment in fantasy speaks for their intimate desire to avoid the Real of *jouissance*.[31] In this sense, the question of censorship is irrelevant, just as that of class consciousness. It is not that the lovers do not have sex because of the censor; rather, they do not do it because they are scared of losing the obdurate fantasy that binds them together. Sex, as such, would not lead them directly to unbearable enjoyment, for the sexual act itself is immersed in and sustained by fantasy; however, it would open the way to it, forcing them to truly face the loved one. In the final analysis, what they refuse to confront is not sex, but love, insofar as love entails the enigma of how a subject succeeds in 'negotiating a fragile balance between the sublime image of the beloved and her real presence, so that the flesh-and-blood person can continue to occupy the sublime place and avoid the sad fate of turning into a repulsive excrement' (Žižek 1997: 67). From this perspective, the key character is Laura's friend Myrtle (Joyce Carey) whom we see at the beginning of the film (in narrative terms, its ending) as she joins them at the train station and starts chatting to both, oblivious to their misery, spoiling their last minutes of intimacy: what does this character represent if not the materialisation of the two lovers' unconscious desire *not* to come too close to each other?

Part II
Variations on Feminine Enjoyment

4
In the Beginning was Enjoyment: the Emergence of Feminine Desire in Bergman and Antonioni

On 30 July 2007 Ingmar Bergman died; Michelangelo Antonioni followed him within a few hours in what seemed an event staged in a sublimely ironic scenario. The uncanny coincidence of these deaths resonates with both truth and fiction, as if truth and fiction could not be told apart. It is precisely this coincidence that I investigate here in connection with the cinematic representation of femininity. The main argument centres on the assumption that in femininity the exclusionary logic is absent. Femininity undermines the masculine field by abolishing the fracture between the Symbolic and the Real, thus depriving the Symbolic of its founding excess.

4.1 Woman's not-all

In the feminine position of not-all (or not-whole, both used as translations of Lacan's *pas-tout*) there is simply no exception to the phallic economy, but total identification with it (see Žižek 2003: 68). This question can also be tackled by referring to the status of what Lacan calls *jouissance féminine*. According to Lacan's formulas of sexuation, the inconsistency of the feminine field is characterised by woman's bond with two "objects": the phallic signifier (Φ) and S($\cancel{A}$). Whilst the phallic signifier designates woman's specific fantasy of man, S($\cancel{A}$) represents her relationship with the symbolic field as radically inconsistent, fraught with Real gaps, always-already penetrated by *jouissance*. If in the first case woman constructs her identity and organises her enjoyment through the phallic signifier, in the second she achieves enjoyment 'beyond the phallus' (Lacan, 1998b, 74) – she exposes the phallic economy of "symbolisation-through-the-exception" as not-all:

> when any speaking being whatsoever situates itself under the banner 'women', it is on the basis of the following – that it grounds itself

as being not-whole in situating itself in the phallic function. That is what defines what? Woman precisely, except that Woman can only be written with a bar through it. There's no such thing as Woman, Woman with capital W indicating the universal. There's no such thing as Woman because, in her essence – I've already risked using that term, so why should I think twice about using it again? – she is not-whole. (Lacan 1998b: 72–3)

The fact that woman defines her sexuality through the phallus *as well as* the big Other is an indicator of the peculiarity of her division: 'Woman has a relation with S(Ⱥ), and it is already in that respect that she is doubled, that she is not-whole, since she can also have a relation with Φ' (Lacan 1998b: 81). It is in relation to the big Other that the distinctiveness of the feminine position can be observed. When Lacan claims that 'woman [in contrast to man] is that which has a relationship to that Other', he means the most radical instance of otherness, in other words a space which is *not* sustained by an external point of exclusion, characterised by the fact that 'there is no Other of the Other' (Lacan, 1998b: 81). Since the enjoyment of this otherness is only available to femininity, 'she has a supplementary jouissance compared to what the phallic function designates by way of jouissance' (Lacan 1998b: 73).

An important consequence is that, since woman's supplementary enjoyment is unavailable to man, 'we would be wrong not to see that, contrary to what people say, it is nevertheless they [women] who possess men' (Lacan 1998b: 73). While man is locked in compulsive symbolic identifications sustained by the excluded (and fantasised about) *objet a*, woman has a chance to disengage from the masculine urge to symbolise and, instead, "enjoy" the Real inconsistency of the symbolic field – the fact that "the big Other does not exist".[1] As we have seen in Part 1, man's enjoyment is by definition 'the jouissance of the idiot' (Lacan 1998b: 81), the (masturbatory) phallic enjoyment which never reaches the Other; woman, on the contrary, *can* enjoy the Other. Instead of pretending to have the phallus (the masculine position), woman is the phallus: she fully vindicates the negativity contained in the phallus *qua* signifier of lack (see Lacan 2007: 583). From this perspective, the cliché whereby man is split between instrumental rationality (work, duty, authority, etc.) and sexuality, hits the target, provided we specify that symbolisation depends on its libidinal exception; if we disturb, or remove, this exception (Žižek's '*acheronta movebo*', 2006c: 366), the symbolic order risks disintegrating.

Ultimately, the Real of sexual difference refers to the incompatibility of the masculine and feminine ways to deal with the surplus generated by symbolisation. While masculinity turns this surplus into *objet a*, femininity restores it as Real: as the explosive nucleus of negativity/lack consubstantial with every symbolisation. Such a view of femininity, however, could be seen to confirm the standard feminist critique of phallocentrism. Žižek openly confronts this issue:

> Feminists are usually repulsed by Lacan's insistence on the feminine 'not-all'. Does it not imply that women are somehow excluded from fully participating in the Symbolic order, unable to wholly integrate themselves into it, condemned to leading a parasitical existence? And, truly, do not these propositions belong to the best vein of patriarchal ideology, do they not bear witness to a hidden normativity to the detriment of woman? Man is able to find his identity in the Symbolic, to assume fully his symbolic mandate, whereas woman is condemned to hysterical splitting, to wearing masks, to not wanting what she pretends to want. How are we to conceive of this feminine resistance to symbolic identification? (Žižek 1993: 57)

Žižek replies to these questions with a kind of *reductio ad absurdum*: if every masculine portrayal of femininity is biased, what would the "proper" one be?[2] In other words, can we really account for a "feminine substance" pre-existent and opposed to the masculine one? According to him, this is precisely the way to miss the originality of Lacan's formulas, since they tell us that

> woman's exclusion does not mean that some positive entity is prevented from being integrated into the symbolic order: it would be wrong to conclude, from 'not-all woman is submitted to the phallic signifier', that there is something in her which is not submitted; there is no exception, and 'woman' is this very nonexistent 'nothing' which nonetheless makes the existing elements 'not-all'. (Žižek 1993: 57–8)

Far from plunging us back into the pitfalls of patriarchal domination, insisting on the inconsistency of feminine sexuality means asserting woman's ontological primacy over man. When Žižek reminds us that Lacan's answer to Freud's *Was will das Weib?* ("What does woman want?") is 'a Master whom she will be able to dominate/manipulate', he is actually affirming woman's status as 'a true subject':

> [. . .] does this mean that woman is structurally, formally, in her very definition, immature, an immature subject? Yes – but not in the

simple sense that would oppose her to a 'mature' man who doesn't need a Master to tell him what he wants, who can autonomously set his own limits. What this condition amounts to is, rather, that woman is a true subject, a subject at its most fundamental, while man is a ridiculous fake, a false pretender. (Žižek 2006c: 91)

It is from this angle that we should confront the question of femininity as it emerges in the cinemas of Ingmar Bergman and Michelangelo Antonioni, both expressions of supreme sensitivity towards the issue of sexual difference.

4.2   Deep surfaces

By staging an encounter between Bergman and Antonioni my intention is, essentially, to assess the validity of Truffaut's well-known observation about Bergman's empathy with his feminine characters:

I think he's more involved in the feminine principle than in feminism. Women are not seen through a masculine prism in his films but are observed in a spirit of total complicity. His female characters are infinitely subtle, while his male characters are conventions. (Truffaut 1994: 258)

The key word here is 'complicity', which suggests an attempt, in Bergman, to identify with the specificity of woman's subject position. The 'spirit of total complicity' I explore through Bergman and Antonioni is one involving the specific mode of *enjoyment* materialised by femininity. In these two directors the fascination with feminine desire springs from the painful awareness that relations between the sexes are fraught with a fundamental impasse. Beyond any direct concern with social questions, both use the cinematic medium as a way to explore and partly neutralise their fixation on sexual difference. It is difficult not to notice how, already at an early stage, their cinemas reflect the fact that, for them, the sexual deadlock "cannot stop *not* being written".

It may come as a surprise that, with the exception of a few films like *The Night* (La notte, 1961) and especially *Blow-up* (1966), the Swede did not esteem the Italian's work. The immediate reason would seem fairly obvious: Antonioni's cinema must have appeared too cold and stylised to a passionate director like Bergman, which also explains why he felt a closer affinity with Federico Fellini. In thematic terms, on the other hand, the main difference would seem to concern the way their films

relate to the problem of religion or, more appropriately, transcendentalism. While in Bergman's work one finds an obsession with God, or
rather its absence, Antonioni as a rule avoids dealing with religious or
spiritual themes, his cinema being thoroughly secular. Bergman's self-
proclaimed atheism, not dissimilarly to Buñuel's, is populated by ghosts,
demons, diabolical creatures that would not be able to flourish so prolif-
ically without the reference to a "dark Beyond". However, if we look past
the obvious, we might find that Antonioni's cinema, despite its proud
indifference to religion and its somewhat "scientific" aesthetic rigour, is
also heavily indebted to a reflection on transcendentalism.

We can put this in the familiar terms of the difference between surface and depth. Although critics generally describe Antonioni's work
as focusing on "the surface of things", while Bergman is perceived as
an artist compulsively attempting to cast a glance beneath the mask –
beyond the precariousness of fictions/appearances – it seems to me that
Antonioni's "flat surface" actually expresses a strong concern with depth,
while in Bergman the search for a transcendental truth fulfils itself in the
endorsement of depthless fictionality. In philosophical terms, the paradox is that both directors resolve the central quandary of modernism
by conflating the two contrasting categories at its heart: appearance and
truth, fiction and reality, the relative and the absolute, the particular
and the universal. While this conflation does not make them postmodern directors, it nevertheless allows them to break free from the
modernist stalemate without sacrificing its crucial tenet, the search for
truth. Instead, this search is reconfigured not as a transcendental move
beyond fiction (appearance, relativism, etc.), as in standard modernist
terms, but as a thoroughly immanent enquiry where the gap between
appearance and truth is recast as a gap between appearance and its empty
place of inscription. With regard to this question, Žižek goes as far as to
claim that this gap is the distinctive feature of true art *tout court*:

> The constitutive gap between the explicit symbolic texture and its
> phantasmic background is obvious in any work of art. Owing to the
> priority of place over the element which fills it up, even the most
> harmonious work of art is a priori fragmentary, lacking in regard to
> its place: the 'trick' of an artistic success resides in the artist's capacity
> to turn this lack into an advantage – skilfully to manipulate the central
> void and its resonance in the elements that encircle it. (Žižek 1997:
> 18–19)

In Bergman and Antonioni the persistence of void *qua* empty place of
inscription is not only evident at the narrative level, but it also resonates

through the same signifier: woman. It is the uncovering of a basic imbalance within immanent reality, embodied by woman, which ultimately proves the two directors' affinity. As Žižek has shown, transcendentalism in Lacan is replaced by an ontology of immanence articulated around the correlation between subjectivity and the unconscious – or the Symbolic and the Real. It is therefore at the conjuncture where, in Lacan, the Symbolic and the Real overlap, that we need to introduce woman as the crucial cinematic cipher in Antonioni and Bergman. For both directors woman works as the only legitimate mediator between the polymorphous universe of fictions and the modernist search for authentic reality, which, however, ends with the insight that the beyond of appearance is nothing but the very "appearance of void" constitutive of the fictional domain itself. In their best films woman becomes a special lens allowing the camera to intrude into a domain where fiction is suddenly raised to the status of substance – the very substance that Lacan calls the Real of enjoyment.

In Antonioni and Bergman woman proceeds from "appearance" to the "truth of appearance". As such, she can only be deciphered as Lacan's *femme*, whose mission is to confront us with the *pas-tout* underpinning the network of symbolic exchange. The woman I am going to discuss enjoys a properly ethical status, since her specific economy of desire throws into relief the invisible mechanism upon which our shared order of meaning secretly relies. For Antonioni and Bergman, then, woman is the key to unlock *the mystery of the dissolution of meaning*: if they are both deeply aware that the universe of meaning only arises from fiction, from the way inchoate reality is artificially transformed into a narrative, their staging of femininity tells us not only that this operation relies on some repressed content, but also, more crucially, that its foundations are immensely more fragile than what we are normally prepared to acknowledge.

With regard to the main psychoanalytic implications in Antonioni's and Bergman's representations of femininity, we can identify two dominant patterns. To start with, we have the typically masculine account of woman as *objet a*. As we have seen in Part 1, man desires woman by reducing her to a part of her bodily appearance that remains elusive, perceived as lost, thus prompting a specific fantasy scenario. This has important consequences, for reality itself relies on this fantasy scenario, our own ability to inscribe a distance between us and the object of our gaze. The same with sexual relations: we have a relationship only insofar as between "us two" there is a space filled in by fantasy. My point, however, is that Antonioni and Bergman stage the collapse of this fantasy in connection with femininity. The woman at the heart of their cinemas brings about *a loss of reality*, which is deeply connected with *a loss of fantasy*. The lesson is one that involves a logic of over-proximity: the closer we get to the feminine subject, the more we lose not only woman as such, but, more significantly, our own perception of reality. With woman, as it were, we *do* throw out the baby with the bath water. If these two directors manage to move beyond the strictures of masculine voyeurism is because they do not forsake the traumatic dimension of *objet a*, the void that envelops the object of desire and representation:

> *Objet a* is simultaneously the pure lack, the void around which the desire turns and which, as such, causes the desire, *and* the element which conceals this void, renders it invisible by filling it out. The point, of course, is that there is no lack without the element filling it out: *the filler sustains what it dissimulates*. (Žižek 1994: 178)

When we talk about *objet a* we inevitably raise the question of its empty framework. While most directors, as we have seen, only hint at this question, and then retreat behind the safe curtain of masculine fantasy, Antonioni and Bergman fully endorse it. For them woman is a cause consubstantial with void.

As for the second pattern of my enquiry, it involves the shift from mas-culine to feminine desire: from what woman is for man (*objet a*), to what woman is in herself. The sheer dedication with which both Antonioni and Bergman confront the question of feminine desire – a question that, as is well known, Freud himself was unable to answer – is alone testament to the extraordinary significance of their cinemas. My wager is that at their best, they manage to open up the cinematic image to the enigma articulated in Lacan's claim that femininity has at its disposal a supple-mentary *jouissance*, a mode of enjoyment that is not determined by her place in the relationship but rather aims at the non-existence of the big Other: S(Ⱥ).

In respect of these two psychoanalytic implications concerning the representation of woman, a further parallel between the two directors can be outlined. In both the first move concerns the inscription of woman as object-cause of desire and consequent consolidation of nar-rative consistency. Bergman's early films (roughly from *Crisis*, 1946, to *The Virgin Spring*, 1960) are narratively on a par with Antonioni's work from his first *Chronicle of a Love* (Cronaca di un amore, 1950) to *The Cry* (Il grido, 1959). After that, the enquiry into femininity acquires a much stronger and more disruptive resonance. Antonioni's trilogy *The Adventure* (L'avventura, 1959), *The Night* (La notte, 1961) and *The Eclipse* (L'eclisse, 1962) (with the addition of *The Red Desert*, 1964), essentially pans out as a prolonged meditation on the relationship between femininity and freedom, a concern that is also celebrated in Bergman's trilogy of the same period (*Through a Glass Darkly*, 1961; *Winter Light*, 1963; *The Silence*, 1963), and which has in *Persona* (1966) its most unequivocal statement.

Most of Antonioni's and Bergman's early films share a surprisingly similar intention as far as their narrative dynamics are concerned. These films are generally articulated around a probing masculine fantasy about femininity, which can be summarised with the following three points: (1) woman is introduced as an ambiguous signifier without a clearly identifiable place in the narrative order; (2) she meets man *qua* lover/harasser, his intervention signalling an attempt to inscribe her into the chain of causes and effects, i.e. to graft upon her a specific symbolic mandate; (3) the attempt fails, and the film ends with woman returning to the opacity of her initial position within the symbolic network. The circular loop of these early narratives speaks for the cinematic failure to symbolise the excess of enjoyment with which woman is associated and that serves to set the narratives themselves in motion. In Lacanese, it makes manifest the existence of a cut, a disjunction, between the signifier and the signified: insofar as they are centred on woman, these stories *qua* signifying chains stumble against the feminine Real they unwittingly produce. The coming into being of woman through the defiles of the cinematic signifier threatens to derail the consistency of film as enunciation. Put differently, she occupies here a borderline position that I am tempted to read as homologous to the various anatomical locations where desire is inscribed: lips, eyelids, the vagina, the rim of the anus, the split on the tip of the penis (but also the gaze, the voice, etc). As Lacan claims in "Subversion of the Subject and the Dialectic of Desire", these partial objects 'that have no specular image, in other words, no alterity' (Lacan 2007: 693), are ultimately the very "stuff" the subject is about, insofar as they embody a lack, a *manque à être*. The difference between *objet a* and S($\bar{A}$) on the feminine side of the formulas of sexuation, then, amounts to what Žižek would call a parallax view: from the masculine perspective, woman is *objet a*; from the feminine perspective, i.e. *in herself*, she is the phallus, the signifier of the Other's lack. And my point apropos Antonioni's and Bergman's early films is that while they confirm that for man woman is *objet a*, they also allude to her crucial role in bringing about the lack in the Other.

The above tripartite structure, with woman at its core, also confirms Lacan's notion that the subject occupies the place 'from which "the universe is a defect in the purity of Non-Being" is vociferated', the implication being that such a place, just as much as the defect it calls into question by verbalising it, 'is called Jouissance' (Lacan 2007: 694). Essentially, and before all other determinations, *jouissance* is the very disturbance that brings the world into existence the moment the subject identifies it:

> *Jouissance* is [...] the ontological aberration, the disturbed balance (*clinamen*, to use the old philosophical term) which accounts for the passage from Nothing to Something [...]. Someone can be happily married, with a good job and many friends, fully satisfied with his life, and yet absolutely hooked on some specific formation ('sinthom') of *jouissance*, ready to put everything at risk rather than renounce that (drugs, tobacco, drink, a particular sexual perversion...). Although his symbolic universe may be nicely set up, this absolutely meaningless intrusion, this *clinamen*, upsets everything, and there is nothing to be done, since it is only in this 'sinthom' that the subject encounters the density of being – when he is deprived of it, his universe is empty. At a less extreme level, the same holds for every authentic intersubjective encounter: when do I actually encounter the Other 'beyond the wall of language', in the real of his or her being? Not when I am able to describe her, not even when I learn her values, dreams, and so on, but only when I encounter the Other in her moment of *jouissance*: when I discern in her a tiny detail (a compulsive gesture, an excessive facial expression, a tic) which signals the intensity of the real of *jouissance*. This encounter with the real is always traumatic; there is something at least minimally obscene about it; I cannot simply integrate it into my universe, there is always a gulf separating me from it. [...] Therein lies the primordial 'decentrement' of the Lacanian subject: much more radical and elementary than the decentrement of the subject with regard to the 'big Other', the symbolic order which is the place of the subject's truth, is the decentrement with regard to the traumatic Thing-*jouissance* which the subject can never 'subjectivize', assume, integrate. (Žižek 1997: 49)

Woman's position in Antonioni's and Bergman's early films seems tantamount to a coincidence of naming (which signals the emergence of the narrative frame) and *jouissance* (the signifier that accompanies and derails the act of naming). It is a position that, in the light of Lacan's formulas, only woman has a chance to occupy, since man is by definition subjected to castration, and therefore "names" the world by excluding enjoyment.

The question I would like to explore with regard to the two directors' early work can be expressed as follows: to what extent is the masculine fantasy of woman prepared to undermine its own totalising function and gain an insight into the dimension of freedom implicit in femininity? If these films no doubt stage a masculine fantasy, they are simultaneously not afraid to see through it, at least hinting at the fact that woman is not-all in the Lacanian sense, i.e. inconsistent with any (intrinsically false) subject position that man may wish to impress on her. Ultimately, therein lies the courage of these films. The non-existence of the sexual relationship manifests itself in the discrepancy between the masculine fantasy of woman as *effect* of masculine intervention, and the specific causality of woman who refuses to be defined by cause–effect dynamics.

4.3   From effect to cause

Bergman's *Crisis* (Kris, 1946) already firmly targets femininity, although its traditional narrative structure partly obfuscates the director's fixation. In 1946, one of the first reviews of the film argued:

> there is something unbridled, nervously out of control in Bergman's imagination that makes a disquieting impression. He [...] seems to be incapable of keeping a mental level of normalcy. What the Swedish cinema needs in the first place are not experimenters, but intelligent, rational people [...] (in Oliver 1995: 141)

The patently preposterous claim of this criticism does not prevent it from striking the right chord. What we immediately notice about *Crisis* is Bergman's inability to keep the narrative fully under control, to strike a "healthy" balance between language and enjoyment. It must be said that if there is a director for whom language hits the body like an arrow, immediately impressing upon it the weight of *jouissance*, this is Ingmar Bergman. Already in *Crisis*, the narrative flow often appears overwhelmed by its own unwarranted desire to stage the impossibility of the sexual relationship as well as, albeit more surreptitiously, the explosive core of feminine enjoyment.

Nelly (Inga Landgré), the young protagonist, functions as a magnetic object of desire, the gap in the narrative structure around which everything gravitates. First of all, she is contended by her foster mother Ingeborg (Dagny Lind) and her real mother Jenny (Marianne Löfgrer), both of whom desperately need her to fill their empty lives. At the same time she is craved as a sexual partner by Ulf (Allan Bohlin), her idiotic fiancé, and Jack (Stig Olin), the adventurous, infectiously romantic would-be actor who is also her mother's protégée. Bergman sets up an existential choice for his heroine and by so doing confronts us with the classic question about woman's desire. Nelly's options would seem to be the standard ones: either man *qua* "shattering force of negativity" (Jack, the unreliable adventurer) or man *qua* essence (Ulf, the honest but ultimately tedious family man). This choice is redoubled as far as the film's mother figures are concerned. On the one hand, the safe but stifling option of Ingeborg, the comforting, wise country woman who raised Nelly; on the other hand, the promise of excitement incarnated by Jenny, the Real mother who, having neglected Nelly throughout her childhood, now comes back with the lure of enjoyment, asking her daughter to join her in the big city's high life. In short, the film portrays a young woman torn between the safety and contentment of a traditional lifestyle and the promise of enjoyment.

The wonderful scene of the ball at the town hall, comparable to one of Max Ophuls's ball scenes, is in this respect extremely significant. Here one can appreciate the extent to which Bergman fails to access his female character's psychology. It is a scene that sets up masculine seduction against feminine enjoyment. When Jack and Ulf simultaneously ask Nelly to dance, she impudently chooses Jack, a complete stranger, thereby humiliating her partner (humiliation being one of the key themes in Bergman's representation of sexuality). Shortly after, Jack mesmerises Nelly by staging a licentious rock-and-roll dance show next to the room where a contralto entertains the mayor together with the older and more dignified invitees. The juxtaposition of classical and modern music felicitously sums up Nelly's predicament, and by the time she flees the ensuing commotion holding Jack's hand, we know that she has made her mind up (a similar scenario returns later in *Journey into Autumn*, Kvinnodröm, 1955). Although at the end of the scene Nelly is rescued by Ulf and returns to her safe life under Ingeborg's protective wing, it is clear that she has taken up the role of a feminine Other whose aim is to frustrate contractual coercions.

In Luchino Visconti's *White Nights* (Le notti bianche, 1957), adapted from Dostoevsky's novella of the same name, we come across a similar juxtaposition of seemingly inscrutable feminine desire and the infectious allure of modern music when Natalia (Maria Schell) briefly, unexpectedly, falls under the spell of an unknown dancer (Dirk Sanders) whilst out on a date with Mario (Marcello Mastroianni). The first thing to

note is that this strangely derealised passage does not figure in Dostoevsky's novella, and precisely as the "excessive" narrative segment of
an otherwise fairly faithful adaptation, it materialises Visconti's libidinal
investment in his literary source (since in every adaptation there is usu-
ally at least one "excessive" element that does not fit the original text).
However, far from merely speaking for the director's homosexuality (it
is easy to discern in this passage Visconti's camera's fascination with the
handsome dancer) it effectively shifts the focus from the masculine logic
of courtly love (the dreamer's fantasy in Dostoevsky's story) to feminine
(Natalia's) desire. What matters to Visconti in this spellbinding scene is
the fact that Natalia is caught between a benevolent would-be lover *qua*
father-figure (Mario) and the promise of Real enjoyment embodied by
the seductive dancer.[3] The charm of the scene lies in the honesty with
which it acknowledges the implicitly traumatic character of seduction, as
Natalia eventually recoils, visibly perturbed, into Mario's arms. Lacan's
thesis on the impossibility of the sexual relationship is founded precisely
on the idea that the Real of enjoyment cannot be domesticated, since
it is "in us more than ourselves", it responds to the undecipherable call
of drive.

Unlike Natalia, the character of Nelly in Bergman's film is thoroughly
de-psychologised as well as deprived of idealistic nuances. If she appears
as a young woman intent on rebelling against her secluded provincial
life, the core of her desire remains completely foreclosed. We are merely
told that she leaves the village to join her mother in Stockholm, taking up
a job in her fashionable beauty salon. Her decision effectively surprises
us, if only because it is not substantiated by emotional or psychological
justification. The general point to make is that *Crisis* subtly subverts the
stereotype of the modern woman's desire for independence, which also
explains why it is reductive to see the film as a drama about a young
woman who discovers the dark side of human nature and then shrinks
back. What Bergman suggests in the second part, rather, is that the causal
link (Jenny uses Jack to seduce Nelly and thus provoke her desire to leave
the provincial village) is reversed: it is Nelly, with the ominous opacity
of her desire, who actually stands for a *cause* that produces specific after-
effects on the people close to her. This means that, in Bergman's first
film, the standard logic of masculine fantasy about woman is already
ingeniously destabilised. As Žižek (1994: 119) puts it in *Metastases of
Enjoyment*:

In sexual activity, men 'do certain things to women', and the question
is: *is woman's enjoyment reducible to an effect, is it a simple consequence*

of what a man does to her? [. . .] In the last analysis, the irreducible gap
that separates an effect from its cause amounts to the fact that "not all
of the feminine enjoyment is an effect of the masculine cause". [. . .]
Woman is not fully submitted to the causal link.

As cause, Nelly's role is epitomised by Jack's Hamletic words to Ingeborg,
in the second part of the film: 'Nelly is so real that I become even more
unreal, and start wondering why I live my ghost life at all'. At the heart
of *Crisis*, as in many Bergman films to come, we have a woman who,
by her very nature, *cannot be inscribed in the closed order of causality*, and
consequently turns into an "absent cause" derailing both the masculine
and the motherly economy of desire. The power she embodies can be
measured against the shattering effect it has on Jack, the self-assured
womaniser.

Here we also have, *in nuce*, Bergman's recurrent modernist theme of the
desperate struggle for truth beyond the fleetingness of appearances. Jack,
the cynical seducer who 'talks like a novel' (Nelly), understands *through
Nelly* that it is time for him to drop the mask and confront the core of
his own self. He suddenly feels disgusted by his life as a sycophant and
social parasite. At this turning point the film is already on the same thematic level as, say, *Persona*, the central question having shifted from the
Freudian "what does woman want?", to the more properly Lacanian "are
we ready to endorse what woman wants, when we know that woman
wants Nothing?" Woman for Bergman represents the only chance to
break through fictions (the mask, persona) and stare the void of the
Other in the face. Despite lacking the main features of the classic *femme
fatale*, Nelly represents a radical version of one, since it is the abyssal
elusiveness of her desire that here drives man to suicide.

The same logic is at work, even more obviously despite the accom-
modating finale, in *Port of Call* (Hamnstad, 1948), where Berit
(Nine-Christine Jönsson), the heroine, is first seen attempting suicide by
jumping off the docks, and immediately after protesting angrily against
those who have rescued her. The failure to inscribe a dimension of social
criticism in this dramatic narrative is due to the presence of a feminine
character whose personal misery is, deep down, *causeless*. Bringing into
the equation the gritty atmosphere of Gothenburg's port coupled with
the focus on the conditions of underprivileged people does not pull it
off for Bergman. The problem is that his camera is drawn too close to
the heroine's face, the emphasis being manifestly placed on what he
intimately perceives as *the enigma of her depression*. The attempt to find
sociological answers ultimately seems unnatural and misplaced, which

is what accounts for the film's uneven feel. In truth, there is enough evidence to suggest that we are already dealing with Bergman's demonic obsessions, not only the emphasis on femininity but also the double deadlock of sexual and family relations. The key, however, remains Berit's subtle shift from effect to cause: the elusiveness of her behaviour and her pervasive depression is not to be read as an effect of the unjust social circumstances of her upbringing but as the materialisation of the feminine not-all, which works as the primary cause of narrative development. As Žižek (1994: 122) reminds us, this is how the logic of not-all functions: ' "not-all" of depression results from the causes that trigger it; yet, at the same time, there is no element of depression that is not triggered by some external active cause. In other words, everything in depression is an effect – everything except depression as such, except the form of depression'.

When Berit tells her boyfriend Gösta (Bengt Eklund) about her past experiences with other men, one cannot help sensing a degree of obscene enjoyment in her words, as if to provoke Gösta's resentment. To a degree, she revels in her misfortunes, which is why eventually Gösta, not dissimilarly from Jack in *Crisis*, is driven to despair (the sequence where he gets drunk and abusive is probably the most compelling of the whole film). If man is meant to shake woman out of her misery, the paradox exposed here is that it is nevertheless man who is eventually caught in the whirlpool of feminine enjoyment. The film's happy ending (Berit's best friend, Gertrud, dies, while the heroine optimistically proclaims 'And soon it will be summer!'), then, hardly conceals the enjoyment embodied by Berit, in a way that reminds me of Jean Vigo's masterpiece *L'atalante* (1934), where the motif of water is also strongly associated with feminine enjoyment. I am thinking of the ethereal appearance of Juliette's (Dita Parlo) laughing face underwater, a mocking mirage for husband Jean (Jean Dasté) who foolishly believes she might have committed suicide. The bride, instead, has run off, abandoning her husband for the glittering lights of Paris. Although eventually the couple is reunited, Juliette's disturbingly real enjoyment *beyond her role* remains at the very core of the narrative.

4.4 Feminine depression

In *Crisis*, the cause of Jack's fascination cannot be merely ascribed to *objet a* in its relation to the staging of feminine masquerade, but should rather be looked for in Nelly's inconspicuous and yet defining characteristic: lethargy. Žižek, discussing Michel Chion's reading of David

Lynch, claims that the feature on account of which woman breaks the causal link (and inscribes a gap in the symbolic *without* being external to it) is feminine depression, 'her suicidal propensity to slide into permanent lethargy'. More specifically, 'the elementary structure of subjectivity turns on how *not-all of the subject is determined by the causal chain*. The subject "is" this very gap that separates the cause from its effect; it emerges precisely in so far as the relationship between cause and effect becomes "unaccountable"'. According to this reading, feminine depression is 'the founding gesture of subjectivity, the primordial act of freedom, of refusing our insertion into the nexus of causes and effects' (Žižek 1994: 119 and 122).

To elucidate this thesis, let us call into question a classic of European cinema like Alain Resnais' *Last Year in Marienbad* (L'année dernière à Marienbad, 1961). Perhaps the only way to really penetrate the enigma of this most enigmatic of modernist films is by getting rid once and for all of the pseudo-intellectual sophistications that abound in all its interpretations. What if, in other words, the meaning of the story should not be looked for in Alain Robbe-Grillet's (the film's scriptwriter) fashionable lucubrations about the transposition of the *nouveau roman* into film (modernist openness, challenge to traditional film narrative, game structure, multiple interpretations, etc.) but rather in the way Resnais organises the emotional relationship between X (Giorgio Albertazzi), A (Delphine Seyrig) and her husband M (Sasha Pitoëff)? The most urgent question raised by the film is easily identifiable and does not require us to unpack obscure and mostly gratuitous self-reflexive references. It concerns the typically masculine attempt to shake woman out of her torpor – which, let us insist on this point, does not imply her ineptitude but rather her full immersion, or participation, in the symbolic order. The basic question posed by the film concerns A's desire: how can one understand what she wants if her desire is seemingly lost in a dense mist through which she herself cannot see? The Seyrig character is the true catalyst of the narrative, insofar as her statuesque reluctance to accept emotional challenges, her fatal passivity, is what provokes X to win her over and lead her out of the labyrinthine network of frozen rituals which captures wonderfully the hypnotic, senseless fascination exerted by the symbolic order upon the subject – to such an extent that X is also visibly affected by it. In this context, the "power of love" is also X's ability to make A believe that they had met before, and that he can save her from her own senseless immersion in her world. The violence exerted by X is precisely *the violence of love*, and in this respect the film is a wonderful metaphor for the necessity of the "game" of seduction.

Are we thus allowed to conclude that this film is about masculine intervention into feminine congenital depression? What, however, if the opposite was true? What if A actually controls the entire narrative from the start, and X is nothing but a product of her fantasy, the idealised symbolic authority she needs in order to detach herself from her world? Perhaps, then, it is not so much that he chooses her, but that *she chooses him to choose her*: the initial and crucial choice is hers. This, incidentally, allows us to make sense of Žižek's understanding of the Hegelian notion of "positing the presuppositions", the implication of which is that we choose what we believe in *retroactively*. All the freedom we have is the freedom to invent a fiction which we choose to *have* believed in. Freedom thus conceived is the opposite of a natural propensity towards our "deeper" desires and inclinations: it is the act through which we discard a certain fiction and choose a different one by projecting it into our past.

Back to *Crisis*. Nelly's radical indeterminacy, epitomised by her inability to choose, suggests that she does not exist as a fully constituted subject. Like the Lacanian subject, she is a lost object. Jack's opportunistic attempt to shake her out of her state of lethargy eventually turns against him, as a reminder that the cynical interplay of fictions is *not* all we have. And yet, precisely because he is in overdrive, Jack continues playing his conjurer's tricks. Spinning a heartbreaking tale about his poor self he manages to convince Nelly of his love for her, and is rewarded by the gift of her virginity. The staging of the final act of seduction in the beauty salon is strongly self-reflexive: the strange appearance of an unknown man, the mannequins' heads turned towards the couple as if staring at them, the final discovery that Jenny had witnessed their lovemaking hidden behind a curtain, and even the invasive presence of the theatre next door with the loud, ironic clapping of its audience. It seems clear that everyone around Nelly bears the mark of cynicism and untruth, or the stain of an obscene gaze, while Nelly herself is connoted as a pure and naïve object of erotic manipulation. The role played by the mother is particularly revealing here, anticipating one of the great themes of Bergman's cinema. Jenny's motherly love contains all the ambiguity of every mother–child relationship:

> The child is a real object, in the hands of the mother who, far beyond what is required by her care, can use him/her as a possession, an erotic doll from which she can get jouissance and to which she can give jouissance. Freud had already emphasized the erotic ambiguity of maternal care, from which the subject will have to emerge as the effect of speech. (Soler 2006: 118)

To Jenny, but also to Ingeborg, Nelly is nothing but an 'erotic doll', an object whose function is to regulate their personal entries in the balance sheet of enjoyment. However, as anticipated, it is through Jack, Bergman's alter ego, that the story takes a new, decisive turn. When he walks away from the salon and, a few moments later, shoots himself in the face right in front of the theatre, the game of manipulation is momentarily suspended. The hint is clear: his is the type of "suicide on stage" that echoes Elisabet's symbolic death in *Persona*, effectively conveying the director's resolve to break into the "beyond" of fiction, a dimension of truth that might elude the stifling precariousness of appearances. Are we then allowed to conclude that Jack's suicide represents the Lacanian act that suddenly opens up a truly redemptive dimension? Here I would instead insist that the key position is occupied by woman (Nelly), and not man (Jack). In other words, we are still dealing with Bergman's favourite dichotomy between the masculine urge to symbolise and the feminine Real of enjoyment. How? A naive reading would suggest that Nelly is fascinated by the Real of enjoyment (passion, seduction, high life, etc.) but "gets burnt" and eventually, after Jack's suicide, rejects it, which is why in the epilogue, having faced the prospect of suicide herself, she decides to return to her little village where presumably she will marry Ulf. This reading effectively corresponds to the standard masculine fantasy about feminine enjoyment, since man often fantasises about the very threat he needs to rescue woman from; as such, it is not only hopelessly conservative, but also deeply flawed as it fails to consider the crucial detail previously highlighted: rather than being at the mercy of an external threat, Nelly is an "unnameable" (causeless) *cause*. In this sense she is also "a symptom of man": ' "Woman is a symptom of man" means that man himself exists only through woman *qua* his symptom; all his ontological consistency hangs on, is suspended from his symptom, is "externalized" in his symptom' (Žižek 2001b: 155).[4] What happens to Jack is that he suddenly over-identifies with his symptom.

This is also why, incidentally, *jouissance* does not disappear with Jack's suicide and Jenny's capitulation, but would seem to emerge fully only in the final scene. Far from indicating that Nelly has retreated back into the safe haven of a drowsy provincial life, the ending hints at something much more insidious, i.e. that in its ultimate configuration the Real is *not* to be conceived as the external limit of symbolisation, but as a surplus-enjoyment always-already entangled with the symbolic order. The long shot of the village in the final scene of *Crisis* should be read with the opening sequence of David Lynch's *Blue Velvet*, the implicit idea being that the true and unbearable horror resides in what seems to stand for its very opposite, the over-protective shield of the Symbolic: the deceptive mood of peace and tranquillity oozed by everyday life in a small village, Ingeborg's stifling maternal instinct, Ulf's oppressive closeness, the quietness of the village . . . This is particularly striking in terms of the sexual relationship: although Jack, with his seductive lies, may appear to be more dangerous, the real problem for Nelly is Ulf, the good guy, with his terrifying compulsion to declare his love. With the film's ending we return to the beginning, but instead of concluding that normality is restored, Bergman subtly suggests that, as it were, the real danger lurks on the smooth surface of things.

4.5   Woman as phallus

More obviously than Bergman, the early Antonioni already underscores the importance of the "surface of things", as well as the modernist dilemma concerning the correlation between fiction and reality. Fiction is already designated as the privileged medium to access the concealed core of the extant, while women become fictional subjects *par excellence*, constantly flirting with the negativity of the Real. In *Chronicle of a Love* (Cronaca di un amore, 1950), Antonioni's debut feature, Paola's (Lucia Bosè) role coincides with the inert presence of her white furs and array of luxurious dresses. These are so many emphatic masks working as captivatingly insubstantial envelopes for the emptiness of the self *qua* phallus. Lacan (2007: 699) comments humorously on the link between woman as phallus and masculine desire as follows:

> Such is the woman concealed behind her veil: it is the absence of the penis that makes her the phallus, the object of desire. Evoke this absence in a more precise way by having her wear a cute fake one under a fancy dress, and you, or rather she, will have plenty to tell us about: the effect is 100 percent guaranteed, for men who don't beat around the bush, that is.

As a *femme fatale*, Paola is certainly the strongest of the characters in *Chronicle of a Love*. Antonioni's outlook on the world of Milanese fashion is clearly less a sociological cipher than a fascinated attempt to unravel the strange relationship between fiction, truth, and desire. As with *Crisis*, the female protagonist abandons her anonymous life in the province for the glamour of the big city, where she marries rich Milanese entrepreneur Enrico Fontana (Ferdinando Sarmi). Paola's identity, however, remains an enigma for the husband, who appoints a private eye to find out about her past. The investigation reveals that before marriage Paola was in a relationship with Guido Garroni (Massimo Girotti), an affair ended mysteriously with the couple sharing a good dose of guilt for the death of Guido's girlfriend Giovanna Carlini, who had fallen into an open lift shaft. When they meet again to plan a defence against possible charges, the old passion between Guido and Paola rekindles, and so does their desire to kill. Their target is Paola's husband, who has grown unbearably repulsive to the heroine. However, as with Giovanna, they are unable to carry out their plan as the rich husband perishes accidentally in a car crash.

The interesting question posed by the film, then, concerns the correlation between desire and inaction. Why do the two lovers falter? Or, more pointedly: why is their desire (to kill, to love each other) constantly frustrated? As with most of Antonioni's later films, what comes to the fore here is the inexplicable deadlock of the sexual relationship, which we would be wrong to ascribe (as many critics have done) to class or economic differences. What is truly at stake in the unshakable frustration, numbness, and inertia of the two lovers is Antonioni's awareness that at the roots of desire there is, literally, nothing. This is the unbearably traumatic fact. I would therefore sum up the film's central concern with the previously mentioned phrase used by Luis Buñuel apropos many of his films: "the impossibility of satisfying a simple desire". The profound psychoanalytic truth of this phrase regards the fact that desire is strictly speaking beyond satisfaction, since it constantly shifts on an endless series of metonymical objects, which in themselves are nothing but embodiments of the void that causes desire to emerge in the first place. In *Chronicle of a Love*, as in Buñuel's *The Criminal Life of Archibaldo de la Cruz* (Ensayo de un crimen, 1955), the impossibility of desire has to do with the act of killing, which in turn is related to *jouissance* (interestingly, in Buñuel's film we also have a woman – a nun – who dies in a lift shaft before the killer is able to lay his hands on her).

It is Paola, the film's heroine, who fatally hesitates. In the most famous sequence of the film, the two reunited lovers drive out to the countryside to plan the assassination of Paola's husband in detail. Suddenly, they seem to lose their determination, a change that coincides with the beginning of a four-minute long take of the two characters as they move slowly on a small bridge overlooking a dry canal surrounded by a vast, misty plain. The passage, which echoes a similar long take in Visconti's *Ossessione* (1943), has been rightly hailed as paradigmatic of Antonioni's original use of the landscape in connection with the characters foregrounding it; here, the barren background heightens the sense of realism and, more importantly, emphasises the mixture of apathy and fear that suddenly seizes Paola.[5] The moment Guido slaps her, reminding her that she is fully implicated in the criminal plan, should be read precisely as a typically masculine gesture aimed at shaking woman out of her lethargy and inscribing her into the causal chain. What matters is that the attempt fails. The murderous plan does not materialise and the film ends with Paola withdrawing again into her nebulous self, prey to a sense of apathy which would seem to coincide with a specifically feminine mode of depression. As Žižek (2007a: 161) puts it, this depression alludes to the fact that

> Woman can never be caught, one can never catch up with her; one can either endlessly approach her or overtake her, for the very reason that 'woman in herself' designates no substantial content but just a purely formal cut, a limit that is always missed – this purely formal cut *is* the subject *qua* $.

4.6 Beyond the victim

That woman designates the paradox of 'a limit that is always missed' is even more evident in the vastly underestimated *The Lady without Camelias* (La signora senza camelie, 1953). Here, the central theme of the contamination between fiction and reality is functional to unravelling the painfully empty truthfulness of fiction. As Clara (Lucia Bosè) states apropos her fictional roles: 'I'm scared when I see myself on screen, I have to repeat to myself ten times every minute "it's me, it's me!"'. For her, it seems, the Lacanian "mirror" does not always work, identification vacillates.

With *The Lady without Camelias*, Antonioni starts deploying the conspicuous meta-cinematic resources of his filmmaking for the exploration of femininity, opening up a series of interrogations that will return as the focal point of his cinema. The plot is deceptively sentimental, verging on the melodramatic. Clara Manni (Lucia Bosè), a Milanese shop assistant, is turned into a successful actress of commercial films by rich producer Gianni Franchi (Andrea Cecchi), who also takes her as his bride. Increasingly distressed by his wife's participation in second-rate productions as a scantily dressed *femme fatale*, Gianni concocts to change Clara's image: he forces her to give up her role in a melodrama fittingly called *The Woman without Destiny* to recast her in a new project as a virginal Joan of Arc (in a nutshell, he attempts to deprive her of her enjoyment). This new lavish production, however, soon turns out to be a colossal box-office flop. Her career seriously damaged, Clara unwillingly falls into her new role as a rich but increasingly unhappy housewife, which leads her into an affair with Nardo (Ivan Desny), a playboy diplomat, with whom she decides to elope. The handsome diplomat, however, quickly reveals his true colours: rather than letting a scandal ruin his career, he opts to "return" Clara to her husband. Unhappy with her marriage and rejected by her lover, Clara at this stage decides to fend for herself. With the help of friend and colleague Lodi (Alain Cuny), she begins to study acting, turning down a number of minor jobs in commercial films. Eventually, after a few months away from the screen, she resolves to approach ex-husband Gianni, who in the meantime has managed to get over her and is now financing a big production. Despite not holding a grudge against her, however, Gianni is unable to secure Clara a role in his new film. Instead, he advises her to hang on to her career in undistinguished melodramas, for, as he puts it, 'actresses age quickly'. Dejected and disenchanted, Clara accepts a part in a second-rate costume drama called *The Slave of the Pyramids* and, succumbing to fate, telephones Nardo offering him to resume their dismal affair.

The most obvious interpretation suggests that we read Antonioni's second work alongside Italian films of the same period such as Federico Fellini's *The White Sheik* (Lo sceicco bianco, 1951), whose script was co-written by Antonioni himself, and Luchino Visconti's *Bellissima* (also made in 1951). These films expose the cynicism of the film industry by linking it to the naïvety of young women seduced by the star system. Clara is surrounded by a number of predatory men (most of whom work in the film industry) who endeavour to take advantage of her good looks in one way or another, either for sexual/sentimental reasons (Gianni and Nardo) or for purely financial ones (directors and producers). As a victimised female forced to accept her fate in a world dominated by male power and opportunism, Clara seems to fit perfectly a narrative that indicts what, years later, Guy Debord would dub 'the society of spectacle' (see Debord 1992). Critics have been quick to underline this dimension of social criticism. At a deeper metaphorical level, *The Lady without Camelias* can also be viewed as a reflection on the incongruity between fiction and reality: on the one hand the frivolity and inauthenticity of the fictional world of film studios, on the other the trials and tribulations of everyday life. However, as with Bergman's debut feature, my task here is to develop a counter-intuitive reading which resists the temptation to search for explicit messages.

To start with, let us observe how we are again confronted with the masculine endeavour to mould woman into an effect of his intervention: Clara's husband literally turns her into an actress "out of nothing" – that is to say, by pulling her out of the indeterminacy in which she was confined before meeting him. What is more, whilst "turning her into a fictional subject" he also determines to control the content of the fiction, thus objectifying her completely. The result of this "phallic intrusion" is only partly predictable. On the one hand Clara, as a good hysteric, instinctively rebels against the masculine compulsion to "name her" by indulging in a love affair; on the other, it appears that she eventually accepts it.

The very observation that Clara is presented as a victim should instantly set our alarm bells ringing, for from a psychoanalytic angle every discourse of victimisation hinges on the displacement of a deeper and more decisive kernel of knowledge. To circumscribe this displaced knowledge we should take into account one of Antonioni's central stylistic features, namely his use of *temp morts*, 'chronological gaps of considerable duration' (Chatman 1985: 31) that disrupt the linear development of the narrative. Once we start focusing on these cinematic "knots", Clara's identity as victim can no longer be taken for granted.

Let us consider the substantial temporal gap between Gianni's marriage proposal to Clara and the sudden reappearance of the newly-wed couple on the set of the film she was playing in: what the ellipsis suppresses is an account of Clara's decision to accept Gianni's proposal, especially if we bear in mind that earlier on she had seemed reluctant to do so. From this angle, Clara suddenly "sheds her sacrificial skin" and, to an extent, becomes the cause of her downfall. And yet, on this evidence, to claim that she marries Gianni out of opportunism amounts to an oversight. What remains untold about Clara's identity is, rather, something that *is and remains unaccountable*. Not only is the audience denied access to the reasons behind most of Clara's decisions (such as her choice to marry Gianni); it is *Clara herself* who is not fully aware of them. The general point to make here is that Antonioni, not dissimilarly from Bergman, sees women as being much more readily in touch with the big Other *in its full extension*, i.e. including its gaps. The parallel with Bergman's *Crisis* is in this sense self-evident: just as Nelly was, as it were, "the causeless cause of her effect", it would be misleading to claim that Clara is simply manipulated by the males around her. Her position of victim does not coincide fully with the effect of these manipulations; rather, she is also the cause of everything that happens to her insofar as this cause remains foreclosed.

With the early Bergman and Antonioni, then, the question of woman already comes full circle. Woman *qua* effect of masculine stimuli turns into woman *qua* original cause of man's despair and even impotence; from this angle, man's manipulation of woman cannot fail to appear as a desperate and ultimately failed strategy to inscribe her in the causal link. The subject of these films is the not-all of feminine enjoyment that frustrates the masculine gaze, a *jouissance* that coincides with the unfathomable and inconsequential weariness that seems to pervade female characters such as Nelly and Clara, telling us that, unlike men, they *enjoy* the possibility of an insight into the elementary inconsistency of the symbolic order. It is this insight that makes them threatening figures. Feminine *jouissance* (or feminine depression) is perceived as a threat because it reveals the insignificance of our attachment to the socio-symbolic order, to "our world". This is also why for these female characters actual narrative progression is minimal. In *Crisis*, Nelly ends up where she had started, that provincial village which functions as a topological extension of the feminine not-all, a space that "refuses" to be fully included in the "great chain of progress"; in *The Lady without Camelias*, Clara remains a second-rate actress, choosing *fiction* as the place for her identity. The remarkable event is the birth of subjectivity proper through woman *qua causeless cause*.

A similar logic is at work in Bergman's *Prison* (Fängelse, 1949), a classic film about filmmaking which in its self-reflexive structure reminds us of Truffaut's *Day for Night* (La nuit américaine, 1973), despite going a step further in endorsing the truthfulness of fiction. The explicit reference to fiction (the making of a tragic film about the prostitute Birgitta Karolina, played by Doris Svedlund) is meant to validate the film's central existential thesis that life is "hell on earth". This thesis is put forward in the opening sequence, set in the studio where the film about the prostitute will be shot. The two fictions then start intertwining, mirroring each other, until the story-lines, the two different levels of fictionality, merge into the same narrative. The point is very subtle: the original, "seamless" fiction is redoubled in an overtly artificial fiction whose ultimate role, however, is to prove the initial thesis of the hellishness of life on earth. By the end of the film we realise that hell is once again directly linked to the unavailability of the female heroine to the male gaze. Birgitta Karolina is in turn prostitute, idealised lover, and finally suicide. In its demonic aspiration to cast its gaze beyond the realm of appearances, Bergman's camera already stumbles against the arid nothingness of the human condition, where there is no anchoring point that might convince us that the big Other (God, the symbolic order) exists. Again, it is by "observing woman" that Bergman gets to the heart of his existential investigation. Most of Bergman's films bear the mark of obdurate feminine *jouissance* in the face of man's futile hyper-activity. An unlikely but striking example of this comes from his most underrated comedy, *The Devil's Eye* (Djävulens öga, 1960), where it is left to Don Juan (Jarl Kulle) himself, sent by the Devil (Stig Järrel), to experience the unavailability of woman (Britt-Marie played by Bibi Andersson).

4.7   Freedom in fiction

At this stage I am going to embark on a brief digression into the "shockingly masochistic" behaviour of Lisa (Joan Fontaine) in *Letters from an Unknown Woman* (1948), a film made by Ophuls during his Hollywood period. This classic romantic fable of doomed love between Lisa and Stefan (Louis Jourdan), set in late nineteenth-century Vienna, delivers much more than just a lush, tear-jerking costume melodrama. At a young age Lisa falls in love with Stefan, a handsome but self-serving and hedonistic pianist with whom she has a fleeting relationship. When he disappears without explanations, Lisa realises that she is pregnant with his child. From this moment on her life develops as a long series of disappointments, during which she desperately hangs on to the hope of meeting her lover again. When, indeed, the magical moment of their reunion arrives, Stefan sets about seducing her for the second time, leading her to realise in horror that *he has not recognised her.* A Lacanian reading based on the notion of misrecognition is particularly helpful here, for again it allows us to see through the logic of victimisation. Stefan's failure to recognise Lisa alerts us to the deepest mechanism at work in communication. What we exchange in communication is always a fantasy of what we are, and the big Other, the agency which mediates between every act of communication, can therefore be visualised as a perfectly blank space inundated with fantasies. This explains Lacan's dictum that desire is always the Other's desire: strictly speaking, our desires are not the expressions of our deeper self, but are instead articulated by the other; contrary to what is normally believed, my desire does not provide an answer to the question "What do I really want?", but instead it allows me to neutralise the disturbing message inscribed in questions such as "What do *others* want from me?", "What am I for these *others*?" My desire emerges when I am looked at by others, exposed to their inquisitive gazes, and I need to come up with a successful strategy that might secure me a place in the socio-symbolic order. The primary function of desire is therefore to sustain the fantasmatic screen that makes communication possible: I invent the fiction of what I want (and thus of what I am) in order to enter the symbolic arena. What is at stake in desire is the process of subjectivation that seals the formation of my identity, which I then exchange in communication.

The key to Ophuls' film lies in realising how it frames Lisa's desire as a narcissistic fantasy-construction that allows her to be seen. Her voiceover reading of the letter, which accompanies the narrative from start to end, confirms that everything we see in the film, until her death, is mediated by her gaze, that is to say, by her fantasy. As with all of Ophuls' great heroines, she exists insofar as she *knows* that she is looked at, that she is a spectacle. Until the moment of misrecognition, everything that happens to Lisa, including her misfortunes, is part of this libidinally-invested fantasmatic framework. From a psychoanalytic viewpoint this means that her desiring Stefan, no matter how painful an experience it might be, is ultimately functional to the narcissistic assertion of her subjectivity.

It is interesting to see how by failing to acknowledge Lisa's identity, thus undermining her most intimate and precious fantasy, Stefan effectively comes to occupy the position of the analyst. By "not seeing her", he deprives her of the fantasy that regulates her own universe. Put differently, he turns into the Lacanian gaze, the impossible point of view from which the subject (Lisa) *cannot see herself* – the implication being that the moment Lisa is reminded that Stefan *qua* gaze cannot be included in her fantasy, her subjectivity collapses. Stefan proves to Lisa the Lacanian thesis according to which there is a substantial gap between "subjectivity" (the identity we construct for ourselves and others through fantasy) and "subject" (what we are "in the Real"). To put it somewhat jokingly, he does not see Lisa because, as a true womaniser, he sees her only in the Real of *jouissance*. Also, as the metaphorical bearer of the analytic discourse, he imposes on Lisa the *traversée du fantasme*, which entails an encounter with lack. Like the analyst, he pleads *docta ignorantia*: 'the analyst has wisely learned not to know, and in so doing he opens up a way for another to gain access to what determined his or her subjectivity' (Verhaeghe 1999: 114).

The moment of radical misrecognition, then, brings to the fore the Real gap between subjectivity and subject: Lisa falls out of her fantasy and into this gap where her symbolic persona suddenly loses its consistency. What, however, if even this trauma was part of the staging? At the beginning of the film Lisa seems to acknowledge the existence of a gap between subject and subjectivity (or between the Real and the Symbolic) when she comments on her first encounter with Stefan:

> I think everyone has two birthdays, the day of the physical birth, and the beginning of his conscious life. Nothing is vivid or real in my

memory before that day in Spring when I came home from school
and found a removal van in front of our building...

This passage provides a useful description of that crucial step towards the
formation of one's identity that Lacan calls "symbolic castration":
the 'second birthday' marks the subject's division and its entrance in
the symbolic order via fantasy and desire, telling us that subjectivity is
always at least minimally decentred or alienated. If Lisa was always aware
of this, then perhaps we should refine the analysis of her masochism
and suggest that she *purposely* lives her fantasy through to the bitter end,
i.e. to the point where fantasy as a protective screen turns into Lacan's
fundamental fantasy, the masochistic scene that Freud captured with the
expression "a child is being beaten". We should not be afraid to acknowledge that the staging of this masochistic scenario whereby subjectivity
collapses into the empty framework of the subject marks the intervention of freedom. As with Clara, it would be misplaced to reproach Lisa for
her childlike immaturity. Instead, we should note that her unshakeable
belief in the Other of fantasy eventually leads her to confront freedom
qua traumatic disattachment, or separation. It is by fully identifying with
the Other – the "naïve" belief that there is nothing outside fiction –
that Lisa uncovers the Other's inconsistency, the gap where her fantasy
becomes Real. Lisa dies unable to complete her letter to Stefan; the letter is eventually sent to him by a nurse. There we find the meaning of
Lacan's motto "a letter always arrives at its destination": the symbolic
content of the letter (Lisa's fantasy world) carries a Real message (the big
Other does not exist!).

Back to Antonioni. In the last scene of *The Lady without Camelias* Clara
meets Gianni at the Cinecittà studios and asks him for a part in his new
production. How are we to account for this decision? Is she being merely
opportunistic? Those who criticised the film for its confused melodramatic plot and overall lack of clarity miss the crucial point. The fact that
we cannot answer the above questions proves that we have located, led
by Clara (a name by no means meant ironically), the unconscious side
of the narrative. In the light of this final scene, her determination to
re-invent herself as a professional actress can only be explained as a desperate attempt *to secure her own identity in fiction*, within the supremely
fragile jurisdiction of the image. Consequently, her final decision to
accept a role in a second-rate film appears in a much more ambiguous
and deceptive light than we might have thought: Clara has not just reluctantly accepted "the way of the world", the fact that she lacks proper
acting talent; on the contrary, her choice suggests that, strictly speaking,

depth and superficiality coincide – that the most profound point in the subject is its automaton-like dimension.

Clara's acceptance of a mediocre role ought to be seen as *the very form of her choice*, a gesture aimed at sanctioning her fictional status. The final shot tells us that the heroine has renounced looking for an opening beyond fictions and has accepted the *radical closure* of the fictional domain. To fully comprehend her gesture we need to grasp its meta-cinematic significance, in as much as it permits Antonioni to assert the paradoxical superiority of appearances over reality. Clara steps from one symbolic role to another: she is a shop assistant, an actress, a wife, an unfaithful wife, a drama student, and eventually she is forced to acknowledge the futility of her search for the proverbial "true identity". In this respect, the final shot where she is flattened against the cheap and artificial set of her new commercial film sums up Antonioni's conviction that truth is *hidden on the surface*, and that woman is the most likely of the two sexes to reveal it. Antonioni's specific enjoyment as a film director has to do with this congealment of the feminine image, the shift from the notion of woman's fully constituted subjectivity to the empty formal framework of her being caught on film. The reference to acting is, in this respect, extremely significant, confirming Lacan's insight into the coincidence of femininity and masquerade. What the ending of *The Lady without Camelias* makes absolutely clear is that, if the idea of masquerade inevitably prompts us to fantasise about a "feminine secret" behind the mask, this secret is *the non-existence of the secret*, the absence of a deeper cause responsible for woman's unfathomable behaviour.

5
About Nothing, with Precision: Femininity Unbound from Ophuls to Antonioni

When Antonioni told painter and personal friend Mark Rothko that his pictures were, like his own films, 'about nothing, with precision' (in Chatman 1985: 54), he hit the right chord: the ultimate aim of his filmmaking is to show how visual representation hinges on a short-circuit between what we see and what we do not see, what we look at and what is already looking back at us. In this section I focus on this short-circuit, or dislocation, discussing a number of female characters whose desire pushes them to flirt with the void of the cinematic image.

5.1 Ghosts

Marie (Maj-Britt Nilsson), the heroine of Bergman's *Summer Interlude* (Sommarlek, 1951), is a close relative of both Clara and Lisa for at least the following two reasons: firstly, her predicament is similar to Lisa's in highlighting the narcissistic roots of victimisation; secondly, her final lesson can be compared to Clara's insofar as it involves the elevation of fiction to the status of a Real beyond reality. After the accidental death of her young lover Henrik (Birger Malmsten), with whom she had spent a memorable summer on an island near Stockholm, Marie decides to withdraw into herself, embracing a cynical attitude to life that reminds us of Julie's reaction to her husband's and daughter's deaths in Kieślowski's *Three Colours: Blue* (Trois Couleurs: Bleu, 1993). In so doing she becomes the first self-proclaimed atheist in Bergman's cinema: 'I don't believe God exists. And if he does, I hate him, and I'll never stop hating him. If he stood before me, I'd spit in his face'. By 'building a wall' around her, however, she becomes 'locked up', totally desensitised to life. For twelve years she keeps working harder and harder as a ballerina at the Royal Opera in Stockholm in order to forget the fateful summer she spent with her first love Henrik. Then one day (actually, the beginning of the film, which for most part is told through flashbacks like *Letter from an Unknown Woman*) Uncle Erland sends her the diary Henrik had kept during that summer, which leads her to revisit the island and reminisce nostalgically that idyllic period of her life. Once she is back to the theatre, however, she seems to sink even more deeply in her stultifying melancholy, fully aware that the best period of her life has gone forever, while now she is condemned to hide her ageing face behind the mask of make up she wears as a ballerina.

It is at this point of seemingly irredeemable despair that we are given a chance to grasp how similar her dilemma is to Lisa's in Ophuls' film. As she leafs through the diary for the second time, it is the ghost-like image of her young self, her smiling face, that is superimposed to the pages – and not, as when she first opened it, Henrik's. This suggests that the object of her melancholy is not the young boy she had first "tasted life" with, but actually *herself*. In other words, the attachment in question is revealed in its true narcissistic colours. At this point we realise that, exactly like in Lisa's case, the "story within the story", i.e. the flashbacks narrating the blissful love affair on the island, was completely structured around Marie's ego. What we saw was the way in which *she* remembered those days. This explains why Henrik himself, in flashback, is depicted as a gullible young man totally dependent on Marie's whims. The older Marie is attached to the diary image of herself as an adolescent full of life and, most of all, craved as a sexual object by both Henrik and Uncle Erland; what she has lost with Henrik's death is nothing but the image of her idealised self, and this is what hurts.

Here we should refer to the difference between "object of desire" and "object-cause of desire". While the former is simply *what we desire*, the latter brings into the equation the fact that desire is caused by *objet a*, i.e. by an elusive attribute, generating surplus enjoyment, that we see in the other. If it is obvious that Henrik works as object of desire for Marie, then the crucial point to stress is that the *cause* of her desire, the feature on account of which Marie desires Henrik, is *Marie's own desire to be desired*. Henrik, for her, represents a sort of prism through which *she can see herself as an object of desire* – as possessing the "thing" on account of which she perceives herself as worthy of the Other's desire. What is at stake is Lacan's "mirror", the self-directed act of sublimation through which the subject enters reality. Marie's narcissistic loop corresponds to the basic displacement of myself *qua* void into myself *qua objet a*, which provides me with an identity through the other's desire. This narcissistic attachment, which is at the heart of the process of subjectivisation, is challenged for the first time when Marie mistakenly calls David, her new boyfriend whom she claims she does not love, by the name of Henrik, for it is through this slip of the tongue that she realises how there was nothing unique about her old lover – and, consequently, nothing unique about herself.

The second, crucial step occurs when, a few moments later, she gives David the diary to read: by acknowledging her symptom, indeed by letting David appropriate its libidinal value, she is suddenly released from the burden of her narcissism. Again, the parallel with *Blue* strikes a chord, for Julie also relinquishes her narcissistic tie to her dead husband by giving her new suitor, Olivier, a "share in the symptom", the concerto for the unification of Europe that Julie and Olivier eventually bring to conclusion together. Both these acts are tantamount to identifications with the knot of *jouissance* (Lacan's *sinthome*) responsible for the subject's melancholy. By giving the diary away, then, Marie effectively dissolves her symptom and, magically, is able to desire again. In the last, moving sequence of the film, we see her performing the lead in *Swan Lake*. During an interval she kisses David with the same sparkling look in her eyes she had during that long-gone summer.

Overall, and despite Marie's mystification with regard to the lost object, *Summer Interlude* provides a clear exemplification of the limit of melancholy. What Marie, the melancholic subject, misperceives in her attachment to the lost object is that the object in itself, i.e. *objet a*, was always-already lost. The problem with melancholy has been accurately described by Žižek (2001a: 143):

The mistake of the melancholic [...] is not simply to assert that something resists symbolic 'sublation' but, rather, to locate this resistance in a positively existing, albeit lost, object. In Kant's terms, the melancholic is guilty of committing a kind of 'paralogism of the pure capacity to desire', which lies in the confusion between *loss* and *lack*: in so far as the object-cause of desire is originally, in a constitutive way, lacking, melancholy interprets this lack as a loss, as if the object lacking were once possessed and then lost. In short, what melancholy obfuscates is the fact that the object is lacking from the very beginning, that its emergence coincides with its lack, that this object is *nothing but* the positivization of a void/lack, a purely anamorphic entity which does not exist 'in itself'. The paradox, of course, is that this deceitful translation of lack into loss enables us to assert our possession of the object: what we never possessed can also never be lost, so the melancholic, in his unconditional fixation on the lost object, in a way possesses it in its very loss.

This implies that both Henrik and the image of the young, smiling Marie, are nothing but fantasmatic embodiments of a primordial lack. The subtle narrative shift from Henrik to Marie suggests that this irretrievable lack, the missing object, is none other than the subject itself. By the end of the film, then, Marie learns to avoid the illusion that she ever possessed the missing object. The fantasy needs to be traversed, since it is through fantasy that she stages the mythical narrative of her loss of enjoyment. The key Lacanian point is that this enjoyment *is never possessed* by the subject, and consequently never stolen either (by the Other, or by God, as implied by Marie). The fantasy, despite holding together the subject's inner sense of self, is always profoundly sterile, it is founded upon a strong dose of sublimation and self-deceit. However depressing this may sound, the lesson of psychoanalysis is that fantasy is profoundly stupid, although simultaneously absolutely vital, for without it the subject would not be able to achieve any identity. It is often reported that for a period after Pier Paolo Pasolini's premature death in 1975, his mother Susanna, with whom he had spent all his life, still behaved as if her son was alive. When somebody paid her a visit, she would quietly welcome the guest with words like 'Pier Paolo is in his room, I'll go and tell him you're here', or 'please don't make too much noise, Pier Paolo is asleep'. As Žižek (2001a: 144–5) suggests through the example of the dead wife, melancholic identification comes to the fore precisely when, after the death of a loved one, we are overwhelmed by his or her ghost-like *presence*: 'For this reason, melancholy is not simply attachment to the lost object, but attachment to the very original gesture of its loss'.

Back to Bergman. Perhaps the ultimate lesson of *Summer Interlude* can be summed up with the enigmatic words of the grotesquely made-up ballet master (Bergman's alter ego?) from the previous scene in the dressing room: 'You dance and that's that. That's what you do. Stick to that Marie, or you'll get into trouble'. As with the ending of *The Lady without Camelias*, we should turn around the seemingly pessimistic content of this warning to stick to one's fictional role. Bergman's cinema is a testament to this message: it is in the illusion itself (of cinema) that we might experience that intense attachment to life, mixed with a sense of utter release, which qualifies the Real.

This is also the message of one of Bergman's most exhilarating films of the 1950s, *The Magician* (Ansiktet, 1958), which, much like Ophuls' *Lola Montès* (1955), reverses the standard critique of spectacle as noxious divertissement or deceit. *The Magician* cannily demonstrates that even in its *revealed* deceptiveness, the illusion is nevertheless *more Real than reality*. In other words, it provides a formula that captures the essence of cinema itself. The film shows that even after Albert Emanuel Vogler (Max Von Sydow) is unmasked as a charlatan who conceals his ineptitude, or existential despair, behind the mask through which he fools people, the illusion is still more powerful than reason alone. The "truth in the illusion" is laid bare in the second part of the film, when pompous Dr Vergérus (Gunnar Björnstrand), who had previously ridiculed Vogler by revealing his impotence, becomes a victim of a superbly staged trick played by Vogler himself after he was thought to have died. Bergman's point seems to be that the illusion of a miracle is more powerful than the belief in the supernatural quality of miracles. To him, as he had already made more than explicit, "God is silent": hoping for a transcendental revelation of truth, in other words, is utterly useless. However, instead of dispensing with the idea of truth *tout court*, with films like *The Magician* he suggests that our only chance to cast a glance behind the curtain of deceitful, ever-changing, unsatisfactory appearances, rests on what we might call "the practice of fictions", which implies that the Real can only emerge from the illusion. In this respect, the central scene where Vogler makes fun of Dr Vergérus by pretending to incarnate a ghost is truly brilliant, for it exemplifies to perfection the Lacanian axiom whereby the very existence of the symbolic order (the order of Logos embodied by Dr Vergérus) relies necessarily on a fantasmatic Other Scene, a pseudo-material space inhabited by spirits. The position of Dr Vergérus, the cynic, can also be explained through Lacan's *Les non-dupes errent* ("those in the know are wrong"): the more he resists the illusion, the fiction staged by Vogler, the more he is mistaken, "duped", since he overlooks the efficiency of the symbolic fiction, the fact that reality itself is structured around fictions. Significantly, he betrays a hint of self-awareness when, confronted by the real Vogler, without his mask, he refuses to acknowledge him: 'I liked his face better than yours!'

5.2 To be seen or not to be seen...

The European film that manages to focus more intensely on the notion of woman as "total spectacle" is without a doubt the previously mentioned *Lola Montès* (1955) by Max Ophuls. That Ophuls' last and most famous work was to become one of Fassbinder's all-time favourites says a lot about the latter and, as we have seen, his particular appreciation of (feminine) masochism. Like most of Ophuls' films, *Lola Montès* is a supremely ambiguous work, particularly in the way it comments on woman by placing her emphatically, and literally, in the spotlight. The pressing question is: to what extent can we class her as a victim? The film is based on the real life of Elizabeth Rosanna Gilbert, known by the stage name of Lola Montez, the Irish actress who died in 1861, at the age of 40, having led a scandalous life as an exotic dancer and a courtesan throughout Europe, United States and Australia. Amongst her lovers were Franz Liszt, Alexandre Dumas and none other than King Ludwig I of Bavaria. She was particularly renowned for her highly immoral "spider dance", a performance during which she raised her skirt so high as to let the audience appreciate that she did not wear any underpants.

As with the real Lola, what strikes us about Ophuls' heroine is her awareness of the choices she makes, choices which eventually turn her into an object of voyeurism, to the extent that the inexpressive acting of Martine Carol in the role of Lola Montès paradoxically works well, as it contributes to rendering the character's objectification. Precisely as object, then, Lola exposes the type of psychoanalytic truth already highlighted apropos Lisa in *Letters from an Unknown Woman*: she exists insofar as she is looked at. This would explain why Ophuls was very fond of a story about an acrobat who had fallen and broken his leg because, during his show, he had for a moment thought that *the audience might not be watching him*. As with Lisa, this moment of radical misrecognition, though only hypothetical, is by definition traumatic, since it pushes us back into the vertiginous abyss of the Lacanian subject out of which, once upon a time, our identity was formed. This abyss is what Lola's final vertigo, as she is about to jump, is about: what if, she must have thought, they are not watching? The success of her dive, like Accattone's dive into the river in Pasolini's eponymous film (*Accattone*, 1961), means that the character has survived the vertigo of its own void. Or does it? Perhaps the lesson of the film is more subtle. What if Lola's mission is self-destructive in a different way, i.e. insofar as it entails the endorsement of the scopic drive, the Lacanian "making oneself seen" which relies on *fully* accepting the "rules of the game", on the fact that reality as such is always radically voyeuristic? In her wish to become spectacle, indeed pure spectacle, Lola gives body to the very void brought about by the scopic drive in its exhibitionistic dimension – which, we should not forget, coincides with the subject's freedom. Thus, one is entitled to understand Ophuls' cinema as a phenomenology of void *through* woman, mediated by femininity. As the director commented to Danielle Darrieux, who played the heroine of *Madame de...* (1953), 'through your beauty, charm, elegance and intelligence, which we all admire, you should represent the void, the non-existence. You must not fill out the void, but represent it' (in Von Bagh 2003: 130). This is why Ophuls described Danielle Darrieux as 'une femme totale' (in Annenkov 1962: 69).

It is then in this phenomenology of void that we should recognise the political potential of Ophuls' work. By turning woman into a commodity – a very pressing theme indeed in today's universalised *société du spectacle* – Ophuls effectively redefines Marx and Engel's observation that woman is the barometer of social emancipation, for he unravels the repressed truth-content of the commodity. In *Capital* Marx (1990: 163) had claimed that '[a] commodity appears at first sight an extremely obvious, trivial thing. But its analysis brings out that it is a very strange thing, abounding in metaphysical subtleties and theological niceties'. Žižek, who is particularly fond of this passage, rightly infers from it that the 'secret' of the commodity lies in its form, rather than in 'the determination of its value by the quantity of the work consumed in its production': 'In other words, classical political economy is interested only in contents concealed behind the commodity-form, which is why it cannot explain the true secret, not the secret *behind* the form but *the secret of this form itself*' (Žižek 1989: 11 and 15). True commodity fetishism implies the awareness that the secret of the commodity is entrenched in its appearance, the fact that 'it really appears to you as a magical object endowed with special powers' (Žižek 2006c: 351). The same can be said about Ophuls' woman. His criticism of our society of spectacle, represented by the fixity and morbid curiosity of the audience in *Lola Montès*, is embedded in the deeper awareness that, in the final analysis, *there is nothing to see*. The only, real scandal voiced by Lola, of which she seems to be aware, is that by debasing and humiliating herself, she becomes this Nothing. In Lola, sacrifice and victimisation break through the retributive logic of narcissism to become a form of "absolute narcissism" founded on the recognition of one's own non-being, radical inconsistency. Ophuls' women are their own executioners, and only as such can they be seen as victims. Through death-drive, they manage to visualise an extraordinary overlapping of voids: their own inner void *qua* subjects and the void of the big Other they inhabit. The fixity with which they stare at the world reflects the world's meaninglessness, it is a 'vide dans le vide' (in Annenkov 1962: 67), as Ophuls said about Louise in *Madame de...* This is why the truly traumatic event for Ophuls' heroines is the abrupt intervention of the gaze, the Lacanian gaze, signalling the fact that there is a point where *they cannot see themselves looking at themselves* (through the other). Depression for them corresponds to the absence of the look of the Other. In *Madame de...*, but even more explicitly in the novella by Louise de Vilmorin from which the film is adapted, the image of this depression is the empty beach on which the protagonist strolls melancholically, an image that recalls the long shot of the empty Irish beach on which Rosy (Sarah Miles), at the beginning of David Lean's *Ryan's Daughter* (1970), walks in patient wait for her other, Charles Shaughnessy (Robert Mitchum), to appear and recognise her.

In *Madame de...*, his penultimate film, Ophuls chronicles the twin stories of the film's heroine, the Countess Louise de..., and her diamond earrings, the glittering little object she resolves to sell to pay the debts she ran up through her extravagant spending. The charm of the story resides in the way it proves the inseparability of the frivolous protagonist from her earrings, for after a whirlwind of vicissitudes and fortuitous circumstances involving Madame's husband, his mistress, and Madame's lover, the luxury object returns to its original place, to the obvious bewilderment of the nameless heroine. The moment of this return is key to understand Ophuls' attempt to establish his idea of the "encounters of voids", his 'vide dans le vide'. What it effectively affirms is both the impossibility for the subject to get rid of her constitutive excess, and, consequently, the actual coincidence of subject and object *qua* meaningless, dispensable "thing" that functions as object-cause of desire. This return of the empty cause around which everything rotates – including Ophuls' ever-gliding camera – is the shattering event which de facto determines the heroine's death. For when Baron Fabrizio Donati (Vittorio de Sica), her lover, presents her with the wandering earrings, Madame is confronted by the hard, impenetrable, soulless materiality of her own self. She realises that she cannot get rid of the object because the object is, in all its superficial opacity, *in herself more than herself*.

5.3 Formal fetishism

At different points in his writing, Lacan claims that the deadlock pertaining to sexuality is not as apocalyptic as it might seem, and can indeed be overcome in the Symbolic. In *Seminar III* he states: 'It is insofar as the function of man and woman is symbolized, it is insofar as it's literally uprooted from the domain of the imaginary and situated in the domain of the symbolic, that any normal, completed sexual position is realized' (Lacan 2000: 177). He refines this stance at the end of *Seminar XI*, where he claims that 'any shelter in which may be established a viable, temperate relation of one sex to the other necessitates the intervention – this is what psycho-analysis teaches us – of that medium known as the paternal metaphor' (Lacan 1998a: 276). Lacan's point is that the drama of sexual dissymmetry can only be staged in the field of the big Other: it is "out there" that the couple can attempt to dodge the Real by externalising it into 'a viable, temperate relation'.

What comes to the fore in Antonioni's early films is that his "paternal metaphors" fail miserably: older husbands such as Enrico (*Chronicle of a Love*) and Gianni (*The Lady without Camelias*) cannot provide any viability or relief to the relationship. Not only do Antonioni's couples fail to find a conciliatory solution in the big Other; normally, these relationships are also tragically truncated when one of the two either commits or threatens to commit suicide. Nonetheless, we should not overlook the fact that what is missing at the interpersonal level is recuperated at the structural level, "absorbed" by the very act of narrativisation. Antonioni's strategy is in this respect fairly canonical: confronted with the dilemma of how to deal with the deadlock of sexual difference, he resorts to displacing it onto a well-defined narrative framework. While the sexual fracture is clearly not recomposed, its impact is deflected onto the structure and the ideological preoccupations it purports.[6] Eventually, however, it is clear that this attempt at narrative symbolisation fails, to the extent that Antonioni's early cinema could be said to provide a perfect illustration of the return of the repressed: what is foreclosed by the process of symbolisation returns to haunt the very consistency of the structure. And my thesis here is that this "ghost of the Real" manifests itself through what I would call "formal fetishism".

The primary stylistic features of Antonioni's cinema have been meticulously and eloquently described. His much-praised modernism can be summed up with what French critics called *de-dramatisation*, a general avoidance of grandly spectacular and over-dramatic gestures, coinciding with a penchant for extraneation, detachment, understatement, intellectual coldness and rigour. Even when engaging with a melodramatic plot like *The Lady without Camelias*, Antonioni's camera carefully prevents us from identifying with the dramatis personae, or from indulging in sentimentalism. It would be improper and intellectually sluggish, however, to liquidate the question of Antonioni's style with the tautological remark that "this is his method". I would rather suggest that his stylistic detachment functions as a symptom of a deeper anxiety concerning the impossibility of the sexual relationship, the key theme of his cinema. More exactly, it functions both as a defence against the deadlock of the Real, and as a way to negotiate a compromise with it, which results in its sublimation into autonomous formal configurations delivered from narrative development.[7]

Furthermore, if we apply Hegel's concept of reflexivity we could maintain that, since it is through form that Antonioni manages to "strike a deal" with the foreclosed dimension of his filmmaking, the filmic content inevitably sets itself up as a grandiose metonymy of form: what is the treatment of such themes as existential aimlessness, lack of purpose, social inertia and stagnation – all characteristic of Antonioni's portrayal of the postwar bourgeois universe – if not a metonymical prefiguration of the director's obsession with form which will explode with *The Adventure*? Just as Antonioni's narratives cannot be fully reconstructed without taking into account their formal excesses, so are these excesses always-already registered in the narrative content.

Let us pick a symptomatic shot of *The Girlfriends* (Le amiche, 1955), whose simple function appears to be that of linking unobtrusively one sequence to the next. In the second part of the film, Cesare (Franco Fabrizi) pays a visit to his fickle lover Momina (Yvonne Furneaux), who had lured him over with a veiled promise of sexual gratification. On his arrival, however, he finds his lover busy entertaining some friends. When the two are finally alone, Antonioni cuts to an external shot of the flat, suggesting his intention not to intrude on the intimacy of this encounter (a few years later, his camera would have certainly remained in the flat). The point, however, is that this external, deceptively unassuming shot takes on a noir significance of its own. The camera is placed outside in the evening dusk, slightly tilted upwards, framing the lit window of Momina's flat, through which we catch sight of the silhouettes of the two lovers. Suddenly an unknown man enters the frame, looks up at the window, and slowly makes for the entrance of the building. Perhaps as a result of this unwanted gaze, Cesare moves towards the window and pulls the Venetian blinds, a peremptory gesture which creates an uncanny visual effect, as the shadow of his silhouette is suddenly skewed into a distorted dark blotch and then instantly disappears.

Such a seemingly inconspicuous shot tells us more about Antonioni's (early) filmmaking than endless discussions about its sociological content. Anticipating *Blow-up*, the impossibility of the sexual relationship is here expressed by way of a hint to the radical inconsistency of the subject *qua* object of the scopic drive. This is indeed one of the first opportunities we have to realise the extent to which Antonioni's cinema concerns itself with *the erasure of the subject*, whether we choose to look at this issue from a formal or content-related perspective. From a formal angle, the apparently meaningless vanishing of Cesare's silhouette foreshadows Antonioni's fatal attraction to the blind spot in the picture (the gaze). Here, in fact, the voyeurism of the camera is already fully operative, for what the camera gets back from the object is the negativity of the gaze: the camera looks, keeps looking, and its visual drive is reciprocated by a flash of pure semblance (the skewed silhouette) embodying the negative capacity of the gaze. This early Antonioni already underscores the importance of the "surface of things". To him reality *is* an image, on condition that this image expresses a potential to uncover the enigmatic presence of the gaze, the repressed kernel of our representation of reality itself. In *The Girlfriends* the "realness" of Rosetta's (Madeleine Fischer) love for Lorenzo (Gabriele Ferzetti) – so overwhelming that it drives her to suicide – originates in the immaterial image of her portrait: 'I started to love you as you were painting my portrait [. . .] I've never felt like that before, you were painting my face [. . .] and it was as if you were caressing me, without realising it'. Fiction here is already designated as the privileged medium to access the concealed core of the extant, while women become fictional subjects *par excellence*, constantly flirting with the negativity of the Real.

In *Chronicle of a Love*, the most flagrant example of formal fetishism can be found in the sequence where, whilst Enrico is testing a fast car on a country road, Guido and Paola, who are waiting inside another car on the side of the road, for the first time after their reunion kiss passionately. The rebirth of their love-story is accompanied by an uncanny element in the mise-en-scène: two publicity posters placed on each side of the road and shaped as two enormous bottles of a 1950s Italian liqueur ("amaro Cora"). As Cuccu (1988: 36) notes, while these posters are historically realistic, at the same time, given the specific emotional tension of the passage, they cannot fail to appear odd, mysterious and even disquieting. The reason for this effect, I would add, is that they speak for Antonioni's fetishistic fascination with non-symbolic figurations, particularly with the spectrality of modern urban shapes and architectural patterns that, in their purely affirmative efficacy, function as a metonymical sublimation of the non-figurative Real. This is why these enormous bottles play the role of *objet a*: their presence is correlative to the trans-semantic excess that runs through the entire narrative.

If we recall Marx's theorisation of commodity fetishism as previously discussed, the most fundamental connotation of a commodity is, paradoxically, its uncanny aura, not its material status as embodiment of the social relations of production. Marx's key intuition is that the essence of the commodity belongs in its exchange-value rather than in its use-value. This allows me to consolidate my argument on the existence of a "Marxist nerve" in Antonioni's cinema. In terms of commodity criticism, Antonioni is closer to Marx than he would have envisaged himself, for he

makes visible how the true secret of the commodity, its irresistible coop-
tative power, dwells in its form (its *Schein*) rather than in its content. It
was Adorno who took the question of the formalistic essence of the commodity to its extreme consequences, when he claimed that the degree
of abstraction at work in great art is coterminous with the abstraction of
the commodity form; which, in turn, is what prompts Jameson (1990:
167) to claim that 'the absolute work of art [...] coincides with absolute commodification', insofar as 'the overwhelming objectivity of the
commodity form [...] is syncopated with that objectivity of the work
of art which is prior to living subjectivity'. In this respect, the insistence on commodity *qua* pure form, one of the distinguishing features
of Antonioni's cinema, can be said to target nothing less than the secret
mechanism that propels today's late capitalistic ideology.

In equating the fundamental dimension of modern art and the commodity form, Adorno emphasises the so-called "predominance of the
objective" – which is in effect the theoretical backbone of his entire philosophical production, amounting to an attempt to reconcile materialism
with the idealist theme of the subjective mediation of objective reality.
Perhaps, however, we should give Adorno a Lacanian twist, that is to say,
interpret his "object" as *objet a*, the elusive feature that is not only "other"
in the sense that it belongs to the impenetrable opacity of matter, but in
the more specific sense that its alterity represents the disavowed abstraction stealthily operative in any field of knowledge. Hence, the "Cora"
bottles in *Chronicle of a Love* represent both the abstraction underscoring
the consubstantiality of art and commodity, and the very sublime object
that deceptively "bolsters" the space of narrativisation. This formalised
feature unravels the mystery of Antonioni's fascination with "the surface of things": what we encounter on this surface is the imperceptible
blot that makes cinematic fiction possible. The supposedly hidden content, the enigma of the narrative, is always-already condensed in a tiny,
elusive detail right in front of our eyes.

The most effective way to tackle the central critical concern of Antonioni's formalism is to translate it into proper philosophical terms:
Antonioni's reliance on form, it would seem, is akin to a sort of Kantian transcendentalist strategy, positing the object of his visual desire as
an unreachable Other (Kant's *das Ding*), whose elusiveness can only be
accounted for in terms of an a priori loss. And, accordingly, this logic
would seem to entail a fundamental melancholy, since it breeds the
notion that every empirical object will never coincide with the Thing. Far
from being of secondary importance, this question can be regarded as the
common theoretical denominator between German idealism, Lacanian

psychoanalysis and Marxism. In Lacanian terms, Kant's transcendentalism cannot be disjointed from the problematic of a Real always-already enmeshed with the Symbolic. In this respect, Žižek holds that transcedentalising Lacan is equivalent to 'a celebration of failure' (Žižek 2002c: xii). His thesis is that the Lacanian Real does not simply amount to an out of reach Other regulating the symbolic field from its unapproachable distance. Rather, it ought to be conceptualised as a traumatic event in the precise sense that encounters with the Real do happen, but any attempt to integrate them into a symbolic economy is destined to fail. Thus, asserting that *the Real is impossible* is not enough, for it leads us to a neo-Kantian, deconstructionist, Levinasian/Derridean logic of Otherness, elevating the Other into an unattainable target (with a regulative function). One should instead accomplish the opposite analytical operation and state that *the impossible is Real*.

Within these parameters, my aim is to establish whether Antonioni's formalism actually contrives to impinge upon the Real. As suggested, on first impression the director would seem to be trapped in the transcendentalist logic of desire and the elusiveness of the object of representation, which implies that the encounter with the Real is endlessly postponed as fundamentally impossible. In Antonioni, as in Ophuls, one of the clearest metaphorical figurations of this attitude is the image of the staircase, a recurrent visual reference suggesting a kind of "winding up" of the subject around its own unreachable and empty kernel. The point, however, is that this empty kernel re-emerges as the sublimated image of his visual drive right from his early production, finding an outlet in a series of highly formalised objects situated on the surface of the world – such as, for example, the commodity. In any event, another "formalised object" starts stealing the scene in these early films: woman.

5.4   If Eros is sick, let's fuck!

In Antonioni's cinema the attempt to represent the elusiveness of feminine desire often turns into a hypnotic fascination with void pure and simple, with the meaninglessness of the image, the point where superficial appearances magically coincide with the shocking emptiness of the subject and its environs, the 'any-space-whatever, which Antonioni in turn pushes as far as the void' (Deleuze 1986: 123).

The Adventure (L'avventura, 1959), generally regarded as Antonioni's modernist masterpiece and most innovative work, marking the beginning of his mature period, provides us with the most captivating example of the director's attraction to the void called Woman. More pointedly, here for the first time Antonioni fully endorses that fatal fascination with void which confers upon his mature cinema the frighteningly frozen, modernist aspect of a self-contained universe inhabited by immaterial ghosts rather than traditional, rounded characters.[8] For the first time he inscribes this void into the open wound of the sexual relationship, a central preoccupation of his cinema since its inception.

The Adventure tells us that the impossibility of the relationship is caused by the "monstrosity" of the partner, since to speak about the partner is ultimately to speak about the partner's own inability to embody the principle of causality. It is therefore an adventure into the abyss of the subject *qua* partner; the vertigo that emanates from this adventure is, to say it with Adorno (2000: 33), 'an *index veri*' (an index of truth). Perhaps no other European film manages to embody the deadlock of the sexual relationship as radically as *The Adventure*. Anna's (Lea Massari) disappearance represents the single narrative event that forces us to confront the deadlock of the relationship, speaking for the uncompromising radicality of Antonioni's position. It is a soundless and unexpected disappearance, a strange implosion, and yet, with hindsight, one can see how it is embedded in the narrative from the very beginning. If we consider the first part of the film, the enigma surrounding Anna's desire (what does she want from her relationship with Sandro? What is the reason for her discontent?) is primarily an enigma for Anna herself. A sublime hysteric, Anna questions not only other people's motives, but most of all her own. Her mysterious vanishing from the small island of Lisca Bianca demonstrates that the question she poses to her partner, her friends, and ultimately to us, is intimately self-reflexive, and can only be truly answered with a painful act of self-erasure. Others (males) attempt to rescue her from her lethargy and indeterminateness; she, on the other hand, digs deeper.

It is not simply a decision to escape, to flee a certain world in order to occupy an alternative one. The merit of Antonioni's film is to make it absolutely clear that he is not interested in the postmodern problematic of escapism but rather, as most of his films testify, in the void that emanates from the subject and is reflected in its environs. Ultimately, Anna's disappearance has to do with her unbearable knowledge about the empty core of her desire, and the breach inscribed in the cinematic text by her absence is effectively what the Antonionian subject is about. Anna can thus be seen as the matrix from which the director moulds his understanding and representation of subjectivity, insofar as she radicalises feminine hysteria, paving the way for later characters as diverse as Lidia (Jeanne Moreau) in *The Night* (La notte, 1961), Vittoria and Giuliana (Monica Vitti) respectively in *The Eclipse* (L'eclisse, 1962) and

Red Desert (Il deserto rosso, 1964), or even Thomas (David Hemmings) in *Blow-up* (1966).

Incidentally, *Blow-up* occupies a crucial position in Antonioni's filmography. The David Hemmings character, an arrogant fashion photographer in the ebullient microcosm of mid-1960s London, cannot but strike us as a wonderful exemplification of the lesson femininity can teach its masculine counterpart. The photographer's existential journey of self-discovery (from fullness to lack, from presence to absence, from desire to drive, etc.) effectively confirms Anna's lesson in *The Adventure*. More to the point, it brings to fruition Antonioni's previous reflections on femininity (his quartet from *The Adventure* to *Red Desert*) in what retrospectively one can see as an attempt to emancipate man from his condition of closure in the symbolic order. Unwittingly imitating his female predecessors, Thomas' enquiry into the nature of his (visual) desire culminates in his endorsement of a drive that brings him face to face with his own subjective inconsistency. Eventually, he is erased from the text – another piece of evidence supporting the fact that cinema can evoke negativity *by subtraction*, as a "being there" that becomes aware of its "never having been there", of its absence to itself.

Significantly, in *The Adventure* it is Anna's father who first brings up the theme of the impossibility of his daughter's relationship with her fiancé Sandro (Gabriele Ferzetti). The brief exchange between father and daughter in the opening sequence suggests both the father's loss of symbolic authority over Anna as well his scepticism towards her relationship with Sandro: 'that guy will never marry you'. When Anna replies that *she* has refused to marry him, he concludes acerbically 'it's the same thing'. What we have here is the first hint to the alleged sociological dimension of the film, i.e. the critical reference to an ancient morality between the sexes that survives in modernity, which Antonioni addressed in full in his Cannes speech in 1960. Antonioni's criticism of modernity concerns modern man's inability to reinvent new moral attitudes that could replace the old ones and therefore reflect more closely humanity's technological and scientific progress. Let us just take a look at the final paragraph of Antonioni's statement:

> For even though we know that the ancient codes of morality are decrepit and no longer tenable, we persist, with a sense of perversity that I would only ironically define as pathetic, in remaining loyal to them. Thus, the moral man who has no fear of the scientific unknown is today afraid of the moral unknown. Starting out from this point of fear and frustration, his adventure can only end in a stalemate.

The visionary core of Antonioni's position should not blind us to its ultimate ambiguity. If Antonioni was critical of his characters' inability to abandon 'a heavy baggage of emotional traits' close to 'those that prevailed in Homeric times', this probably means that he was hoping for a future development of gender-coded morality that could lead to overcoming that sexual deadlock so convincingly, and obstinately, represented in his film(s). As anticipated, my argument is that Antonioni's cinema is from its very beginning *fraught with the anxiety of sexual difference*, to such an extent that, perhaps unconsciously, the director resorts to two main strategies in order to neutralise its traumatic impact: he gentrifies it either through a strong reliance on narrative consistency (his films up to *The Cry*) or through formalism and aestheticisation (from *The Adventure* onward). What *The Adventure* allows us to appreciate is Antonioni's own fascination with the problem he consciously denounces, the couple's inability to overcome their sexually-coded difference: Sandro as the epitome of masculine symbolic authority and as such a replacement (surrogate?) of Anna's father; Anna as the hysterical female subject characterised by the inconsistency of her desire. The first time we see them together, in Sandro's flat, the evidence of their sexual difference is so painstakingly obvious that one almost sympathises with Anna's sudden decision to demand sex. Despite Antonioni's conviction that in our times 'Eros is sick', i.e. that excessive eroticism is a symptom of a profound epochal malaise, this passage should be seen as clarifying a different and perhaps more enlightening function of sex. It is not that by taking her clothes off in front of Sandro 'Anna directly expresses female desire' as part of her search of 'authentic existence' (Brunette 1998: 34). The opposite is true: sex functions here as a stopgap preventing the annihilating encounter with the Real of desire, or sexual difference, exactly like in the final sequence of Kubrick's *Eyes Wide Shut* (1999), when Alice (Nicole Kidman) tells Bill (Tom Cruise) that what they urgently need to do (so as to stop thinking about the traumatic incompatibility of their fantasies) is 'fuck'.

A similar argument applies to Pasolini's *Theorem* (Teorema, 1968). The fact that every member (including the maid) of the bourgeois Milanese family is overwhelmed by an irresistible desire to be possessed by the mysterious guest, played by Terence Stamp, is definitely *not* a reflection of the spirit of 1968 and its climate of sexual liberation; it rather amounts to a desperate strategy they adopt to avoid the annihilating confrontation with the void embodied by *objet a*. Sex, in other words, is their way of dealing with the tremendous anxiety generated by the over-proximity of the stranger in his role of object-cause of desire. This is confirmed in the second part of the film, when the stranger unexpectedly leaves and the family members are incapable of coping with his absence. The point is that through sex they were able to circumvent the very void/lack he stood for. Here we could risk claiming that the Terence Stamp character personifies nothing less than the Lacanian analyst, the 'subject supposed to know' (see Lacan 1998a: 230–43), who, through his imposture (he occupies the place of the impossible Thing), aims at bringing the analysand (the bourgeoisie) face to face with the Real of his/her desire. What the second part of the film successfully demonstrates is not only that the fascination with the object-cause of desire is fundamentally an illusion, but, more crucially, that *this illusion is Real, and has traumatic effects*:

> To 'unmask the illusion' does not mean that 'there is nothing to see behind it': what we must be able to see is precisely this *nothing as such* – beyond the phenomena, there is nothing *but this nothing itself*, *'nothing' which is the subject*. To conceive the appearance as 'mere appearance' the subject has effectively to go beyond it, to 'pass over' it, but what he finds there is his own act of passage. [...] the subject is the void, the hole in the Other, and the object the inert content filling up this void; the subject's entire 'being' thus consists in the fantasy-object filling out this void. (Žižek 1989: 195–6)

To put it differently, we could argue that after the stranger's departure the bourgeois characters "traverse the (bourgeois) fantasy", coming to occupy the Hegelian place behind the 'curtain of appearance' (Hegel 1977: 103), where they experience the lack constitutive of subjectivity.[9]

In *Theorem*, Pasolini's use of sex as a last-ditch attempt to avoid the trauma of subjective destitution allows us to see what is wrong with Bernardo Bertolucci's *Last Tango in Paris* (L'ultimo tango a Parigi, 1972). The film's main weakness lies in the couple's attempt to build a relationship *outside* the symbolic order, without knowing each other. By the end of the film, of course, Bertolucci makes his Freudian point, acknowledging that such a rapport outside civilisation is (tragically) impracticable. Paul (Marlon Brando) dies in the foetal position, reminding us that he embodies unconscious drives, and that these drives must be repressed, as indeed confirmed by Jeanne's (Maria Schneider) last words: 'I never knew him, I don't know who he is, he just wanted to rape me'. From a Lacanian viewpoint, however, what remains highly suspicious is the very *positing of a realm beyond the symbolic order*, symbolised by the anonymous room where the two characters meet. The naïvety of the film, which in many ways reflects the naïvety of 1968 sexual liberation movements, concerns the intrinsically idealistic positing of a "freedom-in-sex" dimension beyond societal constraints.

5.5 There aren't any Ladies

In gender terms, Antonioni's couples are all rather stereotypically incompatible. His males are characteristically alienated, i.e. split between their phallic function (their predatory instinct towards women) and symbolic role (their career, economic and social status, moral and intellectual convictions, etc.).[10] Whether his male characters are intellectuals like Sandro (*The Adventure*), Giovanni (Marcello Mastroianni, *The Night*), Riccardo (Francisco Rabal, *The Eclipse*), or modern professionals like Piero (Alain Delon, *The Eclipse*), their universe remains rigidly divided into the sexual and the symbolic. Antonioni's female characters, on the other hand, are generally depicted as hysterical individuals with a strong tendency towards psychosis. With *The Adventure*, the schism of sexual difference becomes particularly prominent, every couple effectively providing evidence for it: Sandro and Anna, Sandro and Claudia, Giulia and Corrado, Raimondo and Patrizia, the Sicilian pharmacist and his wife. It is with the following *The Night* (1961) and *The Eclipse* (1962), as we shall see, that this schism acquires a properly compulsive magnitude.

My over-arching point is that the sexual deadlock is actually the Real substance of Antonioni's art, the disturbing and yet fascinating "stuff" to which his filmmaking cannot avoid compulsively returning. With regard to *The Adventure*, this formless, annoyingly unshakable Real materialises in Anna's self-erasure from the text, an act truly beyond narrative comprehension whose ultimate aim is to encroach upon the subject's as well as the text's unconscious truth.

From a Lacanian angle, the only plausible answer to the question "where has Anna gone?" is that "she has fallen into the film's unconscious", that is to say she has identified with the lack (the gaze), that structures the image. All other attempts at explaining this event, including those given by the characters, are to be regarded as mere fantasies whose primary aim is to conceal the founding narrative deadlock (fantasy always comes into play where interpretations fails). Even the (generally unnoticed) detail of the small boat leaving the island immediately before Anna's friends become aware of her disappearance would seem to work as a false clue, typically in contrast with the standard detective-story tradition that Antonioni here sets out to subvert (instead of leading to the solution of the mystery, the clue confirms the impossibility of achieving some stable knowledge about the missing character).

Perhaps for the first time in the history of cinema a character fully *comes to be where the cinematic unconscious is*, over-identifying with the lack that sustains the filmic system of symbolic representations, and thus with the symbolic order *tout court*.[11] Roland Barthes was right when he mentioned 'fragility' as one of the three modernist characteristics of Antonioni's work (see Chatman and Fink 1989: 212; Barthes 1988), but only as long as we regard this fragility as the effect of a *stricto sensu* psychotic intervention into the vertiginous void of the image. The way in which Antonioni's females reflect reality is, ultimately, *by matching void with void*, by "coming to be" where the Real is. What better reading of Anna's gesture of self-contraction than Lacan's statement that 'if the sexual relationship doesn't exist, there aren't any ladies' (Lacan 1998b: 57)?

At this stage it becomes evident that Antonioni's intention in *The Adventure* is definitely *not* that of deploring the alienating power of contemporary society, nor of lamenting the audacity of modern individuals who have grown insensitive towards the tragic. His intention is rather to criticise the modern subjects' *inability to forget* (in the Nietzschean sense of the term).[12] In his criticism of the romantic attitude of guilt, melancholy and nostalgia, Antonioni shows how his cinema hinges on the anti-humanistic rejection of the traditional vision of man as a fixed entity anchored in reason and morality. If there is essentialism in Antonioni, it is the essentialism of the unconscious, of the absolute impenetrability that qualifies the most intimate core of the subject. Perhaps it is from this angle that we should read the previously mentioned Cannes statement. The 'moral unknown' to which Antonioni refers is the empty core around which his films (starting from *The Adventure*) explicitly rotate, prompting us to endorse a traumatic encounter with the Real of sexual difference that, alone, can unlock the stalemate. The standard view of Antonioni as a quintessentially modernist director whose artistic sensibility depends on the classic hermeneutic deadlock (the impasse between the aspiration to truth and the impossibility of reaching it) needs therefore to be reviewed. Far from being a melancholic pessimist or a cold aesthete cynically embracing a deterministic vision of the world, he is driven by a passionate search for the truth, provided we conceptualise truth as the unacknowledged element that *ex-sists* in (any) symbolic representation. Let us take the case of Antonioni's use of actors. When he claims that 'the cinema actor must not understand, he must be' (for 'the more his effort is intuitive, the more he will appear spontaneous', in Tinazzi

1976: 49), is he not reiterating, almost *verbatim*, the Lacanian theme of the separation between "thinking" and "being"? The reason why his characters are not instructed about the plot can be found in Lacan, who tells us that "thinking" pertains to consciousness and non-being, whilst "being" is a prerogative of the unconscious.

A few years after Anna's exemplary move, another famous lady made her appearance in European cinema, showing us the way to feminine *jouissance*. Luis Buñuel's *Belle de jour* (1967) opens *in medias res*, at a point where Séverine's (Catherine Deneuve) being has already given in to traumatic unconscious enjoyment. This is why, after all, she is frigid: her enjoyment is completely absorbed by unconscious fantasies of humiliation and degradation, fantasies which Buñuel, of course, readily elevates to the status of primary narrative material. Leaving aside the question of Séverine's masochism in relation to her bourgeois marriage, a question which has been explored in Part 1, let us just ponder the magnificent spectacle of her entranced approach to Madame Anaïs' brothel. Well before Henri Husson (Michel Piccoli) knowingly mentions this place of perdition, Séverine has been won over by its obscene charm. Once she learns about its location, she is driven there as if sleepwalking, against her best intentions. The Real of enjoyment is what awaits her, and Buñuel's merit is that he makes it absolutely clear that the door to this Real is open to woman alone, for it is woman who has a chance to assume the inconsistency of the universe of sense. Anna's disappearance at Lisca Bianca and Séverine's journey of self-degradation have therefore the same structure, insofar as they represent the feminine act of over-identification with the repressed underside of the Symbolic, which undermines the latter from within.

It is easy to see how the structural focus of *The Adventure* is the invisible line that separates the "before" from the "after" of Anna's disappearance. What happens in between Anna's last words to Sandro, her fiancé, and the beginning of the next sequence, when the remaining characters slowly come to realise that she has gone missing? The trap to avoid is to think that she has gone missing *somewhere in the actual text*. Instead, it is much more fruitful to bring the analysis to the meta-cinematic level, suggesting that *she has slipped in between the junctures of the text*, in those underlying "cracks" represented by editing whose invisibility opens up the space for representation. Let us examine the episode of the shark. Why does Anna, whilst swimming with her friends, suddenly shout that she is being threatened by a shark if, as she tells Claudia a few minutes later, that danger never existed in the first place? Despite all the metaphorical interpretations that the figure of the shark may evoke (as we know from many a reading of Steven Spielberg's *Jaws,* 1975), and despite the fact that Anna is effectively a bored and spoilt bourgeois who might well be "looking for kicks", the fantasmatic shark is quite simply a symptom of Anna's unconscious desire *to disappear from the text.*

5.6 Inadequacy of the imagination

This brings us to the titanic challenge of Antonioni's cinematic desire: how to represent absence. In the sequence that follows Anna's vanishing, the director recurs to what Kant, in the *Critique of Judgement,* calls the *dynamically sublime in nature,* that is to say, the immeasurable might of nature whose manifestation causes in man a feeling of helplessness so great and boundless that it defies imagination. Antonioni's sublime is exactly of the kind discussed by Kant, as Anna's absence coincides with a sudden worsening of the conditions of the sea, followed by a violent thunderstorm and hurricane.[13] Kant, of course, resolves the failure of aesthetic imagination vis-à-vis the natural sublime by bringing into contention the moral law, with its ability to absorb the shock of this failure and recoup it in the unbearable pressure of the moral injunction to do one's duty. Precisely because the feeling of the sublime conjures up the impossibility of reaching the Thing, we must submit to the moral law. Contravening the solution indicated by Kant, Antonioni sticks to the very negativity introduced by the Kantian "inadequacy of the imagination". Let us remind ourselves that, in its sensuous connotations, Kant's sublime acquires the shape of a miraculous object through which the impossible dimension of the Thing shines – as Žižek (1989: 203) explains in the following passage:

> The Sublime is therefore the paradox of an object which, in the very field of representation, provides a view, in a negative way, of the dimension of what is unrepresentable. It is a unique point in Kant's system, a point at which the fissure, the gap between phenomenon and Thing-in-itself, is abolished in a negative way, because in it the phenomenon's very inability to represent the Thing adequately *is inscribed in the phenomenon itself.*

Given therefore the coincidence of the sublime with *objet a* (insofar as, to say it with Lacan, it represents *the paradox of an object elevated to the dignity of a Thing*), in *The Adventure* the truly sublime object, the mediator between the phenomenal world and the impossible Thing, is Anna herself. In other words, the miraculous connection with the Thing is engendered by Anna, who disappears and thus brings about... what, exactly?

At one point in Eric Rohmer's *The Green Ray* (Le rayon vert, 1986), Delphine (Marie Rivière) seems about to emulate Anna in her suicidal confrontation with the sublime of nature (the film is punctuated by images of her solipsistic immersion in nature). A young Parisian secretary unable to establish satisfactory relationships with her peers, and particularly with men, Delphine spends the summer travelling to different locations, half hoping, in vain, to find relief from her solitude and anguish. After a few days in Cherbourg and a quick visit to the French Alps, she decides to spend some time in a friend's flat in Biarritz, where, however, her existential malaise worsens to the point of saturation. In one of the most poignant scenes of the film, for instance, we see her hysterically run away from the company of Lena (a Swedish girl who bathes topless and tries to convince her to "enjoy life") and the two males with whom Lena had engaged in a typically idiotic conversation. Before this incident, Delphine had briefly walked down under Biarritz's lighthouse, by the actually existing "chambre d'amour", a cavern where one can contemplate the roaring of the Ocean as its waves hit the hollow space in the rocks. Rohmer (2004) himself commented on this passage as a kind of 'descent into hell', hinting at the possibility of his heroine's suicide. For a brief moment, therefore, Delphine's destiny seems to run parallel to Anna's.

However, as a rule Rohmer's heroines (and heroes) do not disappear, in the sense that they stay well clear of any kind of Real encounter that could bring them face to face with the traumatic substance of their unconscious desires. In fact, the reference to the Kantian sublime in *The Green Ray* (the roaring of the sea) is quickly transmuted into its gentrification, the "green ray" of the title. The green ray is a rare atmospheric phenomenon described by Jules Verne in his novel of the same title as a flash of green light in the setting sun that supposedly allows one to gain an insight into one's true self. It seems to me that this reference functions here as an aestheticised utopian stand-in for both the Real of the sexual relationship and the void of the (feminine) subject. If Antonioni's heroine fully endorses this void, Delphine aims to avoid it, for instance anchoring her hysteria to obdurate superstition and new-age spirituality (her belief in cards, vegetarianism, etc.). As for her final epiphany (she meets a young man, a carpenter, and with him experiences the spellbinding "green ray" phenomenon, which hints at the possibility of love and thus true communication), it deserves critical attention, especially if compared with the endings of Roberto Rossellini's great 1950s films, particularly *Stromboli* and *Voyage to Italy*. If from the point of view of the heroine's desire Rohmer's film seems ambiguous, the transcendental solution marks a substantial difference with both Rossellini and Antonioni. On the one hand Delphine's existential journey into the invasive superficiality of the modern world (despite the time gap, a very similar world to that of *The Adventure*) is marked by an attitude of uncompromising refusal, which is necessary for the opening to the New; on the other hand, however, Rohmer fails to inscribe Delphine's "No!" into the perspective of a true act: her final encounter with the "ray of hope" is clearly less the endorsement of a liberating fall into the void of her desire than an ingenious way of masking such void through a reference to Grace. Despite the mixture of joy and terror on her face as she witnesses the miraculous optical phenomenon of the green ray, hope prevails rather too comfortably here, a sign perhaps that this type of spiritualism does not quite account for the necessity of the Fall.

Not so in Rossellini's *Voyage to Italy*, where the dimension of love, as we have seen, emerges *by subtraction*, i.e. at the point where husband and wife are confronted by their own radical insignificance; and even less in *The Adventure*, which is characterised by Antonioni's indifference towards transcendentalism. More to the point, Anna's effacement places the powerful Christian topos of the Fall in the midst of an entirely immanent universe, with the result that this universe suddenly reveals its empty core. Anna functions therefore as a kind of umbilical cord connecting subject and substance in their fundamental negativity. One only needs to mention the predominance of empty spaces that characterises Antonioni's mature cinema – or rather the vertiginous and invariably aestheticised feeling of emptiness evoked by an open space. The series is practically endless: parks, deserts, backgrounds filled with fog. . . In every instance, Antonioni attempts to connect figuratively with the gap in the big Other – and, of course, his favourite ally is woman.

5.7   Woman in the cities

There are moments in Antonioni's films of the early 1960s where, to use Lacan's phrase about Joyce, the female heroines "manage to cancel their subscription to the unconscious" – unlike their male counterparts, who are condemned to be traversed by the signifier and therefore are unable to free themselves from the spell of the unconscious. More and more in Antonioni's mature cinema, the impossibility of the sexual relationship is externalised onto diegetic elements progressively deprived of their narrative function and frozen into non-symbolic, highly formalised images mostly organised around the feminine gaze. The link between form and the sexual deadlock is already evident is the credit sequence of *The Night*, where the main characters, Lidia and Giovanni (Marcello Mastroianni), descend the Pirelli Building in Milan in an external lift, entering what Lidia aptly calls 'the domain of the living dead'. This "descent into hell" will be accomplished with the couple's participation in the opulent party thrown by a wealthy Milanese industrialist, where their emotional crisis will finally explode. In this respect, the deadlock of sexual difference is still partly readable against the historical background of the film, which by and large confirms the critical view that Antonioni's early 1960s cinema should be understood as a comprehensive attempt to screen the reification of human relationships in late-capitalist Italy. The credit sequence is finely balanced between its metaphorical significance (the couple's descent into hell) and its mesmerising formalism (the reflection of the cityscape on the glass of the modern lift). The point to note is that the content-related "excess" of this sequence, namely the couple's crisis, finds an outlet in the formalism of the image, a strategy that is pursued even more emphatically in the following sequence of Lidia's solitary walk through Milan. Where is Lidia heading to? What is the aim of her meandering? As in Anna's case, the *cause* of Lidia's desire remains foreclosed, strictly off-limits. However, contrary to the classic case of the *femme fatale*, whose elusive libidinal position is thoroughly mediated by the male hero, Lidia's desire is available to us *directly*, disclosed in a completely unmediated way. The meaning of this sequence, then, is that we should not look for its meaning, since what we have in front of our eyes is *the non-phallic essence of feminine jouissance in all its hypnotic insignificance*. Symbolic interpretations are clearly insufficient here. Visibly distressed by an unspecified sense of dissatisfaction with her husband, Lidia heads off aimlessly through the streets of the modern city like a Benjaminian *flâneur*, casting her gaze around, establishing visual connections that in vain we attempt to decipher. There is nothing to decipher, except this nothingness which materialises Antonioni's endeavour to frame "traces of void" through his heroine's gaze. What we have in this sequence is a kind of "perambulating *jouissance*", expressing itself through Lidia's organ of sight, which, it must be added, functions exactly like Antonioni's camera. If in *Blow-up* Antonioni uses masculinity (the photographer's gaze) to demolish the male-coded belief in symbolic knowledge, in the early 1960s films he aligns his camera firmly behind his women, sharing their viewpoint, enchanted and complicit with their contemplation of the world.

The Eclipse pushes this formalism to the extreme. Here Antonioni's typical shot *di spalle*, from behind the female character, not only creates a baffling distance between her and the viewer, but more crucially stresses her strange complicity with the object of her gaze. This underlying intention emerges in full in another highly stylised opening, where the slowness and unnatural movement of both cameras and characters create a feeling of stasis aimed at *derealising* the two lovers, at turning them into *lifeless shapes*. This intention becomes particularly poignant when the back of Vittoria's head, forming a semicircle at the bottom of the shot, is juxtaposed to Riccardo's figure as he is sat facing her, his face pale and expressionless. Apart from the metaphorical reference to Riccardo's inability to empathise with Vittoria, this shot prompts us to question *the actual existence* of the characters. Not only are we forced to perceive the fragility of the modern subject (particularly Riccardo), but most of all we witness its evanescence, which is clearly connected with sexual difference.

Later on in the same scene Vittoria draws the living-room curtain to look outside, unwittingly creating a composition that sums up Antonioni's understanding of femininity. Vittoria's figure is framed against a wide rectangular window, rigorously from the back, while outside looms an oddly shaped water tower resembling a still of the mushroom effect created by the explosion of the atomic bomb. The symbolic meaning is fairly obvious: Vittoria's outward gaze suggests her attempt to escape the claustrophobic atmosphere in Riccardo's flat, the impossibility of their relationship, but all she finds is a reminder of atomic danger, a particularly pressing threat at the start of the 1960s.[14] Yet, apart from reinforcing the no-escape symbolism, this shot also testifies to Antonioni's obsessive preoccupation with form. For a few seconds Vittoria's silhouette is flattened out and situated right next to the water tower, suggesting a mysterious correspondence between the shape of her body, her invisible gaze, and the abstract architecture outside.

This crucial shift from male to female desire is what both *The Night* and *The Eclipse* are about. The long scene of the summer party, in *The Night*, is aptly conceived against the background of the radical dissymmetry between masculine and feminine desire. Whilst Giovanni is busy courting Valentina (Monica Vitti), the rich Milanese industrialist's daughter, Lidia remains aloof. Later she is told about the death of Tommaso (the intellectual whom she had visited at the start of the film), she mourns him quietly and, all of a sudden her mood changes: she starts enjoying the party, to the extent that she happily consents to sneak away with Roberto, a perfect stranger who had been eyeing her up since her arrival.

Despite the fact that after sustained flirting on his part she turns down Roberto with the classic 'I'm sorry, I can't', we are left in the dark as to what actually happens between them, since Antonioni cuts back to Giovanni's affair, suturing Lidia and Roberto back in the narrative only at a much later stage. The point is therefore obvious to see: if Giovanni's *jouissance* is spelt out as pertaining to the phallic kind, i.e. linked to a type of enjoyment only available under the condition of symbolic castration, Lidia's remains enigmatic right through to the very end.

Again, we should relate this state of affairs to *The Adventure*, the true matrix of all Antonionian enquiries into femininity. If Anna falls into the Real/void whose dislocation sets up the big Other, her successors Lidia and Vittoria learn to survive by way of a minimal but vital act of sublimation, whereby the void is transformed into a *mysterious mimetic correspondence with the outside world in its fundamental meaninglessness*. The void is still there, but this time it makes itself available to the camera as a minimally gentrified object, the minimally sublimated image of feminine *jouissance*, insofar as this *jouissance* is 'a good that is not caused by a little *a*' (Lacan 1998b: 77). In fact, I would suggest that the common denominator of *The Night*, *The Eclipse*, and *Red Desert* is their hypnotic fascination with the abyss opened up by Anna's disappearance, although the heroines of these films manage to stop just before the precipice.

With the following *Red Desert* (Il deserto rosso, 1964), Antonioni's strategy changes only slightly. It is important to stress that this is his first colour film, which however does not mean, as many have argued, that formalism becomes his sole concern. Rather, the question is: how does he link sexual difference with the new technical possibility of exploiting colour? The main difference from his previous three works is that the female character's mimetic relationship with the external world is now expressed chromatically. And yet, Antonioni's is not simply an hyperformalistic vision of the world, and even less an escapist one. By focusing on form and femininity, rather, he is able to uncover the basic mechanism that sustains the functioning of the socio-symbolic order. Giuliana (Monica Vitti) is threatened by the dreary modern wasteland around her as well as by the deeply unsatisfactory relationship with her husband Ugo (Carlo Chionetti), an engineer, to the point that the two threats (the greyness of the industrial landscape and the greyness of her husband) become interchangeable. As in *The Eclipse*, Antonioni focuses on feminine hysteria, which produces the anxiety of being controlled and overwhelmed by the other's desire. Giuliana's problem is how to overcome this anxiety. After Anna's psychotic choice in *The Adventure*, Antonioni's solution and ultimate *raison d'être* of his cinema is to be sought in the previously mentioned minimal sublimation of feminine *jouissance*. As far as *Red Desert* is concerned, sublimation is subtly inscribed in the very first sequence of the film. After failing to connect verbally and emotionally with a group of workers on strike, Giuliana is pitched against the ghastly industrial horizon, as usual from behind, her gaze completely hidden. What is she looking at? The camera – the eye of Antonioni's *feminine camera* – provides the answer by zooming in on the splash of reddish flame that intermittently blasts out of a huge pipe. It is by focusing on such uncannily aestheticised objects that Antonioni manages to evoke feminine *jouissance*. If after *The Adventure* his women have learnt to avoid the lethal threat of psychosis, a trace of the latter survives in the enjoyment of the gaze. In fact, Antonioni's obsessive focus on non-symbolisable objects – his "about nothing, with precision" – is psychotic, totally immersed in *jouissance*. Thus, feminine enjoyment becomes *his* enjoyment.

Another way of putting this is by claiming that Antonioni's "objects" correspond to what Lacanian psychoanalysis knows as *sinthomes*, inert condensations of non-symbolisable enjoyment. In psychoanalytic terms, a symptom is not merely a sign revealing some deep-seated disorder, but more precisely *a sign of disavowed enjoyment*, a reference to some kernel of libidinal investment that has to be repressed if the field is to function smoothly. In Lacan's later work, symptom becomes *sinthome*, a term intended to capture the purely libidinal status of the psychoanalytic symptom as 'the way in which each subject enjoys the unconscious, in so far as the unconscious determines him' (*RSI*, unpublished seminar 1974–75, 18 February 1975). On this evidence, it comes as no surprise that Lacan devotes so much of his unpublished seminar *Le sinthome* (1975–76) to James Joyce, whose art he regards as a perfect example of a successful answer to the failure of the paternal metaphor. To Lacan, who in the later stage of his teachings became increasingly fond of linguistic puns, Joyce exemplifies precisely the position of a writer who *jouis*, who enjoys – or, even better, *il Joyce trop*, he enjoys too much. Lacan saw Joyce's most cryptic works (*Ulysses* and, particularly, *Finnegans Wake*) as attempts to disclose the Real of enjoyment from within the symbolic order of language, a strategy meant to compensate for the absence of the paternal function. More specifically, Joyce's famous epiphanies are regarded as examples of how the subject organises its relation to the Other *without the neurotic loop* (the mediation of fantasy and *objet a*): language unties its knot to the phallic function and assumes a thoroughly "suspended" position with regard to the big Other. And this position of course exemplifies Lacan's definition of feminine *jouissance* beyond the phallus.[15]

6
In Film Beyond Film: the Ontological Primacy of Woman

In this final section we enter a microcosm that is thoroughly delivered from the masculine logic of "knowledge through exclusion". Woman here has no secret anchoring in enjoyment. For her, enjoyment is a ciel ouvert, it overlaps with the enjoyment of the big Other. What elevates woman beyond man is the paradox of a perforated whole, a whole that is not ashamed of revealing its holes, through which she verifies the non-existence of the big Other. For this reason, woman is in film beyond film, both fully included in its symbolic domain and in excess of it, belying the emptiness of its foundations.

6.1 Ontology of void

As argued above, Antonioni perfected his obsessive dramatisation of frames filled with a kind of metaphysical emptiness in his films of the early 1960s. *Blow-up* (1966) does not forsake this stylistic cipher; on the contrary, it refines its use. Antonioni realises that his fascination with void needs to acquire a more strategic role. Rather than risk overwhelming the narrative, it ought to reveal its inner functioning. This is why in *Blow-up* the reliance upon open and vacant spaces is condensed in the crucial shots of the vast expanse of Maryon Park, whereas most of the narrative, by contrast, focuses on the hectic London lifestyle of the "swinging sixties". As noted by Jameson, more than the corpse it is the background that matters here, the peripheral presence of the park with its imposing trees 'shaken with wind as though by a kind of permanent violence, day or night never at rest' (Jameson 1992: 196). Maryon Park is a true "desert of the Real", a really existing and yet unreal place of ghostly apparitions which eventually overlaps with the void of the feminine subject – for, if the subject in question is biologically male (to the extent that many critics have commented unsympathetically on his misogyny), his attachment to the gaze, *objet a* as missing object in the scopic field, teaches him the Lacanian lesson that woman has always known: the big Other does not exist!

The "mystery of the park" is indeed a recurrent theme in Antonioni, also particularly noticeable in *The Vanquished* (I vinti, 1953) and *The Night*.[16] In sharp contrast to the Romantic project of the English garden as *locus amoenus*, a place of idyllic communion with nature away from the corrupting influence of modern civilisation, Antonioni chooses the park to reflect on the enigma of the image itself. In Antonioni's parks the Romantic idyll becomes a nightmare, for what the characters meet there is the inconsistency of their own desires – the same inconsistency met by Odetta (Anne Wiazemsky) in Pasolini's *Theorem* (1968), when she measures out the fraction of the garden occupied by the guest before his departure, the point being that, from the perspective of her desire, *he was never there in the first place*.[17] As for Antonioni, suffice it to recall the final sequence of *The Night*, where Giovanni (Marcello Mastroianni) and Lidia (Jeanne Moreau), walking out into a seemingly endless park at dawn, find the courage to confront the emotional impasse in their relationship. Here Lidia's intentions finally seem to become clear, as she tells Giovanni that she does not love him anymore, that she only feels pity for him. Upon realising that he is about to lose her, Giovanni desperately embraces her. At first Lidia resists, but eventually she appears to give in. As this open ending suggests, however, the truth about Lidia's desire remains concealed, and ultimately it is this fascinating kernel of non-knowledge that Antonioni sublimates into form. In this brilliantly constructed finale, the Real of the sexual relationship is deflected onto two main formal features: two trees, and the jazz piece played by the band in the park. In one of the last shots of the film Giovanni and Lidia are framed in an artificially rigid position next to two tree trunks, whose presence creates the effect of an abstract composition while simultaneously suggesting a metaphorical parallel with the couple, since one is perfectly straight and the other curved, replicating Giovanni's slightly unnatural posture. Then, as the final tracking shot moves from the couple lying on the ground to the haunting emptiness of the park, the jazz piece returns and the film ends. The status of music here could be said to constitute the truly ambiguous element of the finale, since it remains suspended between the diegetic and the non-diegetic. The detail not to miss is Lidia's comment on the band, who have kept playing through the night: 'do they think it's going to be a different day if they continue playing?' The somewhat absurd insistence of this music functions precisely as the medium through which the Real of the sexual relationship uncannily materialises.

One of the main formal achievements of Antonioni's cinema, apart from the previously discussed obsession with non-symbolic objects, lies in the opposite ability to evoke an enigmatic correspondence between the empty landscape and the subjective universe of the character. Both components of this mirroring correspondence are pervaded by an instance of radical detachment, whereby we realise not so much that the world is not real, but that it is *as unreal as the subject*. Let us recall the few pictorial shots of *Red Desert* in which, after the sexual *frissons* in the red shack, Giuliana is suddenly seized by a fit of anxiety at the sight of her husband and their friends standing still in front of her, transmuted by the thick fog into nightmarish silhouettes bearing a closer resemblance to zombies than to human beings. We find a similar passage, although much longer, in *Identification of a Woman* (Identificazione di una donna, 1982), when the heroine Mavi (Daniela Silverio) disappears in the thick fog after a heated discussion with her lover Niccolò (Tomas Milian). As in *Red Desert*, the fog is used to evoke the effacement of the world as we know it, the sudden emergence of the empty core of the image which requires either our fearless embracement of it (Mavi), or our withdrawal from it (Giuliana). Whilst Mavi, like Anna in *The Adventure*, stands for a psychotic entrance into the void of the image, Giuliana, as a neurotic, recoils from its promise/threat of *jouissance*. No matter how appealing this *jouissance* is to her, she can only try to keep it at bay, as when she begs: 'I'd like all the people who ever loved me here, around me, like a wall'.

A crucial consequence of psychosis is the insertion of a fracture in the narrative, a void-effect that Antonioni then proceeds to fill out with spectres, elusive figurations of lack. As in the aforementioned passage from *Red Desert*, in *The Adventure* Anna's friends, while searching for her, are slowly reduced to a cluster of automata mapped out against the backdrop of the island – as if to suggest that Anna's absence has become *their absence to themselves*. Halfway through the lengthy search there come a few uncannily non-cinematic moments when we feel that there is simply no difference between what these human beings are and the breathtakingly barren landscape of the island, with its rocks and vertiginous gorges. As they search for the lost one, *they lose themselves*, flattened out against the landscape, deprived of narrative depth. Antonioni visualises the void opened up by Anna through other characters and their connection with that very landscape that mysteriously swallowed Anna. Such spectral figurations of lack remain utterly extraneous to narrative symbolisation, and yet they are at the pulsating heart of the film.

We should insist on the apparently incongruous fact that what is at stake in Antonioni's attraction to the void of the image is the Freudian notion of death-drive. At one point in *Blow-up*, for instance, the hero's desire clearly turns into drive, a compulsion to dispel his fantasy (the 'what actually happened?') and confront (his) desire's lack of foundations. In *Red Desert*, on the other hand, the duplicity of the image (the gap between its imaginary consistency and the Real) is constantly evoked but also resisted by the main character. As Pasolini (1996: 78–81) had grasped, *Red Desert* lucidly illustrates how in film the representational domain is sustained by the invisible Real. To be more precise, it is because fiction in *Red Desert* is explicitly connoted as Giuliana's profoundly neurotic vision that we can "feel" the effect of the Real. For example, the fact that during Giuliana's fits the colour of certain objects around her actually changes, regardless of whether the shot is a subjective one or not, implies that we are forced to look at the world from her pathological perspective. The outcome of this is the inscription of a gap between the camera and the object, a certain detachment which inevitably triggers the crucial question: if it is clear that we are watching the film from a distorted point of view, where is it that we can find the true, "healthy", or at least neutral perspective?

More or less halfway through the film, Giuliana tells her son an enigmatic parable about a little girl on a deserted island. What this diversion achieves is the supplementation of the main story-line with "another scene", whereby the coldly-observed, even arid narrative about Giuliana's existential malaise in the modern wasteland cuts abruptly to a lyrical tale of seemingly utopian harmony between man and nature. What kind of relationship is there between this isolated sequence and the main narrative? Are we supposed to infer that the originally distorted point of view has now been straightened, so that we are now given a chance to perceive things "as they are"? If it were simply so, there would be something idealistically false about Antonioni's description of this utopian niche outside the modern world. A more attentive reading suggests an alternative interpretation. The point is that this classic "narrative within the narrative" is itself minimally split. Its disavowed structuring core is to be located in the mysterious materialization of an unmanned ship that first approaches the beach, then suddenly turns around and moves away. As we watch the vessel through the young girl's eyes, we realise that *a certain gaze*, in the Lacanian sense, makes a furtive and somewhat distressing appearance, an intrusion emphasised (as Pasolini, again, noticed) by Antonioni's change of lens. Rather than oppose modern alienation and idyllic natural harmony, the scene brings about the gaze as object-cause of desire in the scopic field. We can now understand the overall narrative logic of the film: it first creates a zooming-in or blowing-up effect through an initial instance of displacement (from industrial alienation to nature), and in a second move it radicalises this difference by inserting a "ghost ship" which exposes us to the presence of the gaze. The theoretical point to make is that such a procedure bears a close formal homology with what, according to Žižek's interpretation of Hegel's "negation of negation",[18] defines a true revolutionary intervention, as the latter always relies on a first act of detachment from a given context whose aim is to prepare the ground for a second, more radical move.[19]

An analogous *modus operandi*, although with opposite results, can be observed apropos the surreal orgy sequence of *Zabriskie Point* (1970), the film where Antonioni tackles directly the issue of late-1960s counter-culture. Having reached and explored Zabriskie Valley (a typically Antonionian non-place or limit-dimension), Mark (Mark Frechette) and Daria (Daria Halprin), the two young protagonists on the run from their respective environments, smoke cannabis and then make love. Gradually, as the musical theme begins ('Love scene' by Jerry Garcia), they are joined by numerous other couples (actually, members of Joe Chaikin's "Open Theatre") who, in a surreal fantasy of therapeutic collective sex, perform an erotic show on the dunes of the desert. What is untypical of Antonioni in this scene is precisely the way in which he seems to accord a liberating potential to the sexual act, the gentrification of the utopian potential of libido, which is exactly the reason why the passage does not work. The overall feeling of unproblematic sexual harmony that the love-in evokes (despite its ultimately melancholic feel) is essentially false, for it bypasses the central question of the disruptive potential of eroticism. In contrast to the aforementioned sequence of *Red Desert*, here the first movement of displacement, which coincides with the characters' arrival at Zabriskie Point and the encounter with the death-like emptiness of the desert, is *not* followed up by the showing of the gaze; instead, the narrative break is recomposed by this stereotypically counter-cultural reference to cosmic unity in sex. The relationship between gaze and desert is then revisited at the beginning of Antonioni's next work, *The Passenger* (Professione: reporter, 1975), and particularly in its opening sequence where David Locke (Jack Nicholson), a British television reporter, finds himself stranded in mid-desert whilst looking for a group of African rebels to interview. Here, in a few exemplary shots,

Antonioni shows us how the externality of a field (an out-of-frame point of view) can be successfully inscribed in the field *whilst remaining what it was*, a reference to a lack, a missing link.

6.2 On the Real as virtual

Insofar as they focus on the paradoxical representation of absence, both *The Passenger* and *Zabriskie Point* deal with virtuality. Crucially, this notion is linked to the political question of how to effect radical change. In *Zabriskie Point*, Mark, a college drop-out who attends student counter-cultural meetings but declares himself 'bored stiff' with their rhetoric, buys himself a gun and heads for the campus where the police are about to force a group of students out of an occupied library. There we witness the first proper event of the film, when an officer mistakenly shoots dead one of the students exiting the library, thinking that he was reaching for a gun when he was simply tucking his shirt in his trousers. At this precise point the camera cuts to Mark, who, having observed the whole scene, tries to get hold of his own gun. Then a shot is fired and the policeman falls down dead right in front of Mark's eyes. Who is the killer? Although the action happens very quickly, the attentive viewer will have noticed that Mark has nothing to do with it, for by the time the policeman falls to the ground he has not even managed to grab hold of his gun, which he keeps hidden in his boot. Later on in the film Mark tells Daria, the female co-protagonist, that *he would like to have shot the policeman*, but someone else did it first. His bold statement confirms what by then had become fairly clear, i.e., that he is prepared to fully assume the consequences of an act which he did not but would have performed had he been given the chance. From this moment on Mark embarks on a psychotic journey, progressively detaching himself from his world: he steals a small private airplane, joyrides it through the desert, fortuitously meets Daria, engages with her in a short-lived love adventure at Zabriskie Point, and eventually provokes his own death at the hands of the police.

Within such a seemingly disconsolate portrayal of organised student revolts, what risks going unnoticed is the key question concerning Mark's reaction to the killing of the policeman. As often with Antonioni, we are confronted with a non-subjectivisable event, an act that remains enigmatically deprived of its empirical agent, and which therefore acquires a virtual status (see, for instance, the theme of the virtual/impossible murder in *Chronicle of a Love*). Echoing the standard situation of Buñuel's cinema, a certain desire (to kill) is presented as impossible to realise. In

Zabriskie Point, the virtual status of the act is brought to fruition through a simple logic: since the subject of the act does not exist (at least in narrative terms) anyone who shares the desire to accomplish it (Mark) may well appropriate it, willingly assuming its consequences. More to the point, it is the vertiginous openness of the revolutionary act that occupies a pivotal place in this narrative, a feature recalling Walter Benjamin's anti-historicist apology of Messianic time in his *Theses on the Philosophy of History*. In thesis XVII, Benjamin writes:

> Thinking involves not only the flow of thoughts, but their arrest as well. Where thinking suddenly stops in a configuration pregnant with tensions, it gives that configuration a shock, by which it crystallizes into a monad. A historical materialist approaches a historical subject only where he encounters it as a monad. In this structure he recognizes the sign of a Messianic cessation of happening, or, put differently, a revolutionary chance in the fight for the oppressed past. He takes cognizance of it in order to blast a specific era out of the homogenous course of history – blasting a specific life out of the era or a specific work out of the lifework. (Benjamin 1968: 263)

Benjamin's 'revolutionary chance' against 'the homogeneous course of history' is correlative to the radical openness of the concrete historical situation as subtly vindicated by Antonioni. Mark fully endorses the abyss of the act that suddenly opens up before his eyes by assuming the traumatic content of his desire. Crucial to this is the virtual dimension involved, for had Mark actually killed the policeman, the *representation* of the groundless character of a revolutionary chance would have been partially lost.

The same virtual logic is at work in *The Passenger*. Having failed to contact the rebels, David Locke returns to his hotel to discover that David Robertson (Chuck Mulvehill), a British fellow guest he had previously befriended, has suddenly died, apparently of natural causes. It is at this early stage that the virtual dimension comes into play: taking advantage of his physical resemblance to Robertson, Locke opts to exchange identities with him; he swaps the passport photos, drags the man's body into his room, and calmly proceeds to the reception to report *his own* death. Despite the fact that he will not succeed in becoming his double, what counts is that the revolutionary dimension of virtuality – the zero-level where life and death miraculously coincide – is inscribed in the narrative.[20] As in Mark's case, the protagonist is presented with the opportunity to enter *the domain of virtuality* (represented by the double) so as to change his life radically. If the film is centred on Locke's death-drive, we need to add that such a drive conveys an extraordinary liberating potential, which comes to full fruition in the remarkable penultimate shot at the Hotel de la Gloria. Antonioni himself hinted at the correlation between death-drive and freedom:

> I could say that the desire to die has simply become nestled in his unconscious, unknown to him. Or that Locke begins absorbing death from the moment he leans over Robertson's corpse. But I could also say that he keeps the appointment for the opposite reasons: in fact, it's Daisy he is going to meet, and Daisy is a character from his new life. (in Brunette 1998: 144)

Although never clearly stated, Daisy Robertson, the wife of the dead man Locke identifies with, is none other than the nameless character played by Maria Schneider (the Girl). The implications cannot be underestimated, for they tell us that, as hinted by Antonioni in the above quotation, Locke dies (at the hands of the British secret services who were after Robinson) because he was betrayed by Daisy/the Girl: metaphorically, the impossibility of the sexual relationship is re-inscribed at the heart of the narrative.

Interestingly, when called upon to identify the dead husband, Mrs Locke claims that she never knew him, a phrase that echoes that of the Maria Schneider character at the end of Bertolucci's *Last Tango in Paris*, when she refuses to identify the dead Brando. But perhaps in *The Passenger* we should take the act of disavowal seriously: Mrs Locke effectively *never knew* the new man her husband had managed to become. If this reading is correct, then what takes place at the Hotel de la Gloria is truly a (metaphorical) *glorification* of a human being's ability to radically refashion his existence through the endorsement of the "virtual double", the object that is in him more than himself. In line with what I have argued apropos *Blow-up* and *The Adventure*, Antonioni's treatment of death, or disappearance, in *The Passenger*, is encoded with an intrinsically joyous endorsement of the necessity of the Fall, of an act of "resetting" that may bring about the New. Even more crucially, what this sublime film asserts is *the necessity of betrayal*: the whole idea of Redemption through Fall is supported by the final act of betrayal performed by the Girl, an act that, like Judas', in fact corresponds to the highest form of love. It is for this reason that, unlike Mrs Locke, when asked by the police inspector if she knew the dead man, the Girl replies 'Yes'.

Back to *Zabriskie Point*. The hostility with which the film was received can be explained through Antonioni's lack of interest in the revolutionary mystique of active student organisations. In *Zabriskie Point* he follows the less directly political logic of virtuality, which is operative from the beginning of the film and can be summed up as follows: from the virtual core of the commodity to the virtual core of the act. With particular reference to the commodity, one should not underestimate the visual energy generated by *Zabriskie Point*, particularly with its emphasis on advertising. Far from adopting a moralistic attitude towards the commodification of American life, Antonioni aestheticises the object-commodity, drawing our attention to its form. If the elusiveness of the object-commodity is what fascinates Antonioni's camera in the first part of the film, where he focuses on a breathtaking succession of massive publicity posters flanking a Californian road, by the end this fascination has exploded into a delirious apology of the structural enigma of the commodity. I am referring to the famous sequence of the explosion of Allen's house, shot from thirteen different angles, followed by the minimalistic slow-motion framing of the detonation and disintegration of a series of household products such as a box of Kellogg's Special K, a loaf of Wonder Bread, etc. It is with this deliriously formalistic final sequence that Antonioni's cinema confirms its attraction to the imaginary status of *objet a*.

One should nevertheless be careful not to disregard this attraction as a whim of Antonioni's art. The political significance to be retrieved from the formalistic excesses of *Zabriskie Point*'s final sequence depends on its insight into the very meaning of commodity fetishism: what sustains the commodity, and consequently the logic of late capitalism, is its "virtual soul", the empty core of the (sublime) object that sets desire in motion. Žižek's wager is that the enigma of the commodity-form can only be solved by bringing Lacan's unconscious into the equation,[21] that most fundamental and sublime of abstractions which allows us to perceive ourselves as subjects capable of articulating a certain relationship with knowledge.[22]

The explosion of Allen's house brings together the film's two main themes: on the one hand, the equation between the commodity and its empty kernel; on the other, the virtual dimension of the act. The complicity between Mark and Daria is articulated against the background of virtuality, which explains (and partly redeems) the psychedelic portrayal of their lovemaking in the desert: what if the sudden and imaginary multiplication of couples in this famous "love-in" is simply a way to suggest that love is also a virtual dimension, where the particular miraculously coincides with the universal? Perhaps what this sequence surreptitiously indicates, over and above its falsely idealistic (but also, as the script points out, 'slightly ironic', see Antonioni 1970: 67) connotations, is the founding Antonionian theme of the "impossibility of communication between the sexes", the fact that love between two human beings hinges on a virtual dimension that can be assumed but not fully subjectivised. In short, there seems to be no solution of continuity between the three main moments of the film: Mark's assumption of guilt, Mark and Daria's lovemaking, and Daria's imagined explosion; what unites these moments is the thread of virtuality, the fact that they belong together in a de-realised domain – which, conversely, is exactly what endows them with a subversive potential.

As well as providing an insight into the meaning of commodity fetishism, the explosion of Allen's house also tells us something decisive about Daria, whose story runs parallel to Mark's. The first observation we should make is that the explosion is not a direct consequence (however imaginary) of Daria's incensed gaze, but rather the result of a disarmingly artificial "alliance" between Daria's eye (the way she looks at the house) and Antonioni's camera. The editing of the sequence links Daria's eye to a distorted/virtual perspective (hence the repetition of the shot of the explosion from thirteen different angles) which the cinematic eye has a chance to vindicate. The cinematic eye, in other words, activates the virtual logic of the gaze by identifying the blind spot in the visual field, which brings about a *certain surplus of the cinematic image that derails it*, breaking narrative reliability. Once again, as in the early 1960s trilogy, the camera's best ally is woman. Daria's look suggests that she relates to the world in the same way as Lidia (*The Night*), Vittoria (*The Eclipse*), or Giuliana (*Red Desert*), managing to elicit the world's radical inconsistency. It is crucial to account for the difference between Daria's and Mark's positions. Mark's death, despite being activated by drive, speaks for the masculine inability to truly disturb the symbolic order; the film's finale, on the other hand, implies that all hopes for change are left with the feminine subject. Daria's *jouissance*, epitomised by her de-subjectivised gaze split into 13 autonomous camera shots, carries the corrosive power of feminine enjoyment into the symbolic field. With these shots, each one of them equivalent to the impossible perspective of the Lacanian gaze, Antonioni confirms the main lesson of his cinema: only a drastic suspension of all symbolic activity allows for the inscription of difference, to be understood as the Benjaminian 'cessation of happening'.

6.3   Losing loss

To use Pascal Bonizer's excellent definition, the true meaning of Anna's disappearance in *The Adventure* is 'the disappearance of the disappearance of Anna', provided we read this statement beyond its obvious narrative significance. It is not just that soon after Anna's vanishing the people around her simply forget about the enigma of her absence (actually, this is not even true in narrative terms, as her absence keeps haunting both Sandro and Claudia). Rather, it concerns the paradox of "losing a loss": if a "simple" disappearance means that someone has gone missing and can, at least in principle, be found, "disappearance of disappearance" implies that what has gone missing is Nothing – that the object of the search was always-already missing, primordially lost, embedded in negativity.

There is a remarkable passage in Bergman's *Three Strange Loves* (1949), where a psychoanalyst tries to take advantage of one of his patients, a widow affected by melancholia. Although the analyst (who is writing a book entitled 'Liberating Imagination', which projects us forward to 1968) simply wants to sleep with his patient, he makes an interesting comment. When the widow insists that her marriage was a very happy one, he retorts: 'That's an illusion you cling to. You never loved your husband, not until after his death. You've spun a coat of mail out of it. Admit that your life has been one long mistake... Wake up, woman!'

It is in this paradox of "losing a loss" that resides, Žižek (1994: 170) tells us, the 'ethical beauty' of Kieślowski's *Three Colours: Blue*, since Julie's (Julie Binoche) discovery that her dead husband had a mistress allows her to "lose" her libidinal attachment to *the loss of her husband* (and daughter), thus opening up the possibility, for her, of a new beginning, or rebirth. Kieślowski's great intuition is therefore that *it is necessary to die twice*: the first death elevates the husband into an idealised lost object, while the second "symbolic" death (the discovery of his unfaithfulness) confronts Julie with the original trauma of loss, the unbearable awareness that the other was always-already lost – and the lesson of the film is that this traumatic passage through the underlying negativity of the other *is* freedom: freedom, that is, to radically resignify one's immersion in the socio-symbolic order. To find freedom, the film's heroine has to undergo subjective destitution. When, after the tragedy, she says 'Now I have only one thing left to do: nothing. I don't want any belongings, any memories. No friends, no love. Those are all traps', she means it much more seriously than she thinks! It is not, therefore, that she cannot fully detach from the world, but rather that only this self-contraction, or "passage through zero" *qua* symbolic death, allows her to overcome fully what in psychoanalytic terms would be her attachment to the symptom, the knot of her libidinal investment in loss. *Blue*, then, tells us that through woman we connect with the non-existence of the big Other. Julie's gesture of reconciliation with Sandrine (Florence Pernel), her husband's mistress, signals the intervention of the not-all of feminine sexuality: in a way, Julie becomes a woman with this gesture, i.e. the moment she recognises that the Other was always-already dead.

A very similar conjunction of trauma, loss, and freedom is articulated in Nanni Moretti's *The Son's Room* (La stanza del figlio, 2001). Here the basic narrative situation is surprisingly similar to that of Kieślowski's film, insofar as it confronts us with a family trauma and then focuses on the nature of the lost object: who was Andrea, the teenage son in this ideal middle-class nuclear family? His sudden death produces a ghost, the immaterial, ambiguous fantasmatic image of the son which never corresponds to the real one. The point is, once again, that the real Andrea *never existed in the first place*, for his enjoyment (his relationship with Arianna, his theft of the fossil at the beginning of the film) had to be foreclosed so that the image of the angelic son could emerge within the fantasy space of the ideal family. His death therefore forces the family into the painful realisation that the son, in a way, was *primordially* missing – just like Julie's husband (*Blue*) and Henrik (*Summer Interlude*) *were already missing when they were alive*.

A wonderfully subtle exemplification of this logic can also be found in Carlos Saura's *Raise Ravens* (Cria Cuervos, 1976), Saura's last film under Franco's regime and a complex metaphorical statement about that regime's oppressive patriarchal structure. The story is told by adult Ana (Geraldine Chaplin) and reflects the tortuous swings of her imagination as a nine-year-old child. Ana remembers not only facts about her past, but also how she used to distort them, to the extent that the two identities – Ana as a mature woman and as a child – are strangely conflated. The result is an intricate narrative filled with temporal jumps (flash-backs, flash-forwards) and imagined events (particularly the child's visions of her dead mother). Despite this overlapping of different temporal layers, however, we are able to outline a relatively stable and unambiguous plot. After the premature death of her beloved mother, Ana develops a strong resentment against her authoritarian and adulterous father (a military officer under Franco), to the point that she decides to kill him by dissolving a potent poison in his glass of milk. Indeed the father dies, but as an authoritarian figure within the family he is simply replaced by Aunt Paulina. Ana's existential condition therefore does not improve, as she feels increasingly trapped and smothered within the narrow confines of her home (a clear metaphor for Franco's Spain). Consequently, she develops a strong obsession with death, not only fantasising about killing herself but also her grandmother and, crucially, Aunt Paulina.

It is precisely when she tries to poison her aunt, using the same powder she had used for her father, that the narrative uncovers its central twist, for when Aunt Paulina does *not* die, little Ana realises that she also never killed her father (in fact, he had died of a heart attack). Her magical powder was actually bicarbonate of soda; a flash-back shows how Ana's mother had playfully presented it to her as poison to tickle her imagination. This realisation works as a shock for her as it coincides with the collapse of her fantasy world. Paradoxically, however, this is also the minimally traumatic event through which she can detach from her family and, literally, move on: in the last shot of the film, Ana and her two sisters are shown as they leave their dismal environment and walk out into the vibrant and noisy city. Saura's intuition is that our will is not enough to produce change. First, we have to undergo an experience of self-contraction as a consequence of which we lose everything, *including loss*. That is to say: when Ana's powder loses its sublime/magical status, the girl effectively loses the loss of her mother. The point is that Ana's attachment to her mother, and later to her mother's loss, was the very reason why she could not break away from the family milieu. Since she had moulded her own persona on the image of her mother (Saura emphasises this by using the same actress for both the older Ana and her mother), Ana's attachment to her loss simultaneously meant attachment to Ana's own suffering position within the family. So the real problem for Ana is how to gain independence from this attachment to the mother: what she unconsciously seeks to achieve throughout the film is a distance from her. This is why it is important to stress the function of Ana's powder as *objet a*: when Ana realises that the powder is actually nothing but bicarbonate of soda, and, as it were, "does exactly what it says on the tin" (i.e., it does not kill but helps digest), what emerges is the gap between a normal object and *objet a*, the same object endowed with a sublime quality, the "bit of magic" that makes us stick to it.

Going back to Kieślowski's *Three Colours: Blue*, its great achievement is that it manages to focus with equal precision both on the question of loss and on the consequent necessary attempt on the part of the subject (Julie) to reconstitute a meaningful link with the world. Here Kieślowski applies the metaphor of cinema itself, insofar as after the accident his traumatised heroine immediately starts occupying the position of the spectator, looking at the world around her in a similar way to how the cinema-goer looks at the screen. Julie's problem is that, in order to recreate a connection with the world, that is to say a fiction with which she can identify, she has to start desiring again. And, confirming Lacan's motto that "desire is always the other's desire", she unwittingly turns into a voyeur, fascinated by the presence of enjoyment all around her. First a street-fight, which scares her but also awakens her curiosity, to the point that she ends up locked out of her flat. Resigned to spending the night on the stairs, she sees Lucille, her "loose" neighbour, as she invites the married man next door into her flat; later, she finds out that Lucille does not wear underpants and enthuses about her job as a peep-show actress. And there is also the encounter with the new-born mice that Julie discovers in her flat, and eventually of course with Florence, who is pregnant with her husband's child. All these incidents subtly mark the rebirth of Julie's desire, which is first and foremost connoted as visual desire, the pure cinematic desire to identify with a certain narrative framework. It is important to insist that as a prototypical cinematic gaze, Julie's visual desire is set in motion by the presence of *jouissance*, i.e. life-substance in its raw, throbbing, fascinating-repulsive evidence. Julie literally learns to desire, and therefore to reconnect with the world, through the other's desire. What comes to mind here is, of course, Hitchcock's *Rear Window* (1954), where Jeff (James Stewart), like Julie, finds himself occupying the place of the passive spectator who literally constructs a (crime) narrative through the sheer insistence of the act of looking into other people's lives.

6.4 Sons of a spider-God

Subjective destitution is also the central motif in Bergman's *Through a Glass Darkly* (Såsom i en spegel, 1961). As in Rossellini's *Stromboli*, here the decisive struggle is the one between Karin and God, where the female character named Karin (Ingrid Bergman in Rossellini's film, Harriet Andersson in Ingmar Bergman's) is the means through which the cracks in the big Other become apparent. Karin is affected by schizophrenia, mental disturbance being here Bergman's way of rendering the feminine potential to move *beyond* the domain of the phallus. Ultimately, Karin's condition works as a metaphor for the specific division of feminine sexuality. Emulating Anna in *The Adventure* she brings herself to identify with the rift in her sexuality, thus daring to address God's *jouissance* directly, to the dismay of the three males around her. The deadlock of sexual difference could not be more palpable. In terms of narrative development Bergman's film can be thought of as a quartet, underscored by the intermittent return of Bach's D Minor Cello Suite. It is about three men and a woman who, in the haunting opening shot, emerge from the sea like four aliens, and for the rest of the film attempt in vain to communicate. As with *The Adventure* there are boats and, more importantly, the setting is a deserted island, a place that, like deserts, empty parks and volcanoes, stands for a certain desire, to use Pasolini's words apropos his *Theorem*, to portray a 'reality/stripped of everything except its essence' (Pasolini 1968: 197).

The two older men in *Through a Glass Darkly*, Karin's father and husband, are characterised as irredeemably castrated, i.e. split between duty/work and a *jouissance* that is irretrievably lost (the impossible enjoyment of their beloved). We learn that David (Gunnar Björnstrand), a father who is now paying a visit to his son and daughter after a prolonged absence, had abandoned his terminally ill wife in order to go and finish writing his novel in Switzerland. Martin (Max Von Sydow), on the other hand, Karin's husband, is willing to sacrifice himself for his wife's sake, but he is nevertheless unable to establish a meaningful bond with her. David, particularly, epitomises the failure of the paternal metaphor. His predicament, however, is not simply a matter of lost authority and neglect towards his offspring; rather, like most male characters in Bergman and Antonioni (see for instance Sandro in *The Adventure*), his guilt ties in with his inability to cope with feminine desire. This gender-coloured deficiency is reflected in the short play his children have prepared to celebrate his return: the artist (David's alter ego, played by his son) does not have the courage to follow the dead princess (played by Karin) into eternity. If woman has an insight into eternity – the eternity of a metaphorical death *qua* lack in the Other, equivalent to Lacan's $S(\not A)$ – man is excluded from this wisdom.

Karin's younger brother Minus (Lars Passgård) is the film's third male. A typical Bergmanesque adolescent, he is striving to leave puberty behind and find a stable sexual identity, a "minus" who has not yet zeroed in on life. For this very reason he is the one character with whom Karin can at least attempt to establish a connection beyond the wall of sexual difference. The final hint at an incestuous rapport between brother and sister works precisely as a harrowing encounter with the Real of sexual difference. In this respect, Minus's words to his father apropos the incident with Karin are wonderfully eloquent: 'reality burst, and I fell out'. If the father claims that 'reality is a magic circle from which we exclude everything that might disturb our games', Minus voices the feminine position beyond the masculine urge to "draw circles", i.e. to symbolize. Again, Bergman taps into the gap of freedom, a gap whose main metaphorical rendition are the cracks in the peeling wallpaper of the attic where, from time to time, Karin absconds to talk to God; or, similarly, the cracks in the boat where she hides.

But is there a God after all? In philosophical terms, the film effects the passage from a Kantian to a Hegelian perspective, i.e. from transcendentalism to absolute immanence. From a finite perspective (Kant's phenomenal reality), God cannot fail to appear sublime; however, experienced in itself, it suddenly turns into 'a mortifying horror' (Žižek 2004: 43). Karin's realisation, the wisdom she communicates to her masculine audience of three, is that, as she puts it, 'God is a stony-faced spider' (the image of the spider-God will return in the following *Winter Lights*). As she recounts her vision, which was only *hers*, God *qua* spider tried to penetrate her but failed. Bergman tells us that the encounter with a God that has morphed into a spider is a necessary trauma, a trauma that lies in the subject's realisation – at the heart of Bergman's "Faith Trilogy" (which includes *Winter Lights* and *The Silence*) – that God is silent, indifferent. The philosophical implication is that the fracture between transcendence (the divine) and immanence (the universe of fictional appearances) *is inherent to immanence itself*, i.e. it can only materialise as the minimal difference between the appearance of our everyday world and the appearance of the residual object (*objet a*) that comes to occupy the place of the empty Thing, thus assuming all the weight of the inaccessible beyond. This transcendental beyond, therefore, should be conceived as a gap in our world of appearances. As such, the cracks in the phenomenal world correspond to both the Hegelian appearance *qua* appearance, and the Lacanian *doublure* (the redoubling of the gap between transcendence and immanence into immanence itself):

> What the object is masking, dissimulating, by its massive, fascinating presence, is not some other positivity but its own place, the void, the lack that it is filling in by its presence – the lack in the Other. And what Lacan calls "going-through the fantasy" consists precisely in the experience of such an inversion apropos of the fantasy-object: the subject must undergo the experience of how the ever-lacking object-cause of desire is in itself nothing but an objectification, an embodiment of a certain lack; of how its fascinating presence is here just to mask the emptiness of the place it occupies, the emptiness which is exactly the lack in the Other – which makes the big Other (the symbolic order) perforated, inconsistent. (Žižek 1989: 195)

The common thread in Bergman's trilogy is Christ's dramatic 'Father, why have you forsaken me?', the shocking recognition that "the big

Other does not exist". It is from this recognition that an unbearable freedom emerges. Bergman was explicit on this point, claiming that his God is 'something filled with risk for the human being and bringing out in him dark destructive forces instead of the opposite' (in Cowie 1982: 199). The overarching metaphor suggests that the wall of appearances, the terribly unsatisfactory, finite canvas of illusions epitomised by the novel that David, the neurotic father, cannot finish writing – making small changes in the night, never quite happy with the final product – can be torn down only by woman, because woman alone has access to the (lack of) *jouissance* of the Other (the sexualised God-spider). Or, even more pointedly: Karin's access to the Other's *jouissance* beyond the phallus (beyond her relationship with her husband, father, and to an extent brother) is nothing but *the way she verbalises it*. In the final analysis, it is the *jouissance* of speech, a *jouissance* that relates to a strictly feminine experience. Father and husband, whilst present in the attic, do not see anything – and nor does the audience for that matter, except for the opening of a door engulfed in darkness. This moment, we should add, is truly epiphanic, to the extent that it legitimises the trite finale where father and son manage to establish a symbolic link in language (Minus's famous final line is 'Father has talked to me'). The father's conclusive explanation that 'God is love' cannot but sound false and artificial, in a way that reminds us of some of Rossellini's finales (*Stromboli*, *Voyage to Italy*); however, as in Rossellini's case, perhaps we should read Bergman's ending as an affirmation of *the power of the negative*: it is Karin's experience of God's non-existence – her over-identification with the lack in the Other – that produces love as the irruption of freedom and change in the staleness of the family microcosm. From this viewpoint, *Through a Glass Darkly* is a wonderfully concise summa of Bergman's dark existentialism.

And can we not argue the same point apropos Bernardo Bertolucci's *The Spider's Stratagem* (La strategia del ragno, 1970)? In Bertolucci's metaphorical thriller we witness the same type of denouement: the identity of God *qua* Name-of-the-Father (Athos Magnani, played by Giulo Brogi, the resistance hero allegedly killed by the fascists) is merely the other side of the "spider" who had betrayed the plot to kill Mussolini and then artfully constructed his image as hero through the staging of his own death. The film tells us that the role of master-signifier hinges upon *the crafty concealment of its own inconsistency*, the fact that the place of its inscription is always-already empty. Although it is left to the son (Athos Magnani Jr, also played by Giulio Brogi) to unravel the "spider's stratagem", it is worth noting that the son comes to his task by responding to the call of Draifa (Alida Valli), his father's mistress. Once again, it seems, the inconsistency of the big Other is a spectacle originally reserved to woman.

6.5   Mothers everywhere!

What makes *The Silence* (Tystnaden, 1963) a radical work is, first and foremost, its resolve to do away with the issue of masculinity and place all the stakes on woman – an intention which, as we have seen, had intimately driven Bergman's cinema from its inception. The starting point for any analysis of *The Silence* (1963) must be that we are dealing with a fatherless universe. That is to say, we enter a microcosm that is not structured around the gravitational pull exerted by the phallic logic of "knowledge through exclusion". Instead, we are presented with a feminine universe characterised by the ambiguous presence of the mother–child relationship (a true obsession in Bergman's cinema). This question ties in neatly with Bergman's suggestion that the silence at stake here, as with his previous two works, is God's silence. The specificity of the setting requires us to consider the theme of the journey: at the beginning of the film the three characters enter an utterly foreign space, which they leave, bar one of them, in the last sequence. This space, the Grand Hotel Europa, is off-limits to man; he cannot legislate there. All we have are grotesque caricatures of masculinity (the dwarfs, the lover, the old maître d'hotel, etc.), while the director's attention is firmly placed on the two sisters Anna (Gunnel Lindblom) and Ester (Ingrid Thulin). The magic of the film – the same magic we find in Antonioni's best works – is that the prominence of woman "un-knots" the closure of the symbolic order, thus making it sensitive to its underlying emptiness. The microcosm of *The Silence*, in other words, is emphatically "not-all".

The decline of the paternal metaphor in Bergman is generally accompanied by an enhanced sensitivity towards the issue of motherly love, or lack of it. To say it with Lacan, 'Père, ou pire' (the father, or worse), where the *pire*, however – the prospect of a trauma associated to the mother – should be understood in connection with an instance of liberation. The child in the film, Johan (Jörgen Lindström), is Bergman's natural ally in his arduous journey towards the core of femininity, as if the director here intuits that one of the most fruitful ways to approach feminine *jouissance* is by relying upon the child's "interpreting" skills, since *jouissance* is what is at stake in the discourse that forms him. In *The Silence* the specific knot of feminine enjoyment is reflected in the child's gaze, epitomised to perfection in the opening sequence of *Persona* (1966) when Johan (the same child we see in *The Silence*) attempts to touch the interface image of Elisabet's face, presumably his mother.[23] *The Silence* makes this attempted connection absolutely central. Here, quoting Colette Soler's description of the classic ambiguity surrounding the mother–child relationship, the mother's presence

> signifies, beyond what she says – through her contradictions, her silences, her gaps, her equivocations – everything that she does not say of her desire, but that she allows the young subject's eager ears to hear. This desire may be inexpressible, but it gives itself to be read, while the opacity of jouissance, on the other hand, can only be surprised in furtively perceived scenes. In deciphering this enigma, what the child is seeking is the very place of his being and his final identification [...]. He seeks the answer to the question of what he is for the Other. Love, as much as desire, begins with a lack. (Soler 2006: 119–20)

If there is a difference between being a mother and being a woman, the child is the most reliable interpreter of this difference. In Bergman's film Johan discovers that his mother Anna is not only a source of motherly warmth but also a somewhat oversexed woman. Johan's realisation that his mother's desire is directed *also* at another object (man) opens up for him, through castration anxiety, the *prospect of subjectivisation*. The absence of the paternal metaphor, however, determines from the start of the film a series of incongruous identificatory encounters that accompany his process of self-discovery in the hotel. It is through these strange encounters that Johan begins to detach from his obsession with being his mother's love object, and slowly, laboriously, starts constructing his own sexuality. When he first leaves his room to go wandering in the labyrinthine hotel,[24] he carries a toy gun with which he threatens a man who is on a ladder, attending to the fixing of a chandelier. This typically masculine presumption of *having the phallus* (the obvious symbolism of the gun), however, turns into its flipside, i.e. castration anxiety, the moment he sees the maître d'hotel playing with a sausage and then snapping its head off with his teeth. Significantly, the encounter with the Spanish dwarfs ends with their attempt at dressing him up as a woman, another hint that the struggle for sexual identity has only just started and promises to be a challenging one.

Johan's perception of his mother changes drastically the moment he sees her entering a hotel room with the unknown waiter she had picked up on one of her escapades in town. Undoubtedly, this is the time

Anna goes from being "too-motherly" to being "too-womanly" for him, prompting his decisive entrance into the symbolic order of language. As Lacan claims in his unpublished *Seminar IV* (1956–57), the trauma triggered by the encounter with the "obscene" otherness of Mother is therefore a necessary one for the child if he is to affirm his identity in language. Especially in the case of a fatherless condition, the mother–child libidinal bond has to be broken to avoid not only anxiety but also psychotic repercussions on the child. Once the mother becomes "partially absent" to the child by endorsing her desire, the child needs to symbolise this loss, which is what the ending of the film alludes to: Johan enters the order of language *thanks* to the division he comes across in his mother's *jouissance*. Had he not perceived such division, he would have been trapped in the dangerous illusion of being the phallus for the mother's desire (since anxiety arises when the child/subject is confronted with the difference between his imaginary status as loved object and the rather less exciting truth about what he really has to offer to the mother/other). Ultimately, the problem for Johan is how to give up his position as imaginary phallus.

While the Oedipal question in Bergman's film is never fully developed, a number of European films have caused scandal by confronting the subject head-on, failing to grasp the significance of the link between repression (castration) and symbolisation in the context of the mother–child relationship. Louis Malle's *Murmur of the Heart* (Le souffle au coeur, 1971), for instance, offers an interesting variation on the theme of motherly love. Here the consistency of the bond uniting Laurent (Benoît Ferreux) and his mother Clara (Lea Massari) culminates in a typically Oedipal scenario of incest, although presented as a kind of accident and eventually purged of its traumatic content (the film itself has a comedy feel about it). The father is present, but rather as an insignificant, stolid figure. The mother, Italian, is a free-spirited woman connected with the sexual liberation mood of the time, although the film is set in the 1950s. She is not interested in her older husband and remorselessly embarks on extramarital affairs. By treating the theme of incest as a strangely natural culmination of maternal love,[25] Malle provocatively targets the ultimate sexual taboo of a post-1968 society that had just proclaimed itself "sexually liberated". However, the film's failure lies precisely in what I am tempted to call a "utopian gentrification" of what is *the* fundamentally traumatic event. Malle, fascinated by 1968 utopianism, as well as by Georges Bataille's apology of excess, goes beyond Bergman's various references to the ambiguity of motherly love and yet misses the target by, as it were, aiming at it too directly. What he misses is that the moment the fantasy (of incest) collapses in the Real (of *jouissance*), there can only be one, very disturbing, outcome.

Malle's point about incest is reworked, very sensationally, by Christophe Honoré in *Ma Mère* (2004), which this time is directly based on Bataille's unfinished novella of the same name. After the death of her husband, Hélène (Isabelle Huppert), initiates her teenage son Pierre (Louis Garrel) to a series of increasingly depraved sexual experiences, which culminate with her death and the scene of Pierre masturbating by her corpse (a kind of virtual necrophilia). The taboo that *Ma Mère* sets out to pulverise is not so much incest but the masculine fantasy that "mother is pure". The Isabelle Huppert character's bottomless debauchery is deliberately staged for the gaze of her confused son, whose reaction, however, cannot but appear implausible and misplaced. Instead of gaining a distance from mother, as Johan does in *The Silence*, here the son develops a morbid, properly perverse, attraction to her. Finally there is Bernardo Bertolucci's *La luna* (1979), where the incestuous fervour of Caterina (Jill Clayburgh), is aimed at saving Joe (Matthew Barry), her son, from his heroin addiction (in the infamous climactic passage, she masturbates him to try and wean him off the drug). Again, the father is absent, dead; and again, the problem with the film is that it regards incest as the solution to the boy's anxiety rather than as the very (imaginary) feature which causes anxiety.

In relation to the figure of the mother, Ophuls' excellent noir *The Reckless Moment* (1949), set in American upper-middle-class suburbia, explores the shift from sacrifice to symbolic castration. To preserve her family's comfortable and dignified life in Balboa, California, Lucia Harper (Joan Bennett), a housewife, decides to confront the seedy Ted Darby (Shepperd Strudwick), an ex-art dealer who seduced Lucia's young daughter Bea (Geraldine Brooks) and now demands money to disappear from the scene. When Darby, after a violent quarrel with Bea by her house, topples off the small pier and onto a submerged anchor, the modest housewife is suddenly faced by the distressing prospect of dealing with his dead body. As in Hitchcock's *Rope* (1948) and *The Trouble with Harry* (1955), the trouble *is* the dead body, insofar as it stands for the excess that needs to be eliminated if the smooth economy of the symbolic order is to be preserved. What does this imply for the maternal figure, the unassuming middle-class housewife whose main concerns had so far been shopping and supervising the running of the house? In the protracted absence of the husband, she turns into the active force that protects the family microcosm, the very fiction upon which her identity is constructed. The transformation she experiences is clear: from sacrifice (the mother/wife who remains aloof, in the shadow, sacrificing herself for husband and family) to castration (the endorsement of a traumatic loss as a necessary event to establish symbolic efficiency). But are we really dealing with a transformation here? The point is rather that Lucia's second subject position brings out the repressed truth of the first: mother actually enjoys! The scene where Lucia drags Darby's dead body along the shore before lifting it on to a small boat and dropping it into a swamp is truly masterful in stressing how Lucia has stepped into overdrive. This is confirmed by Ophuls' consummated decision to reduce sound to a bare minimum in this scene, thus emphasising how Lucia experiences a kind of psychotic disconnection from her environment. A question immediately crops up: would the husband have behaved in the same way? Would he have chosen the same risky option? To avoid pointless conjecturing, let us merely observe Ophuls' obvious fascination with the reckless *jouissance* mobilised by this woman as she shifts into "maternal overdrive". The film is effectively about the disturbing excess of enjoyment incarnated by Lucia, which comes to over-determine every aspect of her life, as for example her immoderate smoking.[26]

In comparison to the excess Lucia stands for, the James Mason character of Martin Donnolly, the small-time Irish crook who sacrifices himself for Lucia (for he sees in her an emblem of the family values he never had), is a rather meek figure. If, as Žižek suggests, '[s]acrifice is a guarantee that "the other exists"; that there is an other who can be appeased by the act of sacrifice' (Žižek 2001b: 56), then this definition applies to Mason and his final immolation rather than to Lucia, since what emerges in her behaviour is not so much sacrifice for a cause (the efficiency of the big Other), but rather the excess of drive: the enjoyment involved in her being caught in the loop of repetition, i.e. in the series of unsuccessful attempts she makes to break out of the terrible mess she has got into. With Lucia we can grasp the difference between desire and drive. If her "official" desire is to restore family order, ultimately what emerges through drive is the disturbing enjoyment she experiences at missing the target, at realising that *there is no such thing as family order* (the fiction is always-already empty). This is what her final lines mean: as she speaks to her husband on the phone, after normality at home has been restored, she alludes to the fact that they all desperately need him to be there. Why? If there is anything she is still scared of, and needs to be protected from, it is nothing other than her own excessive enjoyment.

We meet another formidable mother in Bergman's *Autumn Sonata* (Höstsonaten, 1978), a narrative that builds up to a memorable confrontation between mother and daughter in the middle of the night – a confrontation that may well be dreamed rather than actually happening, but for this very reason, as always in Bergman, even more Real. Charlotte (Ingrid Bergman) is a self-obsessed pianist who has consistently neglected her two daughters Eva (Liv Ullman) and Helena (Lena Nyman), indirectly causing the latter's disease. Now she pays a visit to them in Eva's country home, hoping perhaps to make amends. But as Eva's attachment to her turns into hatred and despair,[27] she remains a woman, by choice and by need unable to resolve the conflict between her role as a mother and her dedication to her career, her enjoyment of power, her fame. In the memorable finale, with Charlotte on a train travelling back from her visit, accompanied by her new partner Paul (Gunnar Björnstrand) – as idiotic as most masculine figures in Bergman – the mother is back to her old self, after we had been led to believe that she might have repented and changed. Driven as usual, she comments to Paul that she has always missed being at home, but once she is there, she immediately misses being away. If there is something obscene, immoral, and most of all *dangerous* about this mother, it is the very drive she stands for. Eva's final letter to Charlotte, in typical Bergman fashion, leaves some room for the proverbial ray of hope; it is, however, only a small consolation, which does little to diminish the shattering impact with the Real of femininity. Like Anna in *The Silence*, or Monika in *Summer with Monika*, Charlotte typifies Bergman's fascination with women who are *more than mothers* – with women, in other words, who materialise feminine enjoyment in what we might call a Medea-like drive *beyond* the family.[28]

6.6   On erectile tissue and bodily secretions

According to the standard critical reading of *The Silence*, Anna and Ester are two sides of the same coin, two halves of the same being: the physical and the spiritual, the body and the soul. Anna is defined almost entirely through her physicality, the voluptuousness of her body. We see her wash, anoint herself with perfume and lotions, get dressed and undressed, watch others have sex, have sex. Ester, on the contrary, belongs fully in language, in symbolic exchange, although, paradoxically, her wretchedness derives from her incapability to communicate. She is a translator, constantly surrounded by paper, pens and typewriter, but her words fall into a void. Excessive drinking, smoking and masturbation, in Bergman, are invariably symptomatic of a failure of the basic mechanism in the subject's division that regulates symbolic stability. Her lack of enjoyment is counterbalanced by the imposing presence of Anna, no doubt one of cinema's most successful embodiments of unfettered libidinal drive. Bergman's symbolism could not be any clearer: while Anna, pure enjoyment, is healthy and almost oversexed, Ester suffers from tuberculosis and thinks of sex only as a disgusting matter of "erectile tissue and secretions". She hangs on to words, although her only successful communicative act takes place on her deathbed, when Johan, understandably disappointed by mother, turns to her for comfort. The more she represses enjoyment the more she slides towards self-destruction.

It is here that we should radicalise the interpretation. The advantage of a psychoanalytic reading is that it shows the extent to which these two sides are actually interdependent. If the two female figures can be seen as standing for Bergman's desperate attempt to come to terms with the unreachable otherness of woman, they should not be seen as masculine constructions. The most remarkable event in Bergman's cinema is that, although it cannot but start from conceiving woman as a masculine fantasy, it also manages to encroach upon the feminine stance that Lacan has captured with the formula S(Ⱥ). If Ester, claustrophobically locked in her rancid self-awareness and frigidity, gives body to an extreme manifestation of the barred subject ($), totally and irredeemably castrated, Anna, on the other extremity, has seemingly "cancelled her subscription to the unconscious" and become a continuous outburst of enjoyment. While Ester only exists in language, unable to "enjoy" the exception upon which her position is based, Anna would seem to materialise the painfully liberating endorsement of "enjoyment in language".

The film lends itself to be read according to Lacan's interpretation of Freud's motto *Wo Es war, soll Ich werden*: the self must come to be where the unconscious is, it must attempt to disturb the fantasmatic kernel of fundamentally disavowed enjoyment that an unconscious desire always-already is. In this respect, Žižek argues that the unconscious should not simply be described as an 'objective mechanism that regulates my phenomenal experience', but, more accurately, as the very *fundamental fantasy* of the subject, a place occupied by 'an excessive, nonsignifiable, erotic fascination and attachment' which, because of its inaccessibility, deprives the subject of its most intimate self-experience (Žižek 2004: 96–7). And my point is that the key Lacanian notion of fundamental fantasy designates precisely the deepest, albeit unconscious, kernel of libidinal attachment that explains Ester's position vis-à-vis Anna. Put differently, Anna *is* Ester's fundamental fantasy, the obscene fantasmatic kernel which is "in herself more than herself", and that for this very reason *she can confront only at the price of her subjective destitution*. The standard critical view according to which the film shows us two opposite and indeed conflicting "types" of women needs therefore to be rectified. We do not merely have a rational and decaying woman against another woman impersonating sheer sensuality. If it were the case, Bergman's choice to side with Anna would indeed smack of reactionary "body politics". I do not think, in other words, that *The Silence* should be seen simplistically as a "revenge-of-the-body" type of narrative, for what we witness is the complex metaphorical struggle endured by the subject who knows that, in order to regenerate itself, it has to face the core of its own being, the repressed libidinal attachment responsible for its symbolic existence. Only in this way are we able to fully make sense of the surprising finale. If there is hope in Ester's exchange with Johan, it is firmly rooted in her previous painful confrontation with Anna *qua* Ester's own fundamental fantasy. The message carried by the little boy is simply the consequence of such an encounter.

Here, again, we should highlight Bergman's preoccupation with isolating femininity as an object of both desire and intellectual analysis. In this sense, the setting is the most indicative point of reference we have, for the Grand Hotel Europa, where most of the action takes place, is a striking metaphor for the universe of femininity that fascinates the director's gaze. What is left of masculinity in the Hotel is the slightly demented maître d'hotel and a few other insignificant characters – including, for that matter, Anna's lover, who is simply a pawn in her struggle with Ester. Because the Grand Hotel Europa is bereft of masculinity, Bergman is free to "enjoy" his women. And he does so by attempting to come to terms with that disturbing image of the "mother-*jouisseuse*" that evidently sustains his own vision of womanhood. One cannot avoid the feeling that, in *The Silence*, Bergman is both honest and uncompromising in allowing the character of Anna to take centre stage and eventually destroy her rational double. In Anna's triumph we read Bergman's understanding of sexual difference as a desperate, ultimately unsuccessful attempt to define himself through the feminine other. The central paradox of sexual difference is that every effort to define ourselves depends on our ability to define the sexed other. For Bergman, femininity is the traumatic foreign intruder he has to confront in order to define his own self.

This consideration also leads us to the oft-mentioned question of Bergman's humanism. Robin Wood, amongst others, has argued that, despite its bleakness and cruelty, Bergman's cinema is permeated by a profoundly humanist vision. Along these lines, one of the most insightful comments on Bergman has come from Kieślowski (2000: 423), who apropos *The Silence* has argued the following:

> Throughout this dark, bleak, fearsomely sad film – outside its action and utterances – there pulses a tiny groundless flame of hope. I know where the bright trace comes from in this dark film. From Bergman's profound belief in humanity, even where circumstances or feelings compel the protagonists to be cruel and ruthless. To aver that the hope is associated with little Johan (Jörgen Lindström) – with the presence of the child – would be too facile. [...] It would be even more inappropriate to discern it in the figure of the old maître d'hotel (Håkan Jahnberg), who helps the sick Ester, brings her vodka and food, wipes the sweat from her face and plays with Johan. No, the hope in this film – invisible but ever-present – is hidden much deeper. It is in Ester's delicate, actually fleeting gesture as she watches Anna (Gunnel Lindblom) sleeping naked, with little Johan snuggled up to her, and suspends her hand in mid-air, then withdraws it, fearing to stroke her sister: fearing a gesture that would indicate feeling. It is surely that. Is it love? Yes.

On this point, however, I would simply disagree. The trace of humanism Kieślowski sees in Bergman is of the same kind one can detect in his own work, i.e. a thin layer of hope camouflaging the inevitable collision with the Real. What is normally missed is that negativity is *not* the other pole of humanism in Bergman; it is rather its truth, the truth merely concealed by the very mask of humanism. The price one pays by insisting on the humanist reading is the failure to recognise the opposite strategy, i.e. Bergman's deep-seated awareness that the inhuman, even the monstrous dimension in the human being, needs to be confronted if there is to be change.[29] It is not accidental that the inhuman returns forcefully in many of Bergman's later works, such as, most explicitly, *The Shame* (Skammen, 1968), *The Hour of the Wolf* (Wargtimmen, 1968), and *The Serpent's Egg* (1977), which can legitimately be regarded as horror films. In *The Silence*, then, the turning point is the paradoxical coincidence of inhumanity and freedom, insofar as it is only by playing the card of unredeemable *jouissance* that Bergman turns Anna into an ethical character: a mother who does not give up on her desire. If, as Kieślowski remarks, there is hope in *The Silence*, it is nevertheless the hope inscribed in the hopelessness so wonderfully crystallised in Anna's behaviour, her strange tendency towards self-degradation which signals the triumph of "pure life" over stale rationality. It would be a mistake to perceive this triumph as reactionary irrationalism. Ultimately, Anna is the very limit dimension Ester has to face in order to die and, metaphorically, be reborn: 'erectile tissue and bodily secretions' – Ester's own horrified definition of sex. We should read this phrase alongside Freud's dream of Irma's throat, as the horrible, palpitating life-substance that secretly subtends and traverses desire. Bergman argues for the way of the flesh, but only insofar as the flesh is understood to be Real. With Anna, desire turns into drive, into a disturbing necessity to enjoy beyond the pleasure principle. It is in this horrifying compulsion which delineates the loop of *jouissance* that we should find the properly ethical value of Bergman's film. Ester's journey of self-destruction, as the unbearable realness of her fundamental fantasy approaches, is simultaneously a profoundly happy event.

The scene of the two sisters' hateful confrontation, after Anna's copulation with the bartender, is probably the key passage in the film. It is here that Ester comes face to face with what is in her more than herself, the disgusting stuff of enjoyment that she is not able to assume as her own. To understand how far she is from Anna, let us recall the previous scene where the latter, alone, goes meandering in the foreign city, witnesses a scene of sex in the theatre which clearly disturbs her, and then, instead of recoiling, embarks blindly, like an automaton, on a search for something that might tame her libido. During the brief walk through the city crowded with unknown men, we are reminded of Lidia's solitary walk in *The Night*, or Séverine as she sleepwalks towards the brothel in *Belle de jour*. Anna's silent endorsement of her libido is what profoundly perturbs and at the same time magnetically attracts Ester, who in fact cannot keep from eavesdropping and eventually breaking in on Anna and her lover. In a way, the beauty of this confrontation is that it is presented as staged, pre-arranged – Anna's kisses to her lover are not spontaneous ones but aimed at hurting Ester. Contrary to the theme of incommunicability that runs through the film, everything takes place in language here, similarly to the previous dialogue when Anna lied to Ester about her sexual encounters. We are uncannily alerted to the fact that real sex to Anna is merely a means to obtain a higher form of enjoyment, which implies its staging, the pleasure of telling her sister about it. Man, in the meantime, is as usual relegated to a prop, an idiot who is unable to understand or indeed participate in the dispute of these two formidable women. Again, we should highlight how the confrontation implies some kind of distorted reflection: Ester sees in Anna the object in her that she cannot subjectivise.

6.7   Persona on the couch

In Lacan, as we have seen, "not-whole" (*pas-tout*) means that woman is not defined by the phallic function, and yet, unlike man, she is capable of total over-identification with the symbolic order. It is through woman as *pas-tout* that we should enter the *Persona* universe. The film is fully immersed in feminine enjoyment. As with *The Silence*, it centres on two women, each one wearing a mask (persona). That is to say, it reflects on the existentialist topic of the "mask of the self", which in psychoanalytic terms concerns our identity *qua* imaginary symbolic construction, the fantasy of what we are (the story we tell ourselves about ourselves). There is a conventional mask (Alma, played by Bibi Andersson), and one that denotes intellectual awareness (Elisabet Vogler, played by Liv Ullmann). At the heart of the existentialist tradition so dear to Bergman there is, of course, the enormous enjoyment drawn from a relentless probing of the "hard-wearing" of the mask, of its malleability and consistence. The true testament to this sensibility, however, is to be found in the angst-filled curiosity that accompanies any philosophical venture into the "secret substance" guarded by the mask that each of us needs to wear.

The critical accounts of *Persona* generally miss the significance of its dominant feature: the coincidence of the existentialist quest with the question of femininity. The first thing to reckon with is that in Bergman's universe the cracking of the mask is a purely feminine affair. Those readers who saw and continue to see *Persona* as a story of vampirism risk overlooking its intrinsic political point about the necessity to adopt the feminine stance "beyond the phallus". The two women are not enemies, but accomplices, and the ultimate purpose of their invisible deal is, in Lacanese, to erase the dividing line between Imaginary and Real. What is more, they are Bergman's accomplices: Alma and Elisabet translate Bergman's desire to adopt the feminine gaze in order to try and ascertain what happens once the mask is torn down.[30]

In the most famous shot of the film, Alma's and Elisabet's faces merge into a single distorted image whose elementary function is, it would seem, to capture woman's position "beyond the phallus". This puzzling image, which eludes the standard masculine fantasy about woman, is the key to the entire narrative, as well as its structural core. Let us briefly recall its genealogy. To start with, it concerns the physical similarity between two women. In an interview with Stig Björkman, Bergman recalls that the original idea for the film was related to the following chance encounter: 'One day I suddenly saw in front of me two women sitting next to each other and comparing hands with one another. I thought to myself that one of them is mute and the other speaks' (in Cowie 1982: 228). There are other anecdotes concerning the birth of *Persona*, the most famous of which claims that Liv Ullmann had been introduced to Bergman by Bibi Andersson on a street corner, and at that moment the director was struck by the physical similarity between the two. Whatever the case, these tales seem to confirm the well-known wisdom that a film begins with an isolated, recurrent image which, as it were, becomes so insistent as to demand to be inserted into a narrative. The basic function of the narrative is precisely that of limiting the disturbing effect of this obsessive fantasy. The more obsessive the fantasy, the more necessary the intervention of a storyline. Arguably, the fantasy at stake has to do with the prospect of going beyond the protective wall of the face/mask *qua* imaginary identification to expose, in Deleuze words, 'a nudity of the face much greater than that of the body, an inhumanity much greater than that of animals'. Deleuze's commentary on this shot, which is part of his wider analysis of Bergman's use of the close-up as affection-image, is worth quoting in full:

The close-up has merely pushed the face to those regions where the principle of individuation ceases to hold sway. They are not identical because they resemble each other, but because they have lost individuation no less than socialisation and communication. This is the operation of the close-up. The close-up does not divide one individual, any more than it reunites two: it suspends individuation. Then the single and ravaged face unites a part of one to a part of the other. At this point it no longer reflects or feels anything, but merely experiences a mute fear. It absorbs two beings, and absorbs them in the void. And in the void it is itself the photogramme which burns, with Fear as its only affect. The facial close-up is both the face and its effacement. Bergman has pushed the nihilism of the face the furthest, that is its relationship in fear to the void or the absence, the fear of the face confronted with its nothingness. In a whole section of his work Bergman reaches the extreme limit of the affection-image, he burns the icon, he consumes and extinguishes the face as certainly as Beckett. (Deleuze 1986: 102)

Deleuze argues that Bergman's shot brings about loss of individuation, therefore fulfilling the director's desire to expose the fearfully empty framework of the subject.[31] The result obtained by this shot is a woman's face which is both endowed with beauty (fitting the imaginary coordinates of a story about two fascinating feminine faces), and Real (insofar as it is also, as Deleuze points out, a violently distorted image, asymmetrical, minimally and yet profoundly dissimilar from how we are meant to perceive it). As Žižek (2001b: 140) claims apropos Virginia Woolf's face, anamorphosis and sublimity are linked. Bergman's nihilism would then seem to emerge by striking a fine balance between an imaginary identification that verges on the sublime and the grimace of the Real obtained through anamorphosis. The point, which accounts for the parallel with *The Silence*, is that the void of the face mentioned by Deleuze does not appear as a horrifying/disgusting abyss, but as the almost unnoticeable rift between the sublime perception of woman and her underlying dysfunctionality. More than a 'monstrous double' which may lead us to regard the film 'as a kind of modernist horror movie' (Michaels 2000: 17), the composite image of two faces dwells *in between* beauty and horror, in a liminal location that can only be described as a curvature of space: *objet a* in all its devastating ambiguity. Ultimately, the split-face image signifies the trace of absence (*objet a*) that the subject always-already is, its basic impasse. This is how Bergman (and Antonioni) manages to radicalise the modernist premises of his work: the limit is not the meaninglessness of the world perceived by the subject, but the void of the subject itself, its constitutive "absence to itself". The film's finale would seem to confirm this reading: back in the hospital, Alma asks her patient to repeat after her the word 'Nothing'. If this word can be taken as proof that Bergman, as he himself admitted, could not solve the problems raised by the film, on the other hand it also points to the crucial dimension touched upon by the narrative, the self-relating negativity of the subject.

To investigate the second key aspect of the film, let us now draw on another famous anecdote regarding its conception. In April 1965, exhausted and ill, Bergman decided to book himself into a Stockholm clinic. There, the pressing fantasy about the two women encouraged him to start working on the script of *Persona* which, as he stated later, simply "saved his life". What saved his life, we might speculate, was the silence sombrely engraved in the film itself. In 1965 Bergman tried to imagine what the character of Elizabet Vogler might have written in her diary. He wrote the following: 'There was only one way I could avoid a state of despair and breakdown. To be silent. And to reach behind the silence for clarity or at least try to collect the resources that might still be available to me' (Bergman 1995: 59–60). Silence, as already in previous works, is not merely conceived as the symptom of a profound malaise or neurosis, but actually as *the only possible way out of it*. Whether the "silence of God" or Elisabet's own choice, the silence Bergman tries to invest with cinematic dignity is part of a strategy to break out of an existential stalemate. It is in other words an absolutely necessary silence, which alone may lead to salvation through regeneration. It is, furthermore, a feminine silence that emanates directly from *jouissance*. This is why, as I shall argue below, one of the ways to understand Elizabet's role is by positing that it coincides with that of the analyst. In *Persona* she comes to occupy the position of the analyst as theorised by Lacan, for her silence 'begins to break down Alma's defenses at once' (Wood 1969: 58), driving the latter to confront what was buried inside herself.

That Elisabet metaphorically turns into an analyst, insofar as her silence stimulates the analysand's (Alma's) identification with her symptom, would seem to be confirmed in what is perhaps the most surprising moment in the film, Elisabet's mocking of Alma's "orgy story" in a letter to her psychiatrist. The function of this letter is double: firstly, as it is read by Alma it takes us closer to her enjoyment, since the cruel form of her revenge (hurting Elisabet's foot with broken glass) effectively subverts her ethical role as a caring nurse; secondly, from Elisabet's perspective, it advises us not to take her neurosis too seriously. Perhaps this is what the psychiatrist has in mind when, at the start, she tells Elisabet that her silence is itself a 'role' – not necessarily the narcissistic or arrogant pose implied by her choice, but rather the role of the analyst. As Wood (1969: 60) suggests, we should focus on 'Elisabet's ambiguous smile when Anna at last breaks', for it is a smile that denotes a consciousness much more rigorous than most critics are prepared to endow her with. At times, she is of course deeply affected by Alma's personal crisis. But is this not a classic example of counter-transference? According to the Lacanian understanding of transference, the analyst's role is to sit in as a silent cause for a desire that only the patient is aware of, and which he or she will discover in the time it takes to unravel repressed traumas and impasses. During treatment, the analysand transfers expectations for help on to the analyst, believing that the latter knows how to access his or her psychological domain. The ultimate goal of transference, however, is to undermine the illusion that the analyst possesses a stable base for knowledge, showing how lack is ontological, as it already affects the domain of the analyst. Counter-transference, on the other hand, can be defined as a disturbance of the analyst's normal work caused by his or her own neurotic excesses, normally as a reaction to the analysand's emotional responses. As is well known, Lacan placed great importance on counter-transference, whereas Freud tended to consider it as a danger to be avoided.

From this angle Elisabet's role appears structurally homologous to that of the Terence Stamp character in Pasolini's *Theorem*. Through their silence both characters occupy the position of the "subject supposed to know", forcing the other to face up to their repressed "knots of enjoyment". In *Persona*, we have the famous passage where, during a rainy evening and after a few drinks, Alma tells Elisabet about her participation in an impromptu beach orgy which, although it implied her betrayal of fiancé Karl-Henrick, provided the best sexual experience of her life. Most commentators agree that this is one of the most erotic scenes in world cinema, its powerful sensuality springing from the purely fantasmatic status of the promiscuous events: it simply relies on words, it shows nothing. Elisabet, Alma's silent audience, occupies the position of the analyst. More insightfully, Alma's fantasy leads us directly to feminine *jouissance*, insofar as it is grounded in the inconsistency of language *qua* symbolic order; her narration, in other words, provides evidence for the fact that the communicative field is permanently penetrated by enjoyment, which is precisely what makes it not-all.[32] This is also why the passage does not hide any lesbian subtext, a point that Žižek (2006c: 190) argues apropos Anne Fontaine's *Nathalie* (1999), which involves a similar link between two women:

> The trap to avoid here, however, is to read this intense relationship between the two women as (implicitly) lesbian: it is crucial that the narrative they share is heterosexual, and it is no less crucial that all they share is a narrative. There is no "frustration" in it, no sacrificial renunciation of consummating their relationship "in the flesh", their conversation is not a foreplay endlessly postponing full satisfaction. All the speculation about the lesbian subtext, about the feminine bond excluding the man, and so on, is superfluous here – it merely distracts us from perceiving the crucial role of the fact that the two women realise their link at the level of "mere words", that their *jouissance* is the *jouissance* of the Other through and through.

Bergman both confirmed and refined this reading by commenting on Bibi Andersson's extraordinary monologue: she 'makes the scene so remarkable because she tells the story in a voice which carries a tone of shameful lust, and I've no idea where she got it from' (in Kaminsky 1975: 59). Here we touch on the previously discussed Lacanian topic of voice as love object, the intangible objectification of enjoyment that leads us directly to the Real. Again, we should note the coincidence of enjoyment and "mere words", the overlapping of the traumatic Real and the symbolic network of language captured by feminine desire. It is crucial to acknowledge that Alma's story involves the return of some long disavowed scene. Just before she begins recounting it, she tells her interlocutor that she has never betrayed her fiancé; then, by the end, when she admits to the exceptional pleasure she derived from the orgy, her face is locked in a mixture of terror and excitement, which resolves itself in a liberating burst of tears in Elisabet's arms.

Later, the same coincidence of language and *jouissance* (pleasure in displeasure and vice versa) connotes the two characters' excruciating double confrontation about their failures to fulfil the role of mother, which culminates in the split-face image. As Alma tells Elisabet that she is merely playing the role of the mother, while deep down she hates her child (presumably, the boy we see at the beginning of the film), 'with his thick mouth and ugly body', the actress is overwhelmed by a feeling of horror. Indeed, it is in the non-symbolisable core of Elisabet's libido ('you wished the baby would be dead') that the Lacanian subject emerges in its acephalous monstrosity. That Alma's monologue is repeated immediately after, with the camera now framing her face, suggests that, in line with what I have argued above, we have moved beyond symbolic or imaginary identification and fully entered the Real of feminine enjoyment, for Alma's desperate 'No! I'm not like you, I don't feel like you! I am Sister Alma, I am not Elisabet Vogler!' amounts to a last-ditch attempt to preserve her motherly role (nurse) and avoid the encounter with the Real. Alma's problem here is her painful realisation that "she is in her more than herself", for what she says about Elisabet is most importantly true about her persona: her own *jouissance*, already surfaced in the "orgy sequence", now returns to explode her belief in her symbolic role. (Let us not forget that the beach orgy had ended with her pregnancy and subsequent decision to have an abortion). With Alma's shock-realisation that she is a Woman, we can also add that the analytic treatment has run its course.

It is perhaps starting from this reading that we should tackle the film's experimental quality. What if the many modernist features of the film – such as the difficulty to differentiate between what is imagined and what actually occurs; the strong reliance on space and time discontinuity; the constant mixing of different points of view; the many disruptions to the linearity of the narrative, and so on – are not necessarily the outcome of the film's self-referential intention, but rather the

236 Sexual Difference in European Cinema

result of its deliberate immersion in feminine *jouissance*? What if the systematic thwarting of narrative consistency is less the effect of the then fashionable incorporation of self-reflexive concerns than the non-negotiable formal appearance of the feminine not-all? The modernist incident of the projector's breakdown, half-way through the film, begs the following, if naive, question: did Bergman really need to insert it? Is it not a rather clumsy and ultimately unsuccessful intervention aimed at stressing beyond necessity what is already included in the narrative? Furthermore, does film really need to make us aware of its intrinsic constraints, if we believe in it anyway, despite knowing full well that it is just a fiction? My reading suggests that *contrasting fiction and reality is misleading*, for Bergman's ultimate aim is *not* that of stressing how fiction is unable to capture reality. Quite on the contrary, fiction for him is the only instrument we have to access the Real, the imaginary illusion which is in representation more than representation. Let us take the incident of Elisabet's visit to Alma's room at night – did it really happen? It is wrong to pose the question in terms of dream vs (narrative) reality. Rather, the terms to be opposed are fiction and Real, for we are on the side of Alma's unconscious desire, which is absolutely Real and cannot but concern the analyst: Alma "wants" Elisabet, is fascinated by her silence, to the point that her resentment is the other side of her attraction to her. Similarly, when Alma makes love to Elisabet's blind husband (Gunnar Björnstrand), we are within the Real of Alma's dream, a spectacle staged for Elisabet's eyes only.

Conclusion

In retrospect, the films or cinematic fragments I have discussed in this book can be seen to have a common feature: they all say what they do not mean to say, what eludes their desire to signify reality – but they say it nevertheless, with the strength that comes with obsession and hopeless fascination. As a matter of fact, if there is hope in communication, indeed if communication sometimes magically succeeds, it is because we somehow manage to see through the message we receive from the other and, for the most part unintentionally, locate the excessive enjoyment that "stains" it.

I have focused on enjoyment because it is the key category in Lacanian psychoanalysis, the disavowed substance around which not only films, but our lives and subjectivities are woven. Lacan's enjoyment is properly undead, indestructible, like those cartoon characters whose infinite plasticity miraculously returns them to life after terrible calamities. The more we attempt to get rid of *jouissance* the more it pops up, derailing our illusion of a peaceful and pleasurable existence. In its uncanny density, *jouissance* will not simply disappear, like the proverbial dead body in many a Hitchcock film, or – to take a more pertinent European example – the dead man in Henri-Georges Clouzot's *Les diaboliques* (1955). In fact, if Hitchcock's ultimate lesson is that the corpse *must* at some point disappear (i.e., the excess of libido has to be tamed, at least minimally repressed, if we are to maintain a veneer of sanity), Clouzot's film goes a step further in showing us that it is never really gone.

Michel Delassalle (Paul Meurisse), a sadistic boarding school headmaster, and his bitter mistress Nicole (Simone Signoret) orchestrate a diabolical strategy (which of course is revealed to us only at the end) to eliminate Michel's wife Christina Delassalle (Vera Clouzot). First, Nicole approaches Christina suggesting a plan to kill the brutish husband; after the plan is executed, however, the husband's corpse mysteriously vanishes from the swimming pool where it had been provisionally hidden. Christina, who suffers from a weak heart, becomes increasingly anxious about the whole affair, and when one night Michel reappears in the guise of a ghost (he had never been killed in the first place), she finally topples over... Contrary to the classic Hitchcock situation, what we have here is not the necessary (however problematic) disappearance of the dead body, but *the return of a body that was never dead*. The point to note is that apart from being lethal, Michel is properly undead; more precisely, as a promiscuous and vicious *jouisseur*, he embodies to perfection Lacan's lamella, the organ-libido that refuses domestication. And in its deepest configuration, the Lacanian subject coincides with this undead object *qua* materialised *jouissance*.

From this perspective, the enjoyment I have referred to in this book amounts to a kind of "imp of the perverse": it is a dimension "beyond the good" – beyond any utilitarian logic or principle – and as such it cannot but appear as a devilish curse, a destabilising surplus of sense that suddenly emerges as an alien injunction, radically divorced from our familiar horizon of meaning. With regard to this definition of enjoyment as a disturbing surplus, the ultimate intention of this book – in conformity with the ultimate lesson of Lacanian psychoanalysis – is to show that, precisely as a curse, *jouissance* needs to be confronted if we are to envisage or promote change in the basic coordinates of our lives. Lacan's lesson (an eminently *political* lesson) is that radical change in the symbolic order is never the effect of understanding alone; rather, it requires us to shift the goalposts of our enjoyment, to reconfigure the unreflected, mostly disavowed modalities of our libido – in short, to intervene at the level of the Real.

Throughout this book I have tried to express this necessity to face the objectively other, strictly speaking inhuman core of enjoyment by investigating sexual difference as one of the most accessible contexts in which Lacan unravels the meaning(s) of the Real. The Real of sexual difference as reflected in post-war European cinema can be summarised as the persistence of the impossibility of the sexual relationship over its fragile actualisations in fantasy and desire – something which European cinema has long learned to capitalise on. In Part I, the deadlock of sexual difference has been described mainly in connection with the inadequacies of masculine desire, with the emphasis falling on the old European tradition of courtly love; in Part II, it has emerged through the complex casuistry of feminine enjoyment, with particular attention to the thorny issue of its supposed division between two objects: the phallus and the big Other.

The main ambiguity at stake in Lacan's definition of sexual difference pertains indeed to femininity and can be summed up with the following overarching question: is feminine enjoyment Real insofar as it is beyond speech, and thus resists symbolisation, as Bruce Fink (see Fink 1995: 107) and most of Lacan's commentators have it? Against this persuasion, Žižek holds that Lacan identifies feminine enjoyment with the *jouissance* of speech, and not with an external "act of resistance". Enjoyment of speech effectively corresponds to the Lacanian *jouissance de l'Autre*, and it is precisely this modality of enjoyment that Žižek defends as intimately revolutionary. In *The Parallax View*, for instance, he argues that it is comparable to a kind of endangered species in our contemporary "post-ideological" universe, since in this universe 'what addresses us is a direct "desublimated" call of *jouissance*, no longer masked in an ideological narrative proper' (Žižek 2006c: 188). As a rule, his argument is accompanied by a vivid narrative exemplification which is worth quoting in full:

> Imagine (a real clinical case) two love-partners who excite one another by verbalizing, telling one another their innermost sexual fantasies to such a degree that they reach full orgasm without touching, just as the effect of 'mere talking'. The result of such an excess of intimacy is not difficult to guess: after such a radical exposure, they will no longer be able to maintain their amorous link – too much has been said, or, rather, the spoken word, the big Other, was too directly flooded by *jouissance*, so the two are embarrassed by one another's presence and slowly drift apart, they start to avoid one another's presence. This, not a full perverse orgy, is the true excess: not 'putting your innermost fantasies into practice instead of just talking about them', but, precisely, talking about them, allowing them to invade the medium of the big Other to such an extent that one can literally 'fuck with words', that the elementary, constitutive, barrier between language and *jouissance* breaks down. Measured by this standard, the most extreme 'real orgy' is a poor substitute. (Žižek 2006c: 188–9)

This case illustrates why *jouissance féminine* should be located within, and not outside, the field of symbolic representation. It is not a matter of relying on what is perceived as being excluded from the Symbolic (phallic enjoyment); but rather of identifying fully with the Symbolic (excluding nothing) and as a result eliciting its Real core. In Part II I have attempted to demonstrate this logic through a number of filmic references, especially from the cinemas of Ingmar Bergman and Michelangelo Antonioni, which seem to me particularly suitable to render the "not-all" of woman as coincidental with the non-existence of the big Other.

The political consequences of this book, which will need to be fully drawn out elsewhere, are detectable in the shift of perspective accomplished in the passage from Part I to Part II. More specifically, the claim that radical change depends on an intervention in the underground domain of the Real of enjoyment would seem to imply a shift towards the feminine logic of "not-all". To transform the Real means passing from phallic enjoyment to the feminine *jouissance de l'Autre*, recasting the masculine attachment to a surplus enjoyment that fortifies ideology as the founding feature of ideology itself. Or, put differently: while the masculine field accounts for the tension between a series and its excep- tion, the feminine one shows how 'a series and an exception *directly coincide*: the series is always a series of "exceptions", of entities which display a certain exceptional quality that qualifies them to belong to the series' (Žižek 2000b: 115). By inscribing a political potential in feminine sexuality, one asserts the consubstantiality of the Symbolic and the Real, and therefore the changeability of the big Other.

The conflation of sexual difference and the libidinal economy of cinema as I have tried to unravel it can be summarised in two final references, the first from Eric Rohmer's period piece *The Lady and the Duke* (L'Anglais et le duc, 2001) and the second from Max Ophuls' *Letters from an Unknown Woman* (1948). Concerned with faithfully evoking eighteenth-century Paris and its outskirts, Rohmer resorts to a curious strategy: he shoots the exteriors against enormous tableaux, scenic back- grounds mimicking classic French painting. Though the artificiality of the operation may be obvious, it does not detract from the verisimilitude of the story, and as such reminds us of analogous, even more radical experiments like Von Trier's *Dogville* (2003) and *Manderlay* (2005). Para- doxically, in fact, in Rohmer's film the painted backgrounds are more fascinating than the actual characters. This is therefore not just a sign of Rohmer's legendary sense of economy, nor can it be simply taken as a challenge to realism (especially the bloated realism of today's super- productions) through the imitation of art (painting). Instead, Rohmer's tableaux achieve a much more intriguing result: they manage to focus on the specific dislocation "between two fictions", i.e. between the unfold- ing of the explicit story and its decentred background. While all art effec- tively plays with the gap between representation and the empty place of inscription, cinema, owing to the specificity of its form, is in a particu- larly advantaged position to evoke the uncanny resonance of this gap.

To understand how cinematic fiction can be more Real than reality we need first to acknowledge, with the help of psychoanalysis, that real- ity itself is split between its contingent symbolic meaning, secured by the big Other, and the reservoir of fantasies whose function is to fill in, or "cork", the gaps in the big Other itself. Reality, in other words, emerges as the product of two fictions: the immaterial symbolic network we are born into combined with the fantasmatic background we rely on to avoid being sucked into the primordial void (psychosis). In view of this, the power of cinematic fiction does not only reside in its capacity to generate meaning, but especially in its propensity to capture the discrepancy between surface and background – a discrepancy which effectively mirrors the split in reality. Film, in other words, has a chance to represent what is in excess of symbolic representation and simultaneously cannot be fully covered by fantasy, i.e. the visual correlative of the traumatic break in the signifying network on account of which we can claim that "the big Other does not exist". And it is precisely when it manages to render this uncanny excess of fantasy and symbolisation that film may become Real: an imperceptible and illusory appearance stripped of any symbolic consistency, an evanescent and substanceless *Schein* comparable to Hegel's 'appearance *qua* appearance' (Hegel 1977: 89). Ultimately, this fragile Real emerging from symbolisation is cinematic enjoyment at its purest; as such, it opens up and sustains the space of symbolisation *tout court*, and therefore needs to be confronted in all its traumatic inconsistency if the authority of the big Other is to be challenged and radically reconfigured.

To conclude, the connection between this cinematic Real and the Real of sexual difference can be appreciated in a passage of Ophuls' *Letters from an Unknown Woman*, when Lisa and her lover Stefan take a ride on a fairground train in which the romantic landscape viewed from the carriage window is nothing but an artificially superimposed tableau that changes at will, together with the background music. What we have here is an exemplification of both the artificial character of the sexual relationship (for it depends on the "third" of fantasy epitomised by the fake landscape) and the basic dislocation between cinematic fiction and its fantasmatic background. With this book I have attempted to unravel cinema's distinctive capacity to focus on its own dislocation, which in turn has allowed me to make sense of the universal antagonism called sexual difference.

Notes

Notes to Part I

1. Crucially, this is the way capitalism works: our relationship to the commodity *qua* sublime object is not perceived as the result of a prohibition but as a spontaneous yearning.
2. Significantly, he cannot understand what the girl says as her words are silenced by the noise of the sea. Apropos the status of this noise, what comes to mind – despite the obvious difference that Marcello and Paola are not lovers – is the famous scene of sexual intercourse between Rosy (Sarah Miles) and the English officer in David Lean's *Ryan's Daughter* (1970). Žižek comments on this scene by claiming that 'the depiction of the sexual act in the midst of the forest, with waterfall sounds supposed to render their subdued passion, cannot but strike us today as a mishmash of clichés. However, the role of the absurd sound accompaniment is profoundly ambiguous: by way of emphasizing the ecstasy of the sexual act, these sounds in a way dematerialize the act and rid us of the weight of its presence. [...] In short, the paradox of the scene from *Ryan's Daughter* is that the waterfall sound itself functions as the fantasmatic screen that filters out the Real of the sexual act' (Žižek 2006a: 50).
3. With regard to the "woman/statue theme", examples abound in European cinema. Let us recall Kieślowski's *Three Colours: White* (Trois couleurs: Blanc, 1994), where after being left by his wife, the hero buys a woman's bust to keep next to him at night; or the imposing presence of a bronze statue of a woman in the long apartment scene in Godard's *Contempt* (Le Mépris, 1963), where Paul (Michel Piccoli) and Camille (Brigitte Bardot) start drifting apart.
4. The same metaphor is at work in David Lean's *Brief Encounter* (1945), suggesting that the heroine now has a chance to understand what she really wants (the man who stands in front of her, of course).
5. As anticipated, the role of literature in Truffaut is, ultimately, *therapeutical*, as eloquently summed up by Claude (Jean-Pierre Léaud) in *Anne and Muriel* (Les deux anglaises et le continent, 1971). Having finished his first novel, he comments: 'Now I feel better, it's as if from now on the characters of my book will start suffering in my place'. This consideration also allows me to risk a different reading of *Fahrenheit 451*, which is Truffaut's most explicit statement in defence of books/fiction. What if the burning of books, far from simply amounting to a reference to the Nazis, also functions as an unconscious self-destructive intervention through which, unwittingly, Truffaut gets to the traumatic Real beyond symbolisation? One of the key scenes, in this sense, is the suicide of the woman who sets fire upon herself and all her books with a devilish smile on her face. She cannot be caught, she is beyond reach, precisely because she disappears "beyond fiction", or rather in the Real void that structures/frames fiction itself.
6. Truffaut uses a very similar camera movement at the beginning of *The Woman Next Door* (La femme d'à côté, 1981), where Madame Jouve (Véronique Silver)

talks directly into the camera to introduce the tragic story of *amour fou* between Bernard (Gérard Depardieu) and Mathilde (Fanny Ardant). Here the passage from what seems to be a non-narrative dimension to the properly narrative one also signals the intervention of what Žižek often refers to as 'the grimace of the Real' (see Žižek 2001b: 113–46). The slow frame enlargement shows us Madame Jouve's crippled body, a direct result of her confrontation with the Real of the sexual relationship: as she explains later, she had attempted to commit suicide after a failed love story, but had miraculously survived; the impossibility of that relationship, however, was now forever inscribed on her body.

7. Lacan writes about Antigone: 'Although she is not yet dead, she is eliminated from the world of the living. [...] from Antigone's point of view life can only be appreciated, can only be lived and thought about, from the place of the limit where her life is already lost, where she is already on the other side' (Lacan 1999: 280). In Lacan psychosis and ethics to an extent overlap, insofar as in psychosis we refuse to compromise our desire, i.e. to sacrifice enjoyment.

8. We are, of course, knee-deep in Hitchcock's territory, with the question of the ambiguity of feminine identity clearly recalling *Vertigo* (the rapport between Fergus and Julie is explicitly modelled on that between Scottie – whose surname is, revealingly, Ferguson – and Madeleine).

9. This is the key theme, incidentally, of Michael Powell and Emeric Pressburger's *The Red Shoes* (1948) and Chuck Russell's *The Mask* (1994): both these well-known films make the most of the psychoanalytic insight into the object-*jouissance* that captures the essence of the subject.

10. There is a degree of confusion regarding the final lines of dialogue in the iconic sequence of Michel's death. What I argue is that whether or not the Belmondo character actually says that Patricia is a bitch, this point is made not only by the detective in what may be a misinterpretation of Michel's words, but by the film itself.

11. Put differently, what is at stake in anti-Semitism is the aversion to the constitutive "shapelessness" of the subject: 'At the most fundamental level, anti-Semitism does not associate Jews with corruption as a positive feature, but rather with shapelessness itself – with the lack of a definite and delimited ethnic disposition. In this vein, Alfred Rosenberg, Hitler's chief ideologue, asserted that all European nations possess a well-defined "spiritual shape [*Gestalt*]" which gives expression to their ethnic character – and this "spiritual shape" is precisely what is missing in Jews. And – again – is not this very "shapelessness [*Gestaltlosigkeit*]" the constitutive feature of subjectivity?' (Žižek 1994: 146).

12. In *Salò* we also find a direct quotation from *Rome, Open City*. When, having been caught breaking the rules (i.e. having heterosexual sex) Ezio meets his death with the clenched fist of the Communist salute, one cannot fail to recognise here the same kind of heroic passionate attachment displayed by Manfredi in Rossellini's film. We realise that Pasolini is explicitly referring to Rossellini's masterpiece when the libertines, stunned by Ezio's act of defiance, freeze and step back like their Nazi counterparts in *Rome, Open City* after Manfredi's death – an image that inscribes a moment of vacillation in their otherwise mechanical persistence in evil.

13. Could not we argue the same apropos, for instance, the famous "night of the long knives" sequence in Luchino Visconti's *The Damned* (1969)? Here the director's attention to history is clearly overwhelmed by the homoerotic intensity with which he films the SA party/orgy before their being massacred by the SS.

14. The cinemas of Ferreri and Pasolini would seem to ratify the Lacanian maxim that 'Ce n'est pas à sa conscience que le sujet est condamné, c'est à son corps' (Lacan, 2001: 206: The subject is not condemned to its consciousness, but to its body). Given the current cultural studies fascination with "the body", this notion of bodily *jouissance* cannot but appear as a refreshing radicalisation of an academic cliché.

15. Incidentally, that the decisive tête-à-tête between Jérôme and Claire concerned only Jérôme is made obvious in the final sequence of the film, where, despite Jérôme's advice, Claire and her boyfriend resume their relationship.

16. 'Marguerite Duras is a little like Bergman; her universe doesn't touch me personally, I'm a stranger to it, it's distant' (Rohmer 1990: 16).

17. Also, the fact that Max's ex-Nazi friends decide to eliminate Lucia, since she knows who they are and could jeopardise their attempt to erase their old identities, works as a misplaced narrative filler: in actual fact, Lucia needs to be eliminated because her masochistic zeal undermines the evil sadistic position they still unashamedly endorse. In this sense we can see how different Max turns out to be with respect to the gang of Nazi henchmen he initially cooperates with: the second encounter with Lucia produces a "miraculous" transformation, changing him from an unrepentant sadist to a faithful lover willing to sacrifice his own life for the sake of the loved one (he hides Lucia away in his flat until the day when – isolated and starved to death by his ex-companions, who monitor the flat day and night – he attempts to escape with Lucia, but both are killed).

18. Particularly insightful is Bernardi's reading of the sacred in Rossellini: 'If Rossellini's cinema is realistic, then it is in the sense that it reflects on the state of western culture and evokes, in order to comprehend it, the experience of the sacred not in the religious meaning but in the way that Pasolini (who was deeply indebted to Rossellini) or Bataille spoke of the sacred. There is nothing transcendental, supernatural or divine about the sacred in this sense. It is completely immanent' (Bernardi 2000: 50).

19. The magical charm of this extraordinary sequence reminds me of the passage in Fellini's *Roma* (1972) where, during the excavations for the underground some workers discover ancient Roman dwellings. When a team of archaeologists is called upon, they are faced by the breathtaking spectacle of a number of well preserved frescoes of beautiful and melancholic figures; however, as soon as these paintings come in contact with gusts of wind from outside, they vanish.

20. The movement of Mouchette's arms when she is assaulted by Arsene is revealing: first she flails them clenching her fists, as if to signal resistance, but immediately after she embraces her harasser. Bresson, as always extremely meticulous in directing every movement of his actors' (or "models", as he called them), uses here an expedient of classic cinema to indicate that the assault is only partially rejected by the heroine.

21. This was already a key theme in his first work, *Love is Colder than Death* (Liebe ist kälter als der Tod, 1969), and was a year later developed in *Rio Das Mortes*, although in both films the allusion to a "sexual utopia" clearly functions as a smokescreen only partly concealing pressing homoerotic tension (that is to say, sexual difference is not eliminated but simply displaced onto the homosexual couple).
22. Let us consider the enormous poster of Poussin's painting *Midas and Bacchus* (1629) which covers an entire wall of Petra's flat. Some critics have argued that this overbearing backdrop represents the patriarchal system which underlies, and dooms, the relationship of Petra and Karin. When Karin announces that she is leaving Petra, for instance, the main light is not directed at her but at Bacchus's glowing genitalia which hover over her.
23. The question of sadomasochism does not, of course, apply solely to marriage. In this respect, Joseph Losey's *The Servant* (1963) is one of the most acute cinematic statements on the pervasively sadomasochistic nature of *any* relationship between human beings. Scripted by Harold Pinter, the film features a Master (Tony, played by James Fox) and a Servant (Barrett, played by Dirk Bogarde) forming a fully exploitative relationship which is not only based on (homo)sexuality, but mostly on economic and class difference – and which is ultimately destructive for both parties.
24. Legend has it that upon meeting Buñuel, Hitchcock kept exclaiming 'That leg, that leg!'
25. Žižek's insight into masochism seems all the more pertinent today, with the so-called "decline of Oedipus". The more symbolic authority is being fragmented, diluted and neutralised through a multitude of formal practices of liberalisation and democratisation – whose underlying aim is to de-politicise the social field so as to optimise capitalist profitability – the more it would appear that the only way to antagonise power is by assuming its clandestine surplus-enjoyment.
26. Ultimately, Karol's desire for Dominique, his elevating her to the status of the Lady, overlaps with capitalism (he turns into a capitalist yuppie in post-Communist Poland) as desiring machine. Capitalism functions precisely through this endless postponement of the encounter with the lack that pertains to *objet a*, which allows it to produce endless objects of *jouissance* (commodities) which temporarily occupy the void of the object-cause of desire.
27. 'Had Hélène been able to give him the love he required, one feels sure that the beast in Popaul could have been cured, and the man reborn' (Wood and Walker 1970: 134).
28. The same applies to Von Trier's visually mesmerising TV adaptation of Euripides' tragedy, which he developed from a script by Dreyer (although not very faithfully at all). The ending of his *Medea* (1987), in fact, is even more cruel than Pasolini's, insofar as the sequence of the killing of the children, who here are hung, is highly disturbing: as the mother is preparing to string them up to their deaths, the older son helps persuade his frightened brother to do what she wants them to do, even though it means the end of their lives. What is truly unbearable here is the complicity of the victim.
29. Often, in Truffaut, the impossibility of the sexual relationship is explained through some reference to one of the character's "unhappy childhood" (see

for example the Bertrand Morane character in *The Man who Loved Women* or, more explicitly and didactically, the teacher's final lesson in *Pocket Money*).

30. Is this not the ultimate point made by Bertolucci's *The Dreamers* (2003), where the deadlock afflicting the intimate relationship between Matthew (Michael Pitt), an American student in Paris, and French twins Isabelle (Eva Green) and Theo (Louis Garrel), appears surmountable only if displaced onto the conflict taking place outside, in the streets of Paris during May 1968?

31. The same can be said about Stéphane (Daniel Auteuil) in Claude Sautet's *Un coeur en hiver* (1992), whose refusal to "go all the way" with Camille (Emmanuelle Béart) speaks for his desire *not* to confront the sexual deadlock. *Jouissance*, here, is recuperated and gentrified through Stéphane's passion for music (he is a violin craftsman).

Notes to Part II

1. This is how Lacan describes the feminine *jouissance* beyond the phallus: 'There is a jouissance that is hers, that belongs to the "she" that doesn't exist and doesn't signify anything. There is a jouissance that is hers about which she herself perhaps knows nothing if not that she experiences it – that much she knows' (Lacan 1998b: 74).

2. 'The question that instantly pops up is: what is, then, the feminine "in itself", obfuscated by male clichés? The problem is that all answers (from the traditional eternal feminine, to Kristeva and Irigaray) can again be discredited as male clichés. Carol Gilligan, for example, opposes to the male values of autonomy, competitiveness, etc., the feminine values of intimacy, attachment, interdependence, care and concern, responsibility and self-sacrifice, etc. Are these authentic feminine features or male clichés about women, features imposed on them in the patriarchal society? The matter is undecidable, so that the only possible answer is, both at the same time' (Žižek 1995).

3. A situation that reminds me of the wonderful opening scene of Kubrick's *Eyes Wide Shut*, where a mysterious dancer attempts to seduce Alice.

4. One can also see how the film deals specifically with the question of enjoyment of the other (Nelly) as a self-reflexive strategy. Bergman deconstructs this strategy both in Jack and in Ingeborg. "I could use her as my anchor in reality", says Jack – at which point we start suspecting that he might have read a couple of Lacan's seminars. Later, on the train, Ingeborg also realises, through a nightmarish vision, that she does not love the girl for her own sake, but rather precisely as "her anchor in reality". In Lacanian terms, the displacement of enjoyment is the basic strategy through which the subject achieves a minimal degree of self-consciousness.

5. More accurately, the passage reflects the constitutional tension between content and form that typifies Antonioni's filmmaking: the feeling of void generated by the slow 360-degree long take unobtrusively manipulates our perception of the characters' subjective universe, revealing the emptiness of their bourgeois existence (Paola) and aspirations (Guido); simultaneously, their class-related weariness projects itself on to the landscape, conferring upon it an utterly desolated feel. Antonioni's choices are crucial: rotating on its axis, this single shot determines a remarkably inconspicuous "internal

editing" by following the characters' slow movement and dialogue, while avoiding the dramatic effect of shot-reverse-shots and close-ups.

6. Once again, we should stress how misleading it is to seek an ideological message in these films: ideology, here, clearly functions as a kind of "safety net" for an otherwise potentially explosive, and thus paralysing, encounter with the Real.

7. The ultimate consequence of Antonioni's formalism is that it gets caught in the loop of drive, which leads either to the "catatonic" freezing up of the image typical of films like *The Eclipse*, or, in terms of content, to imaginary psychotic outbursts such as the explosion in the final sequence of *Zabriskie Point*.

8. 'Since *L'avventura*, Antonioni's great project has been the empty shot, the de-peopled shot' (Bonitzer, in Deleuze 1986: 122).

9. For a more comprehensive analysis of *Theorem* through Lacanian psychoanalysis see my *Traumatic Encounters in Italian Film* (Vighi 2001: 38–49).

10. The paradox of the male division is that 'man subordinates his relationship to a woman to the domain of ethical goals (forced to choose between woman and ethical duty – in the guise of professional obligations, etc. – he immediately opts for duty), yet he is simultaneously aware that only a relationship with a woman can bring him genuine "happiness" or personal fulfilment' (Žižek, 1994: 152).

11. The bitter irony is that, while shooting, Lea Massari, the actress who plays Anna, actually *did* "fall into the Real", for she suffered a heart attack that left her in a coma for two days (see Brunette 1998: 28).

12. Claudia, for instance, is horrified by the prospect of forgetting: 'My God, can it really take so little to change, to forget? Only a few days ago, the mere thought that Anna might be dead almost killed me. Now I can't even cry. I'm afraid she might be alive. Everything is becoming so terribly simple, even getting rid of tragedies'.

13. See Kant's famous definition: 'Bold, overhanging, and, as it were, threatening rocks, thunderclouds piled up the vault of heaven, borne along with flashes and peals, volcanoes in all their violence of destruction, hurricanes leaving desolation in their track, the boundless ocean rising with rebellious force' (Kant 1914: 125). Incidentally, the hurricane we see in the film was a real one.

14. The theme of the atomic explosion will be reaffirmed in the last sequence of the film, with a shot of newspaper headlines reading 'The Atomic Arms Race' and 'The Peace is Weak'.

15. Amongst other things, this reference to Joyce proves the non-biological character of Lacan's formulas of sexuation.

16. More specifically, in the third (very Hitchcockian) episode of *The Vanquished* (1952), set in London, we find the same association park-murder that returns in *Blow-up*.

17. This specific sequence denotes the influence of *Blow-up* on Pasolini's film, all the more evident since Odetta had previously taken photographs of the stranger in her garden.

18. 'The immediate negation of A negates the position of A *whilst remaining in its symbolic confines*, so it must be followed by another negation, which then negates the very symbolic space common to A' (Žižek 2001a: 72).

19. This is the way in which Žižek understands, for example, the two Russian revolutions of 1917 (February and October): 'the fundamental lesson of revolutionary *materialism* is that revolution must strike twice, and for essential reasons. The gap is not simply the gap between form and content: what the first revolution misses is not the content, but *the form itself* – it remains stuck in the old form, thinking that freedom and justice can be accomplished if we simply put the existing state apparatuses and its democratic mechanisms to use' (Žižek 2002a: 7).

20. The closest literary reference here is Luigi Pirandello's novel *The Late Mattia Pascal* (Il fu Mattia Pascal, 1904), where the eponymous protagonist takes advantage of a similar chance in the attempt to refashion himself as an entirely new person.

21. 'Here we have one of the possible definitions of the unconscious: *the form of thought whose ontological status is not that of thought*, that is to say, the form of thought external to thought itself – in short, some Other Scene external to the thought whereby the form of the thought is already articulated in advance' (Žižek 1989: 19).

22. Lacan's claim that Marx invented the symptom (see Lacan 1975: 106) retains therefore a surprising significance if we are to grasp the political function of Antonioni's formalism. Perhaps we could even risk suggesting that Antonioni was aware of the clandestine Marxist relevance of his formalism in *Zabriskie Point*, for at one point in the narrative the signifier "Marx" indeed does make a furtive appearance: when a police officer asks Mark for his details, since he suspects him of participating in the campus upheavals, he replies scathingly that his name is Karl Marx (written with a capital C by the police officer, who simply does not recognise the magnitude of the signifier).

23. A scenario we also have in Marco Bellocchio's *My Mother's Smile* (L'ora di religione, 2002, see Vighi 2006: 174–84).

24. This passage reminds me of Kubrick's *The Shining* (1980), for what is little boy Danny (in Kubrick's film) looking for as he explores the corridors of the Overlook Hotel, and especially room 237, if not some (traumatic) freedom from parental over-proximity?

25. 'Maybe that's why incest is so scary, why there is such a taboo about it, because it's so natural for maternal love to turn into something else' (Malle 1993: 83).

26. The point can be expanded on by imagining what Lucia would be able to do at the level of state politics. Within this perspective, Žižek claims that '*the same* femininity which, within the closed circle of family life, is the very power of protective love, turns into obscene frenzy when displayed at the level of public and state affairs... In short, it is OK for a woman to protest against public state power on behalf of the rights of family and kinship; but woe betide a society in which women endeavour directly to influence decisions concerning the affairs of the state, manipulating their weak male partners, effectively emasculating them...' (Žižek 2007b: 3). From this angle, Lucia would truly embody Hegel's notion of woman as the internal enemy of the community, i.e. the individual who exposes the fact that the Law enjoys, that "big Other does not exist".

27. Eva: 'A mother and her daughter. What a terrible combination of emotions and confusion... and destruction. [...] The daughter shall inherit the mother's injuries. The daughter shall suffer for the mother's failures. [...] It

is as if the umbilical cord had never been cut. [...] Is my grief your secret pleasure?'

28. Bergman once said: 'All women move me – old, young, tall, short, fat, thin, thick, heavy, light, beautiful, charming, living, dead. I also love cows, she-monkeys, sows, bitches, mares, hens, geese, turkey hens, lady hippos, and mice. But the category of female that I prefer are wild beasts and dangerous reptiles' (in Truffaut 1994: 255).

29. Wood's conclusion about *Persona* points precisely to this notion of trauma and rebirth: 'He [Bergman] exposes himself fully to the despair and horror that man must confront if there is ever to be a possibility of passing beyond. For all the anguish and the sense of deep hurt, there is a marvellously sensitive feeling, at once dynamic and compassionate, for human potentialities, for the development of consciousness' (Wood 1969: 67). Wood, a proud humanist, intuits here the crucial significance of the inhuman in Bergman.

30. As Susan Sontag put it a long time ago, 'the quality of his [Bergman's] sensibility has only one true subject: the depths in which consciousness drowns. If the maintenance of personality requires the safeguarding of the integrity of masks, and the truth about a person is always the cracking of the mask, then the truth about life as a whole is the shattering of the total façade behind which lies an absolute cruelty' (in Kaminsky 1975: 266).

31. Apropos loss of individuation, Bergman recollected how, in the editing room, Liv Ullman and Bibi Andersson did not recognise their own half of the face (Bergman 1995: 61).

32. The derailment of the communicative field is also at stake in the few historically pregnant images of the film. However, as Sontag points out, these images stand for something other than political awareness: 'Unlike Godard, Bergman is not an historically-oriented filmmaker. The TV newsreel of a Buddhist immolating himself, and the famous photograph of the little boy from the Warsaw Ghetto, are for Bergman, above all, images of total violence, of unredeemed cruelty. It's as images of what cannot be imaginatively encompassed or digested that they occur in *Persona* and are pondered by Elizabeth – rather than occasions for right political and moral thoughts' (266). The point is well-observed but needs to be expanded, for these are indeed images signalling the intervention of the Lacanian Real, the "bone-in-the-throat" where the word meets its inherent limit. Failure of communication, in Bergman, is tantamount to these terrifying moments when the mask cracks and reveals the Real of enjoyment. And the key point is that it is through the eyes of woman that we access the devastating spectacle where the symbolic whole suddenly loses its grip.

Bibliography

Abel, R. (ed.) (1988). *French Film Theory and Criticism: A History/Anthropology, 1907–1939*, vol. I: 1907–1929 (Princeton: Princeton University Press).
Adorno, T.W. (2000). *Negative Dialectics*. London and New York: Routledge.
Adorno, T.W. (2005). *Minima Moralia: Reflections on a Damaged Life*. London and New York: Verso.
Annenkov, G. (1962). *Max Ophuls*. Paris: Le Terrain Vague.
Antonioni, M. (1970). *Zabriskie Point*. Bologna: Cappelli.
Bachmann, G. (1975). 'Pasolini on de Sade'. *Film Quarterly*, 29(2), 39–45.
Barthes, R. (1988). *Cher Antonioni: 1988–1989*. Rome: Ente Autonomo Gestione Cinema.
Benjamin, W. (1968). *Illuminations*. New York: Schocken Books.
Benjamin, W. (1996). *Selected Writings, Vol. 1*. Cambridge, MA: Harvard University Press.
Benjamin, W. (2003). *Selected Writings, Vol. 4*. Cambridge, MA: Harvard University Press.
Bergman, I. (1995). *Images: My Life in Film*. London and Boston: Faber & Faber.
Bernardi, S. (2000). 'Rossellini's Landscapes: Nature, Myth, History' in Forgacs, D., Lutton, S. and Nowell-Smith, G. (eds). *Roberto Rossellini: Magician of the Real*. London: British Film Institute.
Bondanella, P. (1992). *The Cinema of Federico Fellini*. Princeton: Princeton University Press.
Bordwell, D. (2005). 'Slavoj Žižek: Say Anything', www.davidbordwell.net/essays/zizek.php.
Brunette, P. (1996). *Roberto Rossellini*. Berkeley, Los Angeles and London: University of California Press.
Brunette, P. (1998). *The Films of Michelangelo Antonioni*. Cambridge: Cambridge University Press.
Buñuel, L. (1985). *My Last Breath*. London: Flamingo.
Butler, J. (1989). *Gender Trouble: Feminism and the Subversion of Identity*. London; New York: Routledge.
Butler, J. (1993). *Bodies that Matter: On the Discursive Limits of Sex*. London; New York: Routledge.
Chandler, C. (1995). *I, Fellini*. New York: Random House.
Chatman, S. (1985). *Antonioni, or, the Surface of the World*. Berkeley, Los Angeles and London: University of California Press.
Chatman, S. and Fink, G. (eds) (1989). *L'Avventura. Michelangelo Antonioni, director*. New Brunswick, NJ and London: Rutgers University Press.
Chiesa, L. (2007). *Subjectivity and Otherness: A Philosophical Reading of Lacan*. Cambridge, MA and London: The MIT Press.
Cowie, P. (1982). *Ingmar Bergman: A Critical Biography*. New York: Charles Scribner's Sons.
Cuccu, L. (ed.) (1988). *Michelangelo Antonioni 1966/1984*. Rome: Ente Autonomo di Gestione per il Cinema.
Debord, G. (1992). *Society of Spectacle*. London: Rebel Press.

Deleuze, G. (1986). *Cinema 1. The Movement-Image*. London: The Athlone Press.

Deleuze, G. (1991). *Masochism*. New York: Zone Books.

Di Carlo, C. and Tinazzi, G. (1996). *The Architecture of Vision: Writings and Interviews on Cinema*. Venice: Marsilio.

Duflot, J. (1993). *Il sogno del centauro*. Rome: Editori Riuniti.

Faldini, F. and Fofi, G. (eds) (1981). *L'avventurosa storia del cinema italiano, 1960– 1969*. Milan: Feltrinelli.

Fassbinder, R.W. (1992). *The Anarchy of the Imagination: Interviews, Essays, Notes*. Baltimore: John Hopkins University Press.

Fellini, F. (1976). *Fellini on Fellini*. London: Eyre Methuen.

Fellini, F. (1987). 'Fellini oniricon', *Dolce vita* 1(3), 29–44.

Fellini, F. (1988). *Comments on Film*. Fresno: The Press of California University at Fresno.

Fink, B. (1995). *The Lacanian Subject Between Language and Jouissance*. Princeton: Princeton University Press.

Freud, S. (1997). *The Interpretation of Dreams*. Ware: Wordsworth Editions Ltd.

Gallop, J. (1985). *Reading Lacan*. Ithaca: Cornell University Press.

Gillain, A. (ed.) (2005). *Tutte le interviste di François Truffaut sul cinema*. Roma: Gremese Editore.

Godard, J.-L. (1986). *Godard on Godard*. New York: Da Capo.

Greene, N. (1994). *Pier Paolo Pasolini: Cinema as Heresy*. Princeton: Princeton University Press.

Heath, S. (1999). 'Cinema and Psychoanalysis: Parallel Histories'. In Bergstrom, J. (ed.), *Endless Night*. Berkeley, Los Angeles and London: University of California Press, 1999, pp. 25–56.

Hegel, G.W.F. (1977). *Phenomenology of Spirit*. Oxford: Clarendon Press.

Hughes, E. (1971). *On the Set of Fellini Satyricon*. New York: Morrow.

Ingram, R. and Duncan, P. (eds) (2004). *François Truffaut: The Complete Films*. Cologne: Taschen.

Insdorf, A. (1981). *Truffaut*. London: Macmillan.

Irigaray, L (1985). *This Sex Which is Not One*. Ithaca: Cornell University Press.

Jameson, F. (1990). *Late Marxism: Adorno, or, The Persistence of the Dialectic*. London and New York: Verso.

Jameson, F. (1992). *Signatures of the Visible*. New York and London: Routledge.

Kaminsky, S. (ed) (1975). *Ingmar Bergman: Essays in Criticism*. Oxford: Oxford University Press.

Kant, I. (1914). *Critique of Judgement*. London: Macmillan.

Kieślowski, K. (2000). 'Bergman's Silence', in Orr, J. and Taxidou, O. (eds), *Post-War Cinema and Modernity: A Film Reader*. Edinburgh: Edinburgh University Press, pp. 422–5.

Lacan, J. (1975). 'R.S.I.'. *Ornicar?* 4, 91–106.

Lacan, J. (1988). *The Seminar. Book II. The Ego in Freud's Theory and in the Technique of Psychoanalysis*. New York: Norton; Cambridge: Cambridge University Press.

Lacan, J. (1998a). *The Seminar. Book XI. The Four Fundamental Concepts of Psychoanalysis*. New York and London: W. W. Norton.

Lacan, J. (1998b). *The Seminar. Book XX. On Feminine Sexuality. The Limits of Love and Knowledge*. New York and London: W.W. Norton.

Lacan, J. (1999). *The Seminar. Book VII. The Ethics of Psychoanalysis*. London: Routledge.

Lacan, J. (2000). *The Seminar. Book III. The Psychoses.* London: Routledge.
Lacan, J. (2001). *Le Séminaire. Livre VIII. Le transfert, 1960–61.* Paris: Seuil.
Lacan, J. (2006). *The Seminar. Book XVII. The Other Side of Psychoanalysis.* New York: W. W. Norton.
Lacan, J. (2007). *Écrits.* New York and London: W. W. Norton.
Lebeau, V. (2001). *Psychoanalysis and Cinema: The Play of Shadows.* London: Wallflower Press.
Malle, L. (1993). *Malle on Malle.* London: Faber & Faber.
Marx, K. (1990). *Capital, Vol. 1.* London: Penguin.
McGowan, T. (2007). 'Enjoying the Cinema', *International Journal of Žižek Studies* 1/3.
Metz, C. (1975). 'The Imaginary Signifier', *Screen* 16/2, 14–76.
Michaels, L. (2000). 'Bergman and the Necessary Illusion. An Introduction to Persona', in Michaels, L. (ed.) *Ingmar Bergman's Persona.* Cambridge: Cambridge University Press, pp. 1–23.
Miller, J.-A. (2000). 'On Semblances in the Relation Between the Sexes', in Renata Salecl (ed.) *Sexuation.* Durham, London: Duke University Press, pp. 13–27.
Mulvey, L. (1975). 'Visual Pleasure and Narrative Cinema', *Screen* 16(3), 6–18.
Naldini, N. (1989). *Pasolini, una vita.* Turin: Einaudi.
Nogueira, R. (1971). 'Eric Rohmer: Choice and Chance', *Sight and Sound* 40(3), 119–22.
Oliver, R.W. (ed.) (1995). *Ingmar Bergman: An Artist's Journey on Stage, on Screen, in Print.* New York: Arcade Publishers.
Pasolini, P.P. (1968). *Teorema.* Milan: Garzanti.
Pasolini, P.P. (1995). *Empirismo eretico.* Milan: Garzanti.
Pasolini, P.P. (1996). *Il film degli altri.* Parma: Guanda.
Rancière, J. (2004). *The Politics of Aesthetics.* London/New York: Continuum.
Rancière, J. (2006). *Film Fables.* Oxford/New York: Berg.
Rayns, T. (1979). *Fassbinder.* London: British Film Institute.
Rohmer, E. (1990). *The Taste for Beauty.* Cambridge: Cambridge University Press.
Rohmer, E. (2004). Radio Interview in *The Green Ray* DVD, Arrow Films.
Soler, C. (2006). *What Lacan Said About Women.* New York: The Other Press.
Sontag, S. (1964). 'On Godard's *Vivre sa vie'. Moviegoer* (2), 2–10.
Stamp, R. (2007). '"Another Exemplary Case": Žižek's Logic of Example', in Bowman, P. and Stamp, R., *The Truth of Žižek,* London: Continuum, pp. 161–77.
Steene, B. (1975). 'A Biographical Note', in Kaminsky (ed.) *Ingmar Bergman,* 3–9.
Tinazzi, G. (1976). *Michelangelo Antonioni.* Florence: La Nuova Italia.
Truffaut, F. (1994). *The Films in My Life.* New York: Da Capo.
Verhaeghe, P. (1999). *Does the Woman Exist? From Freud's Hysteric to Lacan's Feminine.* New York: Other Press.
Viano, M. (1993). *A Certain Realism: Making Use of Pasolini's Film Theory and Practice.* Berkeley, Los Angeles and London: University of California Press.
Vighi, F. (2001). *Traumatic Encounters in Italian Film: Locating the Cinematic Unconscious.* Bristol: Intellect.
Von Bagh, P. (2003). 'Le prigioni del moderno: celebrità, divismo, pubblicità', in De Giusti, L. and Giuliani, L. (eds), *Il piacere e il disincanto nel cinema di Max Ophuls.* Milan: Il Castoro, pp. 124–32.
Weil, S. (1987). *Gravity and Grace.* London: Routledge.

Willemen, P. (1997). *Pier Paolo Pasolini*. London: British Film Institute.

Wood, R. (1969). *Ingmar Bergman*. London: Studio Vista.

Wood, R. and Walker, M. (1970). *Claude Chabrol*. London: Studio Vista.

Žižek, S. (1989) *The Sublime Object of Ideology*. London and New York: Verso.

Žižek, S. (1993). *Tarrying with the Negative*. Durham, NC: Duke University Press.

Žižek, S. (1994). *The Metastases Of Enjoyment: Six Essays on Woman and Causality*. London and New York: Verso.

Žižek, S. (1995). 'Woman is one of the Names-of-the-Father, or how Not to misread Lacan's formulas of sexuation', *Lacanian Ink* 10, 24–39. All quotations from http://www.lacan.com/zizwoman.htm.

Žižek, S. (1997). *The Plague of Fantasies*. London and New York: Verso.

Žižek, S. (2000a).*The Ticklish Subject*. London and New York: Verso.

Žižek, S. (2000b). *The Fragile Absolute*. London and New York: Verso.

Žižek, S. (2001a). *Did Somebody Say Totalitarianism?* London and New York: Verso.

Žižek, S. (2001b). *Enjoy Your Symptom*. London and New York: Routledge.

Žižek, S. (2001c). *The Fright of Real Tears*. London: British Film Institute.

Žižek, S. (2001d). *On Belief*. London and New York: Routledge.

Žižek, S. (2002a). *Revolution at the Gates*. London and New York: Verso.

Žižek, S. (2002b). *Welcome to the Desert of the Real!* London and New York: Verso.

Žižek, S. (2002c). *For They Know Not What They Do*. London and New York: Verso.

Žižek, S. (2003). *The Puppet and the Dwarf: The Perverse Core of Christianity*. Cambridge, MA and London: The MIT Press.

Žižek, S. (2004). *Organs Without Bodies: Deleuze and Consequences*. London: Routledge.

Žižek, S. (2005). *Interrogating the Real*. London: Continuum.

Žižek, S. (2006a). *How to Read Lacan*. London: Granta Books.

Žižek, S. (2006b). *The Pervert's Guide to Cinema* (DVD).

Žižek, S. (2006c). *The Parallax View*. Cambridge, MA and London: MIT Press.

Žižek, S. (2007a). *The Indivisible Remainder: on Schelling and Related Matters*. London and New York: Verso.

Žižek, S. (2007b). *Slavoj Žižek Presents Mao: on Practice and Contradiction*. London and New York: Verso.

Žižek, S., and Daly, G. (2004). *Conversations with Žižek*. Cambridge, Oxford and Malden, MA: Cambridge University Press.

Index

Adorno, Theodor   58, 70, 187, 189
Almodovar, Pedro
 Talk to Her   81, 118–19
Antonioni, Michelangelo
 The Adventure   142–3, 156, 185,
  188–91, 193–4, 196–8, 201, 202,
  205, 210, 213, 216–17
 Blow-up   26, 93, 152, 185, 190, 199,
  203, 206, 210, 247n
 Chronicle of a Love   155, 166–7,
  184, 186–7, 208
 The Cry   97, 155, 191
 The Eclipse   156, 189, 193, 200–1,
  212, 247n
 formalism   187–8, 248n
 The Girlfriends   185–6
 Identification of a Woman   205
 The Lady without Camelias   168–70,
  171, 174, 175, 179, 184
 The Night   83, 152, 156, 189, 193,
  199–201, 204, 212, 229
 The Passenger   207–10
 Red Desert   156, 190, 201–2, 205–6,
  212
 The Vanquished   204, 247n
 Zabriskie Point   207–8, 211–12,
  247n, 248n, 249n

Barthes, Roland   194
Bataille, Georges   222, 223, 244n
Bellocchio, Marco
 The Conviction   83, 85
 Good Morning, Night   90–5
 My Mother's Smile   248n
 Slap the Monster on Page One   125
Benjamin, Walter   92, 95, 135–6,
 199, 209, 212
Bergman, Ingmar
 Autumn Sonata   119, 224–5
 Crisis   158–61, 162, 164–6, 170,
  246n
 The Devil's Eye   172

From the Life of the Marionettes
  126–8
 The Hour of the Wolf   228
 humanism   228–9, 249n
 The Magician   179–80
 Persona   230–6, 249n
 Port of Call   161–2
 Prison   171
 The Serpent's Egg   228
 The Shame   228
 The Silence   102, 218, 220–3,
  225–30
 Summer Interlude   176, 179
 Summer with Monika   139, 225
 Three Strange Loves   213
 Through a Glass Darkly   216–19
 on women   249n
 The Virgin Spring   155
 Wild Strawberries   102
 Winter Lights   218
Bertolucci, Bernardo
 The Conformist   67, 125
 The Dreamers   246
 La luna   223
 Last Tango in Paris   192, 210
 Novecento   67
 The Spider's Stratagem   219
Bordwell, David   1
Bresson, Robert
 The Devil Probably...   110
 A Gentle Woman   103
 Lancelot du Lac   51
 Mouchette   103, 244n
Buñuel, Luis
 Belle de jour   115–17, 195, 229
 The Criminal Life of Archibaldo de la
  Cruz   167
 That Obscure Object of Desire   26,
  27, 49, 89
 The Phantom of Liberty   89, 105
 Tristana   80, 118
 Viridiana   80, 86, 107
Butler, Judith   13

Cavani, Liliana
  The Night Porter 83, 117
Chabrol, Claude
  Le beau Serge 129
  Les Bonnes Femmes 129
  The Butcher 131–2
  The Cousins 129
  The Unfaithful Wife 129–30
  Web of Passions 129
  Weddings of Blood 130
Chiesa, Lorenzo 104, 125, 132
Clouzot, Henri-Georges
  Les diaboliques 237

Debord, Guy 169
Deleuze, Gilles 71, 97, 120, 122, 188, 231–2
Demy, Jacques
  The Girls of Rochefort 35
Dreyer, Carl Theodor
  Day of Wrath 67–9
  Gertrud 9–10

Fagioli, Massimo 92–4
Fassbinder, Rainer Werner
  The Bitter Tears of Petra von Kant 106–8
  Chinese Roulette 119
  Fox and His Friends 109–11
  Gods of the Plague 106
  Love is Colder than Death 245n
  Martha 114–15
  masochism 105–14
  The Merchant of Four Seasons 111–12
  Querelle de Brest 107
  Rio das Mortes 106
  Why does Mr R Run Amok? 132–3
Fellini, Federico
  8½ 25, 87, 88
  Amarcord 23, 29, 53–4, 76–7, 85, 87
  And the Ship Sails On 55
  The City of Women 25
  La dolce vita 19–24, 87, 88
  Fellini Satyricon 90
  Fellini's Casanova 51–2, 116
  Ginger and Fred 50–1

The Nights of Cabiria 24
  Roma 23, 244n
  I vitelloni 47
  The White Sheik 24, 169
Ferrara, Giuseppe
  The Moro Affair 90
Ferreri, Marco
  Blow-out 73
  Dillinger is Dead 97, 133
Fink, Bruce 238
Fontaine, Anne
  Nathalie 234
Frears, Stephen
  Dangerous Liaisons 47
Freud, Sigmund
  beyond the pleasure principle 71, 123, 133
  counter-transference 234
  drive 55, 123, 206
  Ego and Id 7, 226
  feminine desire 151, 155, 161
  Fort Da 53
  Irma's throat 137, 229
  libido 20, 86, 95, 207, 237
  masochism 105, 112, 114, 120, 174, 180, 195
  the moving image 8, 92
  return of the repressed 67, 132, 184
  theory of dreams 95

Gallop, Jane 13
Godard, Jean-Luc
  Breathless 66
  Contempt 11, 242n
  Numéro deux 128
  Pierrot le fou 129
  Vivre sa vie 109

Haneke, Michael
  The Piano Teacher 121
Heath, Stephen 8
Hegel, Georg Wilhelm Friedrich
  absolute immanence 128
  aesthetics 97
  appearance *qua* appearance 128, 241
  lord and bondsman 121

Hegel, Georg Wilhelm Friedrich –
  continued
  negativity 121, 207
  night of the world 138, 171
  Particular and Universal 138
  positing the presuppositions 164
  reflexivity 134, 185
  woman 138–9, 248n
Hitchcock, Alfred
  Psycho 128
  Rear Window 216
  Rope 223
  The Trouble with Harry 223
  Vertigo 21, 114
Honoré, Christophe
  Ma Mère 223

Irigaray, Luce 13, 44, 246n

Jameson, Fredric 187, 203
Joyce, James 102, 198, 202, 247n
Jung, Carl Gustav 85, 88–90, 136

Kahn, Cédric
  Red Lights 82
Kant, Immanuel
  das Ding 187
  moral law 60–2, 120, 122–3
  sublime 30, 196–7, 247n
  transcendentalism 188, 218
Kaurismäki, Aki
  The Man Without a Past 34
Kieślowski, Krzysztof
  The Double Life of Véronique 63,
    65–6
  A Short Film About Love 77
  Three Colours: Blue 130, 176, 213,
    215
  Three Colours: White 242n
Kubrick, Stanley
  Eyes Wide Shut 63, 191, 246n
  The Shining 248n

Lacan, Jacques
  the act 42, 98, 99–100, 126, 136,
    138, 164, 165, 209, 211
  anxiety 64, 76, 121, 126–30, 137,
    191, 201, 221, 223
  aphanisis 84, 136

between the two deaths 43
counter-transference 234
courtly love 18–20, 30, 47
drive 21–2, 25–6, 42–3, 51, 55, 57,
    63, 69, 71, 73, 76, 93–4, 97–9,
    111–13, 120, 123, 126, 190, 210,
    224–5, 229
exclusion 24
feminine enjoyment 12–14,
    117, 149–51, 155, 202, 238,
    246n
formulas of sexuation 12–13,
    149–51, 157–8
fundamental fantasy 95, 105, 174,
    255
gaze 26, 35, 93, 95, 173, 181–2,
    206, 212
jouissance 4, 60, 97, 125–6, 132,
    154, 157, 178, 237–8
Kant with Sade 66, 120, 122–3
lamella 102, 137, 140, 238
'les non-dupes errant' 50, 180
love 139–41
May '68 94
misrecognition 172–3, 181
objet a 12–14, 20, 22, 24, 26, 41,
    44, 45, 50, 52–5, 74–7, 79–80,
    117, 119, 127–9, 131–2, 140,
    150–1, 154, 156, 162, 177, 186–7,
    191, 196, 204, 211, 215, 232,
    245n
phallus 13–14, 24–5, 149–50, 156,
    166, 202, 216, 219, 221–2, 230,
    238, 246n
symptom 6–8, 67, 76, 79, 93, 96,
    124, 165, 178, 196, 202, 214, 233,
    248n
symbolic castration 19, 68, 174,
    201, 223
transference 233
Lean, David
  Brief Encounter 144–5, 242n
  Ryan's Daughter 183, 242n
Lebeau, Vicky 1
Losey, Joseph
  The Servant 245n
Lynch, David
  Blue Velvet 165

Malle, Louis
  Les Amants 131
  Murmur of the Heart 222, 248n
Martinelli, Renzo
  Five Moons Plaza 90
Marx, Karl
  class 28, 106–9, 128, 136, 145,
    167, 245n
  commodity fetishism 7–8, 182,
    186, 211–12
  proletarian violence 136
Metz, Christian 2
Mulvey, Laura 2

Ophuls, Max
  Letters from an Unknown Woman
    172, 177, 240–1
  Lola Montès 179–82
  Madame de... 181–3
  Le plaisir 55, 116
  The Reckless Moment 223

Pasolini, Pier Paolo
  Accattone 3, 110, 181
  death 179
  Mamma Roma 48–9, 221
  Medea 133–8, 245n
  Oedipus Rex 134, 136
  Pigsty 134, 136
  Salò, or the 120 Days of Sodom
    70–3, 79, 125, 243n
  sub-proletariat 3, 48–9
  Theorem 191–2, 204, 217, 234,
    247n
Petri, Elio
  *Investigation of a Citizen Above
    Suspicion* 123–5
Pirandello, Luigi 248n
Polanski, Roman
  Bitter Moon 116–17
  Knife in the Water 117
Powell, Michael and Pressburger,
    Emeric
  The Red Shoes 243n

Rancière, Jacques 6, 97–8, 100–1
Rohmer, Eric
  Chloe in the Afternoon 61–2, 79

Claire's Knee 46, 74–6, 78
La collectionneuse 57–60, 62
The Green Ray 197–8
The Lady and the Duke 240
The Marquise of O... 80–1
moral law 66–7
My Night at Maud's 60–1
Resnais, Alain
  Last Year in Marienbad 162–3
  Same Old Song 35
Rilke, Rainer Maria 58, 63
Rosi, Francesco
  Illustrious Corpses 125
Rossellini, Roberto
  Francis, God's Juggler 100
  Germany Year Zero 97–100
  No Greater Love 100
  Rome, Open City 69–72, 243n
  Stromboli 216, 219
  Voyage to Italy 82, 101–2, 142, 144,
    198, 219
Russell, Chuck
  The Mask 243n

Saura, Carlos
  Raise Ravens 214–15
Sautet, Claude
  Un coeur en hiver 246n
Scorsese, Martin
  Taxi Driver 98
Soler, Colette 164, 221
Sontag, Susan 109, 249n

Truffaut, François
  Anne and Muriel 242n
  The Bride Wore Black 41–3, 47
  Confidentially Yours 36, 38, 39, 44
  Day for Night 39, 171
  Fahrenheit 451 36, 242n
  Jules et Jim 29–32, 39, 44
  The Last Metro 39, 44
  The Man Who Loved Women 33,
    36, 43, 44, 46, 80, 246n
  Mississippi Mermaid 34, 49, 141–2
  Les Mistons 29
  Pocket Money 34, 246n
  Shoot the Piano Player 37–8, 43–4
  The Soft Skin 44

Truffaut, François – *continued*
  Stolen Kisses 53
  The Story of Adèle H 40–1, 42
  The Woman Next Door 35, 118,
    242–3n

Vigo, Jean
  L'atalante 162
Visconti, Luchino
  Bellissima 169
  The Damned 244n
  Death in Venice 25
  Ossessione 167
  White Nights 159–60
Von Trier, Lars
  Breaking the Waves 116–17, 240
  Dogville 240
  Manderlay 103
  Medea 245n

Weil, Simone 96–7
Welles, Orson
  The Immortal Story 30
Wellman, William
  Beau Geste 76
Wenders, Wim
  Wings of Desire 64
Wertmüller, Lina
  Seven Beauties 32
  Swept Away 84–5
Woolf, Virginia 232

Zulawski, Andrzej
  Fidelity 66
  That Most Important Thing: Love 66

Žižek, Slavoj
  anamorphosis 27, 232
  anti-Semitism 68–9, 243n
  biogenetics 99
  Christianity 110, 218
  commodity fetishism 182, 211
  courtly love 17–18, 20–1, 26–7,
    30, 53
  drive 98, 133
  excess of representation 6
  feminine depression 163, 168,
    171
  feminism 84, 151, 246n
  film theory 1–3, 9, 78, 97
  on Haneke 121
  on Hegel 138, 164, 192, 207
  jouissance 71, 157, 238–9
  on Kieślowski 64–5, 77, 213
  liberation 97–9, 113–14
  love 139–43, 145
  masochism 105, 107, 120–1,
    245n
  masturbation 32–3
  materialism 99, 113, 248n
  melancholy 178–9
  objet a 155–6
  on Pascal 124
  political correctedness 38
  pornography 31
  psychosis 126, 133
  on Rossellini 100
  sacrifice 224
  superego 120, 133
  on Von Trier 117